GAON
Conflict and Cohesion
in an Indian Village

GAON

CONFLICT
AND COHESION
IN AN INDIAN
VILLAGE

BY HENRY ORENSTEIN

PRINCETON UNIVERSITY PRESS
PRINCETON, NEW JERSEY, 1965

Printed in the United States of America
by H. Wolff Book Mfg. Co., Inc., New York

With gratitude and love to my parents
NATHAN AND HANNAH

 Preface

THE field data for this study were collected in the course of two trips to India, first over 1954–1955 and next over the summer of 1961. The 1954–1955 trip was financed by a Fulbright grant, with additional assistance from the University of California at Berkeley. The second trip was undertaken with the aid of a National Science Foundation grant. Assistance from the National Science Foundation and from Tulane University made available the free time required for preparing the data for publication. I thank these institutions for their assistance.

My field work was much facilitated by the suggestions in 1954–1955 of Y. B. Damle. Irawati Karve was generous with her time and advice on both field trips. Much of value in this work is attributable to her. In 1955 J. S. Ranadive acted as assistant in the field research, most efficiently gathering data on religion, and helping especially to collect information on my census and questionnaire. In 1961 I had the very competent field assistance of A. G. Pleasonton, who also was skillful and careful in helping to prepare the tables that appear in this book. The suggestions and advice of others have contributed much toward the completion of this study, especially D. G. Mandelbaum, J. L. Fisher, T. Ktsanes, and L. Reissman. I am indebted to Phyllis Breed for her thorough handling of the stenographic work.

In transliterating Marāṭhi words I have, by and large, followed common usage in the area studied rather than literary standards. With some exceptions, the guide used was Bulletin 31 of the Library of Congress Cataloging Service. However, I have rendered the "sh" as "ś" or, if retroflex, as "ṣ." Nasalization of a vowel is indicated by a succeeding "ṅ." All final "i"s in the Marāṭhi words in this book are long, hence I have omitted the diacritic, "ī." I have used English pluralization for Indian words.

Common place names are rendered in popular form; for example, "Poona," rather than "Pūṇe." Some names of organizations are given as pronounced by villagers, in which case I have used the regular system of transliteration; however, where printed anglicized forms of organization names were readily available to me, I have employed them. The fictitious name of the village, "Gaon," means "village" in Marāṭhi; the spelling here used is derived from that generally found on maps. It is pronounced in a manner similar to the English word "gown."

 Contents

 Illustrations

MAPS

PLATES   *following page 36*

View of the village from the east

The main street in the village, facing north

Women winnowing grain on the ruins of houses

Wrestling matches held during the village fair

Rajput women carrying household deities to the village Goldsmith, who will clean them in preparation for a wedding

Creditor and debtor. An Untouchable beggar and a Brahman donor

Rope Makers at work

Inside a Scavenger house, with a cradle in the foreground. The hut is about ten by fifteen feet

A Brahman kitchen. A Brahman professional cook from Mot prepares food for a feast

Bāil Polā. A procession of bullocks in front of the Hanumān temple

"They won't eat!" A Temple Priest wedding; the couple are too emotionally upset to take part in the feast

Village Potter at work in his courtyard

Part I · Introduction

Introduction

IN THE religious literature of traditional India the village is relatively infrequently mentioned. For example, the sacred laws of Hinduism, the Dharmaśāstras, include many statements on kinship and the family, on the ideal stages of life through which the individual should pass, and, perhaps most of all, on the four *varṇas*, the theoretical origin of all castes. When the village is discussed, it is incidental to rulings on these and other subjects. A similar note is struck in some scholars' conceptions of the actualities of Indian social structure; society is taken to be organized almost solely about kinship and caste, especially caste. Emile Senart, for example, has characterized India as "an immense complexity of mobile organisms," thus relegating the territorial bond to the background.[1] More recently Dumont and Pocock have suggested that "the territorial factor, the relation to the soil is not, in India as a whole, one of the primary factors in social organization. It is a secondary factor in relation to the two fundamental factors of kinship and caste." According to these authors, the village does not possess "sociological reality"; it is an "architectural and demographic" fact rather than a datum of social structure.[2] Others whose concerns have been somewhat differently focused have come to conclusions that have much the same implications. They deny the significance of social solidarity in the village. The model of the Indian village is held properly to be "exploitative"; it is conceived as

[1] Emile Senart, *Caste in India*, E. D. Ross, transl., London, 1930, pp. 16–17.

[2] Louis Dumont and D. Pocock, *Contributions to Indian Sociology*, No. 1, Paris, 1957, pp. 18, 26.

comprising a network of interaction among castes wherein conflict is rife and wherein one group dominates others through
superiority in wealth and numbers. These writers often emphasize class, in the sense of the relationship of a group to the
means of production, which in village India poses the landed
against the landless.[3] What village unity exists is allegedly a
product of "coercive integration."[4] To the extent, then, that
any system is thought to obtain in the Indian village, it is,
according to this perspective, a political rather than a social
system.

There is, however, another perspective. In a number of
studies the data and/or analyses have suggested that the
village does have "sociological reality." All accept the importance of the caste system, but some of the analyses, setting
aside the divisive potentialities of the separate and solidary
castes, have stressed the complementary nature of their differences. Wiser's early analysis of jajmānī, the traditional
economy found in many Indian villages, perhaps overempha-
sized the harmony of caste interaction.[5] Other, more recent
studies, while not going so far as Wiser's, have, however, indicated that the village does have social unity.[6] Yet none de-
nies the existence of coercion or conflict. Evidence and analy-

---

[3] When the term "class" is used in this book, it is to be understood in
this sense. The usage is obviously derived from Marxian thought, although its application to rural life in this manner is not entirely consistent with Marx.

[4] Oscar Lewis and V. Barnouw, "Caste and the *Jajmani* System in a
North Indian Village," in *Village Life in Northern India,* by O. Lewis,
Urbana, 1958, pp. 55–84; Thomas O. Beidelman, *A Comparative
Analysis of the Jajmani System* (Monographs of the Association for
Asian Studies, VIII), Locust Valley, 1959.

[5] William H. Wiser, *The Hindu Jajmani System,* Lucknow, 1936.

[6] E.g., see Morris Opler and Rudra D. Singh, "The Division of Labor
in an Indian Village," in *A Reader in General Anthropology,* Carleton
S. Coon, ed., New York, 1948, pp. 464–496; Harold Gould, "The
Hindu Jajmani System: A Case of Economic Particularism," *Southwestern Journal of Anthropology,* Vol. 14, No. 4, pp. 428–437.

ses, in some instances presented by the same scholars, show
that the village is socially integrated *and* that power and conflict are fundamental in village life. For example, Srinivas has
demonstrated the relevance of the "dominant caste" in the
Indian village, and in a different publication has shown that
the village exhibited general solidarity.[7]

It will be one of the main purposes of this study to show
that solidarity obtains in the Indian village and to demonstrate
the relationship between it and the potentially centrifugal factors of caste, conflict, and power. Those who have emphasized village cohesion have noted the link between it and
caste interaction, a matter which will be further explored here.
But conflict and coercion, admittedly extant, have not up to
this time been related to village cohesion; hence this relationship will be given particular attention.

Many Indian villages are presently in a state of rapid
social change, in the course of which their social identity has
been attenuated (although probably not, in most cases, completely destroyed). The second purpose of this study will be to
investigate the manner in which social change has affected the
village tie, how conflict, inequality in power, and caste interaction have shifted with the weakening of village cohesion.

The data employed in the subsequent analysis were collected over 1954–1955 and in the summer of 1961 in a village
of 1554 people—265 households—which I call by the fictitious name of "Gaon." The village lay in the Marāṭhi-speaking
part of the deccan (or plateau) region of India, in Poona District, about one mile from a market town, which I will refer
to as "Mot." In 1954–1955 Poona District was a part of the

[7] M. N. Srinivas, "The Social System of a Mysore Village," in *Village
India, Studies in the Little Community,* M. Marriott, ed., Chicago,
1955, pp. 1–35; "The Dominant Caste in Rampura," *American Anthropologist,* Vol. 61, No. 1, 1959, pp. 1–16.

larger administrative division of Bombay State. By 1961 most of Bombay had been partitioned into Gujarat and Maharashtra, the latter containing Poona District.

The village, like many others in India, was changing rapidly. The conditions described in Part II pertain to traditional village organization, which was more fully manifested earlier in the century. This organization was still largely intact in 1954, so most of the particulars were gathered by direct observation as well as through informants, although my description of some features is based upon the latter source only. The changes will be discussed separately in Part III. I need hardly mention that the term "traditional" does not signify immobility; change had, no doubt, always been taking place. However, there is a system of mutual expectations and culturally prescribed activities persisting through change—changing, at times, itself, but usually slowly. This is what we will find most instructive for our purposes, both for the consideration of cohesion and as a base-line for the assessment of change.

The question of the representativeness of the village deserves brief mention. Clearly there are some Indian communities completely different from Gaon. A few have but one caste, while Gaon had twenty-four in 1954 and seventeen in the recent past. Some villages have little or nothing of the traditional economic system called "bālutā" in this area, "jajmānī" in northern India. But Gaon is not peculiar. For example, in a survey of 151 villages, it was found that most held from about five to a little over twenty castes.[8] Most multi-caste villages have an economic system similar to bālutā in many respects. The conclusions drawn from this study will

[8] McKim Marriott, *Caste Ranking and Community Structure in Five Regions of India and Pakistan* (Deccan College Monograph Series: 23), Poona, 1960, pp. 22–23.

be applicable to few, if any, other villages in all of their details. But I believe the general position taken here will hold for a good many Indian communities.

The analysis that follows was undertaken from a particular theoretical position, which should, I think, be discussed before getting to the details. I emphasize the problem of the relationship between inequality as expressed in interpersonal domination, conflict, and social solidarity. My observations are based upon the findings of a number of theorists, most notably, among earlier writers, Simmel, Durkheim, and Tönnies, and among recent ones, T. H. Marshall, Alvin Gouldner, and Max Gluckman.[9] But my remarks are not intended to represent a complete theory, only an outline in broad perspective of the theoretical background to the subsequent empirical matter.

We can distinguish, first of all, between different forms of domination and then later attempt to relate these differences to the more general systems of cooperation and conflict of which they are a part.

Domination differs from society to society in many details, but I contend that among the most significant ways in which it may vary is the extent to which it is "socialized." In purely social domination inferiors are valued *as persons* by superiors, and coercion is not of primary importance in the

[9] Georg Simmel, *The Sociology of Georg Simmel,* K. Wolff, transl. and ed., Glencoe, 1950; *Conflict and the Web of Group Affiliations,* K. Wolff and R. Bendix, transls., Glencoe, 1955; Emile Durkheim, *The Division of Labor in Society,* G. Simpson, transl., Glencoe, 1947; Ferdinand Tönnies, *Fundamental Concepts of Sociology,* C. Loomis, transl., New York, 1940; T. H. Marshall, "The Nature of Class Conflict," in *Class, Status, and Power,* Reinhard Bendix and Seymour M. Lipset, eds., Glencoe, 1953; Alvin Gouldner, "The Norm of Reciprocity: A Preliminary Statement," *American Sociological Review,* Vol. 25, No. 2, 1960, pp. 161–178; Max Gluckman, *Custom and Conflict in Africa,* Glencoe, 1955.

relationship between the parties. In social, as contrasted with what we may call purely political, domination, one needs the inferior in order to define oneself as superior—not merely to extract from him the products of his labor, which will be used without reference to him. Social domination exists wherever there is symbolic wealth display; there would be no point to the display without an audience—an audience that matters to the actor, and one to whom he assumes he matters. The continuation of the practice presumes mutual identification. More important, social domination often takes the form of a social "debtor-creditor" relationship. By giving to others more than one gets from them, or rather by sharing a belief that this is the case, one becomes their creditor. The recipient is indebted to the dominant party, and the latter thereby creates dependence upon himself. But the creditor needs his debtor as a person; it would be pointless to have oneself defined as creditor to an irrelevancy. The inferior, by agreeing to the asymmetrical exchange, accepts the role of debtor and, therefore, the enhanced significance of the superior. Dominance and submission in this context are thus social phenomena.[10]

I have used the adjective "political" to indicate a condition opposed to social domination. This kind of domination exists when the superior party is indifferent to the inferior, where the latter is merely a means. Under such circumstances regular interaction will be primarily a product of the exercise of power. A well-known severe example of this is economic ex-

---

[10] It makes little difference if the products or services are in fact produced by the dominated, so long as the latter does not believe that they are "really his." If he does, we have a fundamental disagreement over the terms of the relationship and hence an extreme case of purely political interaction. However, this is not relevant for the data to be analyzed here.

I might mention that the creditor-debtor idea probably underlies competitive gift-giving between near equals, which is common in societies throughout the world.

ploitation in the recent past in the West, where the dominator used the dominated as a means of producing goods and, indifferent to his reaction, gave him less than was received from him. There are other conditions, equally extreme, in which political domination is manifested more obliquely, as for example in race relations in the American South, where one group is obliged through coercion, direct or indirect, to maintain an appearance of debt and dependency. (Because conditions like this are largely political in character but give the appearance of being social, one might, following a similar treatment of the *gemeinschaft* concept, refer to them as examples of "pseudo-social domination.") In these cases political domination is extreme; more frequently it is milder, as, for example, in most employer-employee relations in modern, large-scale industries.

It is apparent that when domination obtains in complex societies, where there is generally a preponderance of secondary relations, it will usually be more political than in simpler societies, where primary relations are more significant. However, this is not invariable, as can be seen, for example, in the existence of political domination in Northwest Coast Amerinds' quasi-slavery and of social domination in some of the elaborate states of aboriginal Africa.[11]

I would emphasize that the existence of social domination does not signify complete absence of the use or threat of force. Power exists in all groups, even relatively egalitarian ones. There is deviation from rules; the possibility of this, if not its actuality, is always present. Hence some form of force will

[11] On the Northwest Coast, see Philip Drucker, "Rank, Wealth, and Kinship in Northwest Coast Society," *American Anthropologist,* Vol. 41, No. 1, 1939, pp. 55–56. For good examples of social domination in African states, see Jaques J. Maquet, *The Premise of Inequality in Ruanda,* London, 1961, pp. 118, 121, 129–135; and E. J. and J. D. Krige, *The Realm of the Rain Queen,* London, 1943, chap. x.

be employed or threatened, overtly or covertly. However, force is not the primary factor in inducing regular interaction except where political domination is approached. Similarly, political domination is not usually pure. It is rare to find persistently interacting parties in which one is held in subordination entirely through naked force and used with complete indifference by the superordinate.[12]

Domination is obviously only a part of a larger system of cooperation and conflict. We might anticipate, then, that the two kinds of domination will be related to different forms of cooperation and conflict. In this connection I find T. H. Marshall's typology of conflict to be useful, especially when considered alongside Durkheim's treatment of social relations. Marshall classifies conflict situations as follows: 1) competition, wherein individuals conflict because they have the same goals and similar means of obtaining them; 2) bargaining, which is conflict over a share of the whole, where the means differ among the parties, but where they share a stake in the maintenance of the system; 3) conflict proper (which I will call "strife"), where there is fundamental disagreement over the rules that regulate interaction.[13] Marshall's first two types clearly parallel Durkheim's mechanical and organic solidarity.

[12] Although the polar concepts I propose are in part based on Tönnies' work, I would not hold with him that "a young man is warned against bad Gesellschaft (society), but the expression bad Gemeinschaft (community) violates the meaning of the word." (*Fundamental Concepts* . . . , p. 38) My personal moral preference is to avoid extremes of either type of domination, but of course this is beside the point. Morality in this sense is not involved in the typology. Except in extreme political domination, there is no necessary rejection of one or the other form of domination even by the participants. From their perspective the interaction should, of course, conform to prevailing ethical standards. Moreover, I conjecture that each kind of domination has in the eyes of the parties involved its own "virtue"; virtuous political domination is, perhaps, impartial and legal, virtuous social domination paternalistic.

[13] Marshall, "The Nature of Class Conflict," pp. 82–83.

They are to be associated with what we here term social domination. The third type, strife, calls to mind political domination, Durkheim's "forced division of labor."

Wherever domination closely approaches the political pole, given the opportunity, there is likely to be open strife between the "legally" powerful and the weak, out-and-out conflict having at stake the very system of rules by which the groups interact. This is basically asocial conflict; in its extreme form it is class war in the Marxian sense. Conflict, however, is not a necessary outcome of political domination. Where a power monopoly exists in fact as well as in law, there will be no alternative for the powerless other than passive obedience. These are not social relationships, properly speaking, but political ones. Solidarity can exist where relationships are political. If they are markedly political, solidarity may still exist within each of the groups involved; if mildly so, there may be, in addition, a looser, vaguer solidarity extending beyond the parties concerned, as in nationalism. Hence the individuals involved in political relationships are not necessarily anomic.[14] But if the political relationship is extreme, it follows from the definition that the parties involved will not identify with one another.

Social relationships, whether of domination or equality, usually involve mutual identification, solidarity. This does not preclude conflict; and conflict, if not too severe, may in turn help provide conditions in which solidarity can prevail. It seems likely that a complete, long-term absence of conflict is either a sign of apathy, the very negation of solidarity, or of the transcendence of political over all other relationships, producing

[14] I believe that an essential determinant of the emotional condition of anomy is the absence or enfeeblement of group ties. There must be some internalized norms, of course; but a bond to a group and acceptance of its laws, although these are not even wholly known, let alone internalized, also lessens the anomic emotional state.

the passive obedience of the utterly powerless. Wherever we find a cohesive group, we will usually find conflict, although it will take place within the rules governing interaction rather than over the existence of the rules themselves.

"Likeness of mind" is essential to cohesion; it produces "mechanical solidarity." Yet Durkheim, who was only parenthetically concerned with conflict, has pointed out that the very fact of similarity generates competition.[15] People who are similar to one another in status and have much the same goals assess their attainments against one another; hence they are prone to rivalry, especially if they interact frequently. Where interaction is less frequent, conflict is less likely, but even here, so long as approximate equality exists, an allegation of inferiority is likely to result in hostility. Thus, within cohesive groups one sometimes finds individual pitted against individual; or "partnerships" are formed, whereby the group is, in some contexts at least, fragmented into smaller units.

Social domination may lessen competition. Another form of alliance found with mechanical solidarity, more frequent, I believe, than that between "partners," contains clearly ranked individuals or groups. People may share means and ends, yet differ in relative position. Where two parties in the same social group are very different in wealth or power, the poorer, weaker one may accept a submissive role, assuming rivalry to be futile, an assumption most likely to be made if he derives benefits from the stronger. He thus accepts a position of social debtor. Rank differences between parties in a solidary group may be culturally prescribed. For example, the statuses of father and son usually involve little conflict so long as rapid culture change does not produce differences of interest between generations. A father was once a son, and a son can see himself as a father, if he is not already one; thus,

---

[15] Durkheim, *The Division of Labor . . .* , pp. 266–268, 365.

identification is present, while the difference in rank discourages competition.

Conditions differ where a division of labor, "organic solidarity," is of much importance. As has been pointed out by many writers, complementary interaction and hence general solidarity frequently result from differences among groups, each of which contains its own solidarity. But, apart from the division of labor by sex, I believe organic solidarity is less firm than mechanical. It is probable that conflict among groups is a greater threat to the system of interaction when each group is itself solidary.[16] However, so long as the conflict is no more than bargaining, so long as it takes place within rules rather than over their existence, it is unlikely to damage the system.

Of course, one must have some mechanical solidarity embracing the whole, some similarity of mind, at least tacitly recognized as such, in order to give the mutual trust necessary for transactions among the groups. If transactions take place within a social context, they must follow persistent rules, but the rules rarely determine all of the details of interaction. There are usually interstices between the rules and there are vaguely defined concepts within them. There are often delays between the provision of goods or services and the remuneration. Hence each party must presume the other to be trustworthy. The persistence of the exchanges in a manner satisfactory, in the long run, to those involved gives evidence of the rightness of the presumption and thus strengthens the social bond.[17] Again, it should be observed that the threat or fear of force, implied or openly stated, helps maintain the rules against the possibility of frequent deviation; but where social rather

[16] This is not Durkheim's position. See *The Division of Labor* . . . , pp. 148–152.

[17] This closely follows Gouldner, "The Norm of Reciprocity . . . ," pp. 174–176.

than political relations prevail, this is not the predominant factor.

The solidarity of each different group involved in a division of labor may threaten the integrity of the whole, but there are a number of mitigating factors. One of these is competition; conflict within the parts often fragments them, thus lessening the likelihood that they will be posed against one another as unified groups. Moreover, because there are fewer similarities among groups in a division of labor than exist within each group, one not infrequently finds that allies are sought in groups other than one's own, in order the better to compete with members of one's own group.

Rank is another factor that may lessen conflict among groups in a division of labor, so long as a complete power monopoly is not involved. Where groups are ranked relative to one another, and where they accept their positions, competition is precluded by definition. The more undefined rank is, the less stable the system is likely to be. This is not invariable. There are ways in which ambiguity of rank may be handled, one of which is, as we shall see, to maintain aloofness regarding rank, to avoid the issue. But wherever one solidary group approaches another in status in an unequivocal manner, as for example when there is social mobility, especially where the groups are similar to one another, we have the same potentiality for conflict that obtains in mechanical solidarity.

While ranking can and sometimes does maintain socially cohesive and conflict-free relationships among different solidary groups, it may have a contrary effect. Because each group is cohesive, identification across group lines is feebler, hence severe political domination and strife can occur. If power is held by individuals in different groups, extreme political domination is unlikely, for differences in group membership act against the formation of a unified power bloc. But when any one group holds a monopoly or near monopoly on power, the social character of the relationship between groups is endangered. The danger is greatest when the dominators and dominated are very widely separated in rank, and especially where their subcultures differ in what are considered important respects. Identification is then often weakened. Symbolic wealth display, for example, may become but a feeble gesture toward the lowest groups, intended primarily for those not so distant in rank. The debtor-creditor relationship may be conceived as so unbalanced and the debtor so dependent, that the latter loses some of his value as a debtor, and he may respond, in turn, with resentment. If these conditions are extreme, there is as likely to be the mere appearance as the reality of social domination. In any event, some disaffection is probable.

It is in this area that the political aspects of group life are likely to be most important. But it is here, too, that conflict, not only among groups but also within them, may play a highly significant role. Domination itself may give conditions that help to socialize domination, for the highest group will often be most prone to rivalry. The group as a whole often claims dominance, but the particular individuals in it who are actually to exercise dominance are not always clearly designated. Hence it is not unusual to find that this group more than any other is rent into subdivisions, each competing with others or resenting them because bested in competition. Due to such intragroup conflict, the rights of the lowest groups are not necessarily threatened with extinction by unified action of the dominant. Moreover, because of the competition, the dominant group is likely to seek outside allies, and these will probably be sought among people least threatening to them, who are often in the lower part of the social scale. In such circumstances the lower group cannot be viewed with complete indifference. Furthermore, when they are sought as allies, their rights within the system will be given additional protection. So long as their rights are upheld, they will probably feel they have a stake in the system. So long as the parties accept the terms of the relationship, and so long as the ideas of debt and dependency exist, mutual identification persists. Solidarity must not be conceived as present or absent, but as manifested to different degrees in different parts of a society.

It is evident from the observations thus far made that interpersonal relations, from this perspective, are not always primarily social in character. They may be, as has been suggested, political. There are other relations, not important from our view, that are almost solely economic, for example "silent trade." [18] From the perspective of this study, one of the most important conditions in which the social bond is attenuated is that of rapid culture change. The rules of interaction and, at times, the social boundaries of the interacting groups themselves are weakening, sometimes being replaced by other rules and new social groups, sometimes not. Under these conditions anomy and/or strife are to be anticipated. Some of those who benefited from the old rules may resist their decline; others may go along or prefer that the rules be changed; hence interpersonal conflict or hostility is not infrequently forthcoming. If all or most of the old norms and ties are attenuated, anomy is the outcome. But rapid social change need not lead to anomy. However rapid the change may be, rules usually do not all change at the same rate; the individual is not necessarily normless, because some of his ties can remain firm, and because new ties to groups, involving new rules, can meanwhile replace the old ones.

[18] See Melville J. Herskovits, *Man and His Works,* New York, 1950, p. 276.

 2

The Village

GAON was situated in Poona District not very far from Poona city. To get to the village from the city required a train ride of about four and one-half hours. An alternative way, slightly shorter, was by bus, but the ride was very rough and, in the dry season, dusty. Both means of transportation took one only as far as Mot; from there one walked or took a tonga. The road from Mot to Gaon was poor, badly rutted and dusty in the dry season and muddy during the rains. During most of the year it was necessary to ford a stream that crossed the road near the village.

The climate of Poona District has been characterized as "continental." Like much of the plateau region of Maharashtra, it is neither so hot nor so humid as the coastal area. There are marked diurnal and seasonal variations in climate. Mean diurnal variation in temperature for all months is from 64.4° F. to 89.4° F. The "cold season" extends from November to February, the "hot season" from March to May, and the "wet season" from June to October. The mean temperature is lowest in December, when the monthly mean variation is from 46.1° F. to 88.8° F. May is the hottest month; the mean monthly variation is from 66.4° F. to 105.7° F. The main supply of rain is from the southwest monsoon, which usually strikes Poona District in mid-June and lasts until the end of October. Yearly average rainfall for the district as a whole is about 35″, usually between 20″ and 25″ for the area around Gaon.[1]

[1] *Gazetteer of Bombay State* (rev. ed.), Vol. xx, *Poona District,* Bombay, 1954, pp. 11–14.

The district of Poona was at the time of this study divided into four parts called *prānts*. One of these was the municipality of Poona. The remainder was further subdivided into administrative areas usually called *tālukās*. There were twelve *tālukās* in the district plus one other administrative unit called a *mahāl*. The *tālukā* in which Gaon was found was named after Mot, its main market town. The most important single government official on the district level was the collector; he had numerous functions, which included supervising tax collection, acting as chief magistrate, and performing quasi-judicial duties. Under him were *prānt* officers, sometimes called assistant collectors, and *māmlatdārs,* in charge of *tālukās*. These exercised within their areas all the powers delegated to them by the collector.[2]

Administratively the name "Gaon" was applied to two separate units, Gaon proper and an offshoot a few miles away, which I call "Vādi." Although Vādi had originally been formed by residents of Gaon, it was the larger community; in 1954 it had about 340 registered landowners against Gaon's 242.[3] The formation of Vādi probably dates back to the earlier part of the nineteenth century. In the 1881 land records, the earliest available in 1954, there are recorded sixty-eight landowners from Gaon and about eighty from Vādi. In the land records, voters' lists, and other official documents, the two communities were merged. The records were kept in Gaon, and residents of Vādi paid taxes to the accountant in

[2] For details on the administration, see *Gazetteer of Bombay State* (rev. ed.), Vol. xx, chap. 13.

[3] Because land records for the two communities were combined, informants were used to distinguish residents of Vādi from absentee landowners. By and large my census data were sufficient to identify Gaon residents, but villagers' assistance was needed in some instances, for example, where "paper" divisions had taken place. Some names, probably mostly absentee landowners, could not be identified by informants.

Gaon. Officials dealing with the village did so with the two communities jointly. In theory this included the village headmen, who were from Gaon proper. However, the headmen rarely visited Vādi. At one time Gaon and Vādi had probably been socially more closely knit; signs of this were still present in 1954. For example, some of Gaon's service castes, in allocating work among their subdivisions, "gave" Vādi to one subdivision, Gaon or a part of Gaon to another. However, this kind of allocation occurred in this area even between two administratively distinct villages when one of them lacked an appropriate service caste. Vādi held its own village ceremonies in 1954, and its members had no more to do with Gaon than with other contiguous villages, apart from their business with the village accountant. Socially it was a separate community, and this study did not include it.

The houses of Gaon varied much in size. Quite a few had but one room, often no more than about twenty by twenty feet; they were sometimes built in rows, sharing walls, but having separate entrances and occupied by different families. A majority of these very small houses were situated east of the main village street, where Untouchables lived. However, most houses in the village had two or three rooms, and some had four or more. The largest houses were built around courtyards, where cattle were kept at night. A few were of two stories. A striking characteristic of the village was that a number of houses, particularly the larger ones, were deserted, for many of the people had left the main settlement and built new homes near their farms. In many of the deserted houses, a number of the stones that made up the walls had fallen out, for the stones were held together by mud and required continuous attention if they were to remain in place. Some of the houses had become mere rubbish heaps, and some showed great gaping holes in their walls. From some approaches Gaon looked rather like a ghost town. Map I conveys the extent of the ruins.[4]

Only a heap of stones remained of what was once the *cāvdi* (a building which housed offices for the village headmen and accountant). In 1954 these offices were situated in two different, privately owned buildings.

There were six important temples in the village. One of these was the Mariai temple, dedicated to the smallpox goddess, and situated in the Untouchable quarters. Near the center of the village was a temple devoted to Viṭhobā, an *avatār* of Viṣṇu, and at its edge was the temple of Hanumān, or Māruti, the "monkey-god." Just outside of what was once the main gate, north of the village, were two temples, one devoted to Śiva and the other to the goddess Bhavāni Devi. The remaining important temple, housing the god Datta, was situated in the fields of Gaon, about a mile from the main settlement. Scattered throughout the area of the main settlement were many shrines and small "temples"—some consisting of stones daubed with red coloring, one being a circle of white-painted stones around a larger carved one, and others statuettes of gods in tiny "houses" of their own.

There were two schools in the main settlement and one a few miles away in the fields for the convenience of those who lived at some distance. The schools were for grades one to six only. For higher grades, children went to schools in Mot.

The main settlement contained three very small shops, sell-

[4] Neither this map nor that of the village castes (Map II) indicates the number of households in the main settlement. The units in the maps were defined by reference to the existence of separate entrances, which do not correspond to households. In some cases one family used two separate houses. These two maps are based upon the work of two engineering students from a college in Poona. They are fairly accurate but not precise.

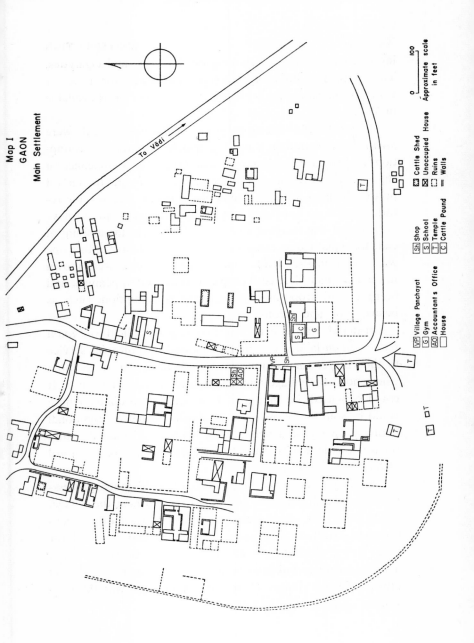

Map I
GAON
Main Settlement

To Vādi

0   100
Approximate scale
in feet

VP Village Panchayat   Sh Shop
G Gym   S School
AO Accountant's Office   T Temple
   House   C Cattle Pound

⊠ Cattle Shed
⊠ Unoccupied House
⊠ Ruins
= Walls

ing items such as soap, cooking oil, matches, and cigarettes. They were used only for emergency purchases, for a greater variety of merchandise at slightly cheaper prices was available in Mot.

The most important crops grown in the village fields were *javari* ("Indian millet"), used primarily for home consumption, and sugar cane, largely a cash crop. The significance of sugar cane had recently been increased, but by far the largest part of the land was still given over to *javari*. Because the return from sugar cane was very high, much more would have been grown, but the government strictly limited the amount of cane to be planted on canal-irrigated land, and most of the cane was grown on such land. Numerous other crops were grown in smaller quantities: cash crops, such as cotton, peanuts, and oranges; and crops mostly for home consumption, such as beans, okra, and onions.

Farmland was either owned outright or held on *īnām* tenure. *Īnām* land was generally allotted in return for service to the village, for example, to village headmen or to those who tended the village temples. No taxes were paid on it. It could be leased, but not sold. Land held on ordinary tenure could be sold, but most looked upon their land as traditional family property, and hence were loath to alienate it. More often it was leased, and the lessor took one-half or one-third of the crop.

Only sugar cane, rice, and wheat required much processing. Rice was brought for polishing to a mill near the village. Sugar cane and wheat were put through diesel or bullock-operated crushers. The same machines could be used for both crops, since they were harvested at different times. There were three bullock-operated crushers and seven diesel crushers in the village. Their primary purpose was the conversion of sugar cane into raw sugar.

Aside from the conversion of sugar cane into raw sugar, village production was on a very small scale and largely, although not solely, associated with traditional caste occupations. There were, for example, iron work, carpentry, gold and silver work, leather work, and rope making. Tools and equipment were simple. The carpenters' tools, hammers, chisels, axes, and so on, were made of untempered steel, which quickly dulled with use. The equipment in iron work consisted of sledges and a hand-operated bellows. Only simple items were manufactured, such as cartwheel rims and harrow blades, not complex items, such as plows. This was the state of things with all village craftsmen.

Some villagers performed services for others, for example, as barbers, water carriers, and butchers. Religious services were performed by village Brāhmaṇs, who acted as family priests; by members of another caste, Guravs, who cared for most of the temples in the main settlement; and by a celibate priest, called *"gosāvi,"* who served in the Datta temple on the farms of Gaon.

Almost all of those who provided goods or services for others also did agriculture, either on their own or on others' lands, and most were primarily dependent upon agriculture for subsistence.

Most of the goods and services available in the community were dispensed to others in return for a portion of their crops rather than for cash. Such exchanges were governed by custom; most service castes were incorporated into the traditional system of economics called the *balutā* system. The details of the system will be discussed later; for the present it should be mentioned that one of its effects was to produce a tendency toward village self-sufficiency, toward isolation from outside forces.

But the village had never been completely isolated. Caste

organization, for example, extended well beyond its borders. Every year a travelling holy man customarily stopped for a day in the village. Some of the more religious residents went on pilgrimages to holy places, especially to Pandharpur. Practically all villagers did much travelling in the general area of Gaon. The most important occasions for travel were weddings and village fairs. People often travelled considerable distances to attend the wedding of a relative. Fairs were held once a year—usually on a religious holiday—by almost every village in the area, and they were attended by many outsiders, people in neighboring villages and kinsmen of village residents. The proximity of Mot was an obvious factor lessening isolation. Unlike many other villages of this region, Gaon did not hold a market day; instead, the villagers went once a week for market day in Mot. Traditional performances were held in Mot, and villagers not infrequently attended them. There were *tamāśās* held there—public entertainments for men— which involved singing and dancing, often somewhat bawdy. A *kīrtan* was held on occasion in Mot. The *kīrtan* was a performance usually presented in a large temple, where a *kīrtankār,* or preacher, gave religious lectures illustrated by stories and jokes and supported by a group of men doing *bhajan,* a type of religious singing. *Kīrtans* were popular with men and women. Government offices were present in Mot and, because so close to Gaon, more readily accessible to these than to most other villagers. Thus, outside factors had always impinged upon the village to some extent.

Within the remembered past the village had constantly been undergoing some change. Recently, however, it had been changing unusually rapidly. This was due to a number of innovations originating outside the community, especially by way of government agencies, and (also through govern-

ment) the introduction of an irrigation canal. These changes
will be discussed in more detail in Chapters 12 and 13, but,
in order to prepare for the ensuing discussion, we must attend
to some of them here.

One of the most important recent changes was in immigration. Outsiders had settled in Gaon in the distant past, but
there had been relatively few of them, and most were kinsmen
of long-standing residents. Recently immigration had greatly
increased, and many of the new residents were only loosely
incorporated into village society. These are best taken up
separately, when the subject of change is considered. However, village records are too incomplete to be used for this
purpose. I have employed generation. Each household head
was asked whether his father had been born in the village, and
the responses were checked with an informant who had been
village accountant about thirty years prior to the study.[5] If a
man's father had not been born in the village, I classified his
household as "new resident." All propositions concerning the
traditional village, including statistical information in Part II
of this book, refer only to old residents, except in Chapter 3
and in other places where specific exception is made.

Of the twenty-four castes in the village, seven contained
only new residents. I give their population and main traditional occupation in Table 1.

One caste of long standing in the village, the Bāgḍi, was
given little attention in the course of my study. They comprised eleven households, totalling fifty-eight people, all living
outside the main settlement. Although they had been based in
the community for a number of generations, the Bāgḍis were
customarily a wandering caste, having the traditional occu-

[5] Women sometimes returned to their natal homes for childbirth,
especially their first; hence further inquiry was necessary in some cases
on whether the respondent's father's father had been a resident of the
village at the time of his father's birth.

pations of cattle breeding and, especially, begging. Because
of their traditional tendency to wander and because they lived
at some distance from the main settlement, they were not considered by other villagers to be a part of the community. Unless specific mention is made of this group, it is not intended
to be included in any statement in this book, statistical or
otherwise.

TABLE 1

Population and Occupation of New-Resident Castes

CASTE	MAIN OCCUPATION	POPULATION	
		Households	*Persons*
Māli	gardener	7	38
Dhangar	shepherd	1	5
Bhoi	fisherman	2	5
Vadāri	earth worker	1	7
Ghadṣi	musician	1	1
Holār	musician	2	12
Māng Garuḍi	cattle breeder	2	7

Of the remaining sixteen castes, two were peripheral to
traditional village organization, the Marāṭhās and the Kaikādis. Kaikādis had originated in southern India, as will be
noted later, and, like the Bāgḍis, had been a wandering group
by custom. Some villagers referred to them as wanderers, and
they were only partly incorporated into the *bālutā* system. But,
unlike the Bāgḍis, some Kaikādis owned land in the village.
Furthermore, because they were situated almost within the
borders of the main settlement, they frequently interacted
with others and were generally considered to be of the community.

The Marāṭhās, apart from giving *bālutā* to service castes,
did not have any traditional role in the village. This was so,
villagers said, because they were not originally from Gaon.
However, everyone, including the Marāṭhās, asserted that

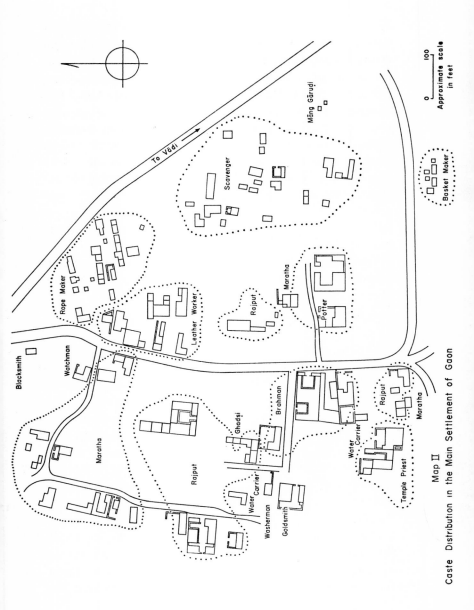

Map II

Caste Distribution in the Main Settlement of Gaon

they had lived in the community since the early nineteenth century. There is evidence that they had resided in the village for a long time. In the 1881 land records there are eleven Marāṭhā surnames listed, a total of sixteen landowners. Land, villagers said, was plentiful in the early nineteenth century, and a group of Marāṭhās, all of one surname, was allowed to settle on village lands outside the main settlement. Affinal kinsmen soon joined these, it was said, and yet more came later. In time, some moved into the main settlement. In any event, many members of the caste were, in 1954, well integrated into village life. They were thought of by others as fellow villagers. This caste, along with the Kaikādis, will be included in future discussion.

Excluding the Bāgdis, there were in Gaon 185 old-resident households, containing 1081 people. In Table 2 I give the

TABLE 2

Population and Occupation of Long-Standing Castes,
Old and New Residents

CASTE	MAIN OCCUPATION	OLD-RESIDENT POPULATION		NEW-RESIDENT POPULATION	
		Households	*Persons*	*Households*	*Persons*
Brāhmaṇ	family priest	5	27	1	4
Gurav	temple priest	4	22	—	—
Marāṭhā	agriculturalist	48	312	26	176
Sonār	goldsmith	1	5	—	—
Kumbhār	potter	9	67	—	—
Sagar Rājpūt	agriculturalist	46	291	11	59
Koḷi	water carrier	2	7	—	—
Nhāvi	barber	1	4	1	7
Lohār	blacksmith	2	10	—	—
Muslim	butcher	2	6	5	34
Parīṭ	washerman	1	6	—	—
Rāmośi	watchman	2	10	1	3
Kaikādi	basket maker	3	12	1	5
Cāmbhār	leather worker	13	73	—	—
Mahār	scavenger	24	117	2	9
Māng	rope maker	22	112	5	43

main traditional occupations and the populations of the sixteen long-standing village castes, divided into old- and new-
resident groups.

These castes were represented in the village for as far back
in time as any villager could recall, and probably had been
there even earlier. It seems that in the past other representatives of some of the castes had appeared in the village from
time to time and then left or died out. For example, it was
said that a Māli woman had once come to the village and then
died, leaving no descendants. The Mālis of 1954 were unrelated to her. The castes given in Table 2 were the stable traditional castes of the community.

In the future, I will refer to long-standing village castes,
other than the Brāhmaṇ, Marāṭhā, Rājpūt, and Muslim, not
by their regular names, but by their main traditional occupations, with initial letters capitalized to signify that the caste
name is intended. Diacritics will be omitted when referring to
Rajputs, Marathas, and Brahmans.

Another recent change that should be mentioned at this
point was a heightened tendency for people to live outside the
main settlement, close by their farms. Again, this had been
done to some extent in the distant past. But it was not frequent. At one time Gaon and other villages in this area had
walls and gates; the remains of the former were still visible in
1954. By 1954 a majority of villagers lived outside the main
settlement. Including both old and new residents, but excluding Bāgḍis, there were 140 households, totalling 934 people,
living on farms. Eighty-eight of these households, containing
596 people, were old residents.

When people settled on farms, they often built their houses
near one another, hence many of the houses formed clusters.
Five of the clusters had assumed sufficient social identity to
have been called by specific names. I will refer to these as

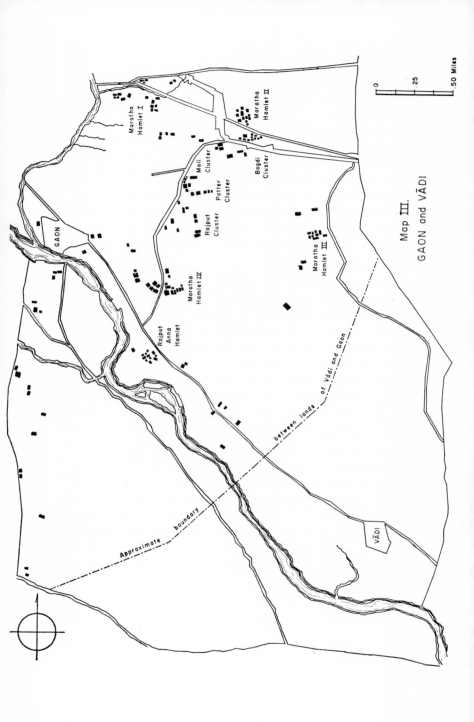

Map III.
GAON and VĀDI

hamlets. The hamlets and clusters are depicted on the map of the lands of Gaon, Map III.[6] One of the hamlets was dominated by Rajputs. It will be designated as the Rajput hamlet or, for reasons to be given later, the Anna hamlet. Four were dominated by Marathas and will here be referred to as Maratha hamlets, with the addition of Roman numerals for specific reference. Maratha hamlets I, II, and III had originally been settled by immigrants, but hamlets I and II had a long history in the village. Villagers asserted that the original Maratha immigrants had settled in the area of hamlet I and that hamlet II was settled soon after that. Hamlet I consisted of ten households of old residents and six of new ones, and hamlet II comprised seven old-resident households, five new. These hamlets were reported to have been in the past as large as, or larger than in 1954. I will refer to them either by number or collectively as the original Maratha hamlets. Hamlet III contained six new-resident households and three old-resident households. It had a briefer history; according to residents of the hamlet, there had been but one household in its present location about thirty-five years ago. Hamlet IV was established by former residents of the main settlement. It contained twenty households, seven of which were new-resident groups. The Rajput hamlet, eleven households, one a household of new residents, was also settled originally by people from the main settlement. Maratha hamlet II contained only members of that caste. The Bāgḍis lived close by but had little to do with the Marathas. All other hamlets contained representatives of at least one caste other than the dominant one.

6 This map is based upon that used by the Revenue Department. Natural features are therefore accurately placed. Houses, however, are obviously disproportionately large, and they are placed approximately, by my own estimation, with the aid of villagers.

Part II · The Traditional Village

 3

The Family

THE family, as contemplated in all schools of Hindu law, is "joint," that is, a patrilocal extended family. It consists of two or more patrilineally related nuclear families living in one household, employing one hearth, and sharing property.[1] Males are co-owners of family property at birth. Women's legal rights to joint family property were somewhat obscure in Poona District, for two schools of law were followed there; however, both schools agreed that females might inherit under some conditions.[2] According to the Mitākṣara, the most important traditional legal work used in the district, men might demand partition of family property during the lifetime of their father, though this was qualified in customary law.[3]

The villagers' generalized conceptions and ideals concerning the family were similar to the legal and customary definitions. In villagers' ideals jointness was preferred for as long as possible, but in village norms, as generally in customary and traditional law, separation of the family was expected to take place at the death of the father.

[1] For a brief discussion of my definition of the joint family, see my article, "The Recent History of the Extended Family in India," *Social Problems*, Vol. 8, No. 4, 1961, pp. 343–344. A family usually, but not always, coincides with a household, i.e., those sharing one hearth. The household can include non-family members, such as servants, and some family members who may be temporarily absent, as for education or business.

[2] N. C. Aiyar, *Mayne's Treatise on Hindu Law and Usage* (11th ed.), revised by Sir V. R. Ayyar, Madras, 1950, pp. 48–49, 58, 600–630, 647–648.

[3] N. C. Aiyar, *Mayne's Treatise . . . ,* p. 520; Arthur Steele, *The Law and Custom of the Hindoo Castes Within the Dekhun Provinces Subject to the Presidency of Bombay, Chiefly Affecting Civil Suits,* London, 1868, pp. 55, 56, 216.

As in English, the terms used for the family were vague. The term *"ghar,"* best translated as "house," was probably most precise, but the word *"kūtumb"* was more frequently used. Strictly speaking, *"kūtumb"* does signify a proper joint family; it is thus that the villagers explained the term when explicit inquiry was made. However, it was used more broadly in ordinary speech. It was often applied to all those who might, *in theory,* live in one joint household, that is, to the *khari bhāuki* or its subdivisions (see Chapter 4). Less frequently it was applied to all close relatives.

The household was conceived to be a community of worship as well as a social and economic entity. Each household had associated with it a number of deities, intended to be worshipped twice a day by the household head. On important occasions he was assisted by his wife, who touched his hand at appropriate parts of the sacrifices, thus participating in the offerings.

All households had two main deities. These were the same throughout the village: Khaṇḍobā, a manifestation of Śiva; and Devi, a vaguely defined female deity. It was thought to be inauspicious to change these main deities; stories were told of men who had substituted another god for Khaṇḍobā and of the ill fortune that had befallen them as a result. But most households had in addition to the two main deities some representation of Bāḷ Kṛṣṇa, as well as a few other gods. The custom of having extra deities was universal, although it was optional in theory, and the additional gods themselves were, in most cases, not considered very important. I was able to discover no villager who knew the names of all the deities in his household. One of these extra deities could, however, take on particular significance in a kinship group. For example, the main *bhāuki* of Rajputs in the village took Datta as one of

PLATE I. The village from the east. Main street of the village, facing north. Women winnowing grain on the ruins of houses.

PLATE II. Wrestling at the village fair. Rajput women carrying household deities to be cleaned. Untouchable beggar and Brahman donor.

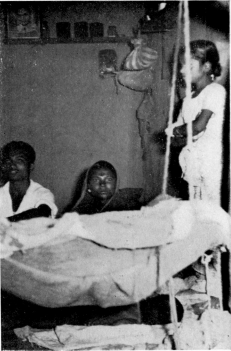

PLATE III. Rope Makers at work. Inside a Scavenger hut, cradle in fore-ground. Brahman professional cook from Mot preparing a feast.

PLATE IV. Bāil Poḷā; procession of bullocks. Temple Priest wedding feast; the couple too upset to eat. Village Potter at work.

their deities and held this god to be among their most important.

Statistically, the joint family was not the prevalent type. Most families were nuclear. There was only one case in which three generations of married men shared one hearth. In Table 3 I list families by type. The criterion employed for

TABLE 3

Incidence of Family Types

	Households	Population	% Households	% Population
Nuclear	174	828	56	56
Semi-Joint	47	308	19	21
Joint	37	360	13	24

distinguishing a family is the use of a common hearth. Nuclear families are so classed despite the presence of the household head's mother. In a number of cases a married man lived with his unmarried adult brothers. This gives the appearance of a "stem family" (wherein the norm requires all but one of a man's sons to set up separate households when they marry). I have called these "semi-joint," for, as we shall see, they were not true stem families. Joint families are classed as such where two or more married brothers shared the same hearth, where three generations of married men shared a hearth, or where men and their married brothers' sons did so. Length of residence in the village is not particularly relevant for family type, so I include all village residents except Bāgḍis in this table and in other tables and statements concerning the family.[4]

[4] There was a slightly higher proportion among new residents of brothers who had separated prior to the demise of their father. There were four of these among both new and old residents. However, there was also among new residents a slightly higher proportion of brothers who had continued joint after their father died, five cases of new residents as against seven of old.

These data make it appear that the norm for joint family living was weak. However, the raw statistical information in the table is misleading. Men often had no brothers, and many had but one married son or none whatever. Joint families are improbable in such cases. Moreover, customary and traditional law—unlike village ideals—did not prescribe that a joint family persist after the demise of the father.[5] Hence we must reconsider the data in terms of appropriate categories, omitting instances in which joint families are not to be expected.

The maintenance of a common hearth occurred in far the majority of instances in which a man had an only son who was married. Of a total of thirty-nine cases, only two lived separately. In one of these, the man's father was away tending commonly owned land in another village. In the other, the man's son was working in a lucrative business in Bombay, in which the man had part interest. Jointly owned land was involved in this instance too. These separations were simply for economic convenience.

Instances of married brothers are organized below in accordance with whether the father was living or dead. The figures refer to groups of two or more brothers. A group is counted as joint only if all members remained together. There were but three cases in which one married brother was separated from others living jointly, and in all three the father was living. Some families appear twice, for example, where a man was separated from his married brothers, but lived jointly with his married sons.

One case is not included in the table. Four married brothers lived jointly, but their father had moved to another village to look after commonly owned lands. Similarly, six of

---

[5] P. V. Kane, *History of Dharmaśāstra,* Poona, 1946, Vol. III, pp. 562–572,

TABLE 4

Incidence of Joint Living Among Married Brothers
by Decedence of Father

	1		2	
	FATHER	LIVING	FATHER	DECEASED
	a	b	a	b
	Non-Joint	*Joint*	*Non-Joint*	*Joint*
Number	8	15	64	12
Percentage of				
a and b	35	65	84	16

the eight cases in column 1a, where the norm for joint living
was violated, were matters of economic convenience. For
example, in one case two of three married brothers had left
their father, one for government work, the other to work as
an engineer in a Bombay factory. (By 1961 the former had
retired and returned to the village.) In another, a man's wife
had inherited land in Gaon, and he moved to the village to
look after it, leaving his father and three brothers, who lived
in a joint family at some distance. The remaining land of this
family was jointly owned. In the other four cases all family
property was owned in common. The separations were considered temporary, although permanent separate residences
had been established.

The two remaining instances were results of conflict. In
one of these the conflict was mild. There were four brothers,
three of whom lived jointly. Land was owned in common by
all four. One of the men estimated his father's age at 105.
This was probably an overestimate, but it was clear that the
father was exceptionally old, so aged that he was unable to
hear or speak properly. He was, in fact, so senile as to be no
longer a distinct personality. The other instance involved
more severe conflict. There were two brothers with different
mothers, and the men lived in separate residences with them,
one with the father.

There were two cases of joint families including men and
their married brothers' sons. These two and the twelve cases
in column 2b show that the ideal to remain joint after the
death of one's father influenced behavior to some extent. But
the ideal did not affect the majority. We may conclude that
men tended to live jointly so long as their father was alive,
but that, if married, they usually separated when he died.

There is reason to believe that such has been the pattern
of joint family living in this area and, indeed, in India as a
whole within the recent past. The average number of persons
per household in the rural areas of Poona District from 1921
to 1951 was as follows: [6]

1921	1931	1941	1951
4.7	4.8	4.2	5.5

I am uncertain of the significance of the increase in 1951—
possibly it was due to an expanding population with limited
housing—but it is clear that there is no evidence of a decrease
in family size. This is consistent with what is known of India
as a whole, as I have elsewhere shown.[7]

Ownership of the land could continue joint after a household partitioned, but in fact the land was usually divided
soon after partitioning. Of the sixty-four cases of separated
brothers whose father was deceased, forty-five owned land,
but only seven of these continued to own it jointly (nine in
law, but seven in fact). In two of the seven the land was rented
and the proceeds divided equally, and in the other five the
produce of the land was equally divided. The divisions were
made in this manner despite differences in the number of people in each household; thus the separate economic position of

[6] Census Commission of India, *Census of India, 1951,* New Delhi,
1953, Vol. IV, Pt. 1, p. 308.
[7] "The Recent History of the Extended Family in India." See note 1,
above.

every household was recognized. As soon as households divided, even if land was kept in common, additional sets of family deities were acquired, and the head of each new household assumed responsibility for their worship.

In village ideals, brothers should have remained joint after their father died, yet, as we have seen, they did so only infrequently. This makes little economic sense. Contrary to some opinions, jointness is not an ideal to which only the wealthy can attain. Partition of a family usually involves division of property, which is uneconomical. It can mean the fragmentation of land into small parcels, sometimes too small to be usefully farmed. Joint ownership of land allows for a division of labor and a pooling of resources which in a marginal economy such as this would be wholly to the advantage of the participants. It is true that where very little land is owned, it would be economically beneficial to transfer the whole to one brother and let the other seek work elsewhere. This occurred in some cases. But, in fact, when land was divided among brothers, they usually remained to work their separate plots, even if these were very small. When a man sold his land, as discussed below, he often avoided selling to his brother.

While economic considerations had some causal significance in the maintenance or partitioning of joint families, I do not believe that they formed the sole or crucial cause. It is probable that the maintenance of a joint family contributed to wealth. Where jointness was maintained, the possibilities for holding on to wealth were greater and also the possibilities, through pooling of resources, for investment and, hence, a further increase in wealth. Jointness thus probably enhanced economic position, not the other way around.

However, although jointness was economically beneficial to almost everyone, it was not so important for the destitute or near destitute; their capital wealth could not support even one nuclear family, so partition made little difference. Hence, where the norm was broken and brothers separated while their father was still living, we should expect to find a high incidence of partition among such people if wealth was a crucial factor. However, partitioning might also be expected to be fairly frequent among the well off, for the survival of such people was not threatened by it. If wealth was the main determinant of family type, one would expect to find joint-ness strongest in the middle groups, weakest at the extremes.

The body of data available to me, because largely limited to one village, is too small to allow a definite conclusion, but the general position taken here—that wealth is not the sole or crucial factor—is supported by it. In Table 5 I give family data by capital wealth.[8] As joint families share wealth, they would appear disproportionately wealthy if the family were used as the unit of analysis. Therefore, I give the data in terms of married brothers and of married men and their mar-ried nephews. I do not include cases of uncle-nephew separate residence, only those of co-residence. These are classed in the row entitled "Father Deceased, Joint." A group of brothers as such has not here been classified (as in Table 4) "joint" or "non-joint"; where one brother separated from two or more others, I have put them in the appropriate categories. In

---

[8] I do not intend capital wealth in the strictly technical, economic sense, but rather as referring to all productive or potentially productive wealth. This included land, animals, and sugar-cane crushers. These varied in price; I have used approximate average market values as of 1954–1955, rounded to the nearest five rupees. Dry land, irrigated land, and land on which sugar cane was grown were valued, respectively, at Rs 300, Rs 750, and Rs 1600 per acre. A bullock was priced at Rs 500, a buffalo at Rs 600, a cow at Rs 250. Donkeys cost about Rs 150, goats, calves, and sheep about Rs 50, and a buffalo calf Rs 75. A chicken, of which three or more were counted. cost Rs 2, a kid Rs 10. A diesel crusher was valued at Rs 10,000, a bullock crusher Rs 2000. Diesel pumps were not counted, for their value was realized in irrigated (as against dry) land.

some instances men had separated from their brothers and left the village. The non-residents are included in the table in the appropriate columns and rows. I do not have data on the wealth of men not from the village, and so have counted non-residents as having capital wealth equal to the average of that of their brothers living in the village. This introduces little distortion, for brothers were usually very similar in this regard. Where land was owned in common by a joint family or among separated brothers, whether or not village residents, I have averaged the total wealth. (If the wealth were divided, it would be allocated approximately equally.) As in Table 4, some families appear twice. The first two columns of Table 5 subsume the destitute or near destitute, those to whom partitioning or jointness was economically not very relevant. The last two columns include the well off, those who were not likely to suffer much economic hardship in the event of partition. The wealth intervals are not equal, but based upon what I believe are the most relevant lines of division between destitution, middle groups, and the well off.

TABLE 5

Joint Living by Decedence of Father and Wealth
(in 1000's of rupees)

| | DESTITUTE AND NEAR DESTITUTE | | MIDDLE GROUPS | | | WELL OFF | |
	1	2	3	4	5	6	7
	0–0.28	0.29–0.59	0.6–2.9	3.0–4.9	5–8.9	9–17.9	18 *and over*
Father Living, Non-Joint	4	0	2	4	2	4	0
Father Living, Joint	8	3	13	2	9	6	0
Father Deceased, Non-Joint	45	13	36	11	21	7	16
Father Deceased, Joint	2	2	11	6	2	5	2

The evidence is best seen where sons partitioned while their father was alive, thus breaking the norm, and where the ideal was upheld and brothers remained together after the demise of their father. In the first row, giving violations of the norm, we find that fifty per cent of the men fall in the middle brackets, where they would least be expected if wealth were crucial. In the fourth row, where the ideal is maintained, there is a high incidence of men, sixty-three per cent, in the middle groups, where they would be anticipated according to the economic hypothesis, but a considerable number in the destitute and well-off groups, thirteen and twenty-three per cent respectively, where they are less to be expected. Considering the data in another way, five per cent of those in columns one and two, the destitute, remained joint after their father had died, while sixteen per cent of the middle groups and eighteen per cent of the well off did so. Five per cent of the destitute separated while their father was alive, the same number as maintained the ideal standard of jointness. Seven per cent of the middle groups violated the norm, and ten per cent of the well off did so. I should not assert that economics was irrelevant. For example, in some cases the destitute separated in order to find work. The fact that a high percentage of well-off families kept to the ideal is probably due to the economic advantage of joint living; jointness probably contributed to wealth. However, it is evident that the economic factor is not the sole or crucial cause of jointness and partitioning.

Brothers did not usually remain together after the death of their father despite the economic advantage of joint land ownership. Men in Gaon insisted that the frequency of partitioning was motivated by quarrels among women. "Brothers know one another and can get along. Their wives are strangers and often fight." "A man may not notice if his older brother gives his [the brother's] children something. Women notice those things." This, the male opinion, is not implausible. As will be observed later, the position of a recently acquired wife in a joint family was the lowest in the group. If she stayed in the joint family, she remained in a low status and in many cases had a sizable burden of the housework for much of her life. If she left the common residence group, she was subject only to her husband in day-to-day living, and even this was limited by the division of tasks within the household. At least in part, however, this explanation is to be understood as a male theory, which served to strengthen men's beliefs in their greater magnanimity and cooperativeness. Women's quarrels could not have been the main motive for partitioning in all cases, for this does not explain why the land was divided after the households were separated. Moreover, girls often married very young, some as young as six or seven; there were few quarrels at that age. The very young wife was frequently treated with consideration and affection at first; later, difficulties were likely to arise. Yet, if the father was deceased, partitioning usually took place as soon as a man married, even if his wife was very young.

In different contexts, when not discussing motives for family partitioning, men frequently made mention of *"bhāu bandaki."* This was explained as meaning "brothers' quarrels," but the term was applied to all quarrels among kinsmen. Quarreling was, in fact, frequent among brothers and other close kinsmen. A group of three informants identified thirty-two quarrels among kinsmen, involving seventy-two men in a list of eighty-nine villagers, all household heads. Sixteen men quarreled with their brothers, and fourteen of these involved much hostility. Eight quarreled with fathers' brothers' sons, and seven of these were very hostile. Five quarreled with fathers' brothers, four with much hostility. Two quarrels were with distant *bhāuki* members, and one with a mother's brother.

People asserted that quarrels usually had economic motives, such as differences over division of land or *bālutā* payments. But hostility seemed to go beyond the point of simple, "rational" economic haggling. Brothers sometimes took their disputes to court and underwent considerable expense, even economic ruin, in an effort to best one another. I give as an example one family, including four brothers. It had had a particularly good economic standing at a time when many others were in debt. During World War II there was prosperity, and many people repaid their debts. But in this family, the father died at that time, and the brothers started quarreling. Partition of the land was demanded, and the problems involved produced more hostility. They went to the courts and there suffered so much from fees that they were unable to pay their land taxes and lost much of their land. Economically all lost in the dispute. Such events were by no means rare. I do not know whether in cases of this sort men realized that they might all lose in the end. I think they had some inkling of the possibilities, but they continued quarreling on principle, and with a bitterness often out of proportion to the small differences under dispute. When a dispute went this far, the breach was not usually healed after a settlement was effected. Indeed, in many cases less severe than this, much overt bitterness persisted after the alleged economic motive for the quarrel had been removed. Even when the dispute had not been severe, brothers not infrequently accused one another of attempted violence or suspected one another of poisoning. When brothers' lands were contiguous, which was often the case, quarrels over animal trespass frequently occurred. Minor bickering, apart from overt quarreling, was very frequent.

INTERPERSONAL RELATIONS IN THE FAMILY

When villagers discussed kinsmen they often assimilated the more distant relations to closer ones. For example, in giving information on kinship terms, informants often mentioned the proper term and then added that the relationship was "really that of" some closer kinsman. Thus, brother's son was assimilated to own son. This was done in many contexts with many different relatives, especially when moral judgments were made about how relatives should be treated. I will call this phenomenon "merging." Merging occurred among all close relatives and will be further discussed later. However, it was most marked among people in a joint family or what would have been a joint family if the group had remained intact. Within this group all relatives but ego's spouse were merged with parent, sibling, or child. Thus, brother's wife was "like a sister," or "should be treated like a sister," son's wife was "like a daughter," and so on. Apart from ego's spouse, this gives three pairs of categories; but there was a further tendency, less universal than this, to reduce these to two pairs, merging elder sibling with parent and younger with child. Thus, elder brother and his wife were "like father" and "like mother."

These distinctions indicated the ideal loci of respect, dominance, and responsibility. A man was supposed to respect and obey his elder brother as he would his father, his elder brother's wife as an elder sister or mother. A woman was supposed to treat her son's wife with the protective care that she gave her daughter, and the latter, in turn, was supposed to look upon her mother-in-law as a mother. Hence, apart from ego's spouse, the lines of authority were, ideally, drawn solely with regard for sex and age or generation. The oldest male of the highest generation was supposed to receive the most respect and obedience, the female at the opposite pole, the most protection and care.

These concepts comprised villagers' ideas about what relationships ought to be like. As we shall see, they did not invariably correspond to social norms or to actions. However, because of the ranking involved in them, they helped to restrain conflict. Merging was, in part at least, a response to any kind of tension latent in kinship relationships; where tension was more likely, it occurred more often.

SPOUSES

Marriage could be delayed by such things as poor economic conditions or a family name of bad repute, and it could be hastened by overanxious or very traditional parents; but the search for a spouse usually started soon before a child, especially a female, reached puberty. When prepubescent girls were married, they were returned to their natal homes repeatedly for periods varying from four months to a few days until they were old enough to adjust. Children of the same sex had to be married in order of age. Thus if parents delayed the marriage of a daughter, they had also to delay the marriage of her younger sister, even if a good match was available.

The delicately wrought balance of proprieties involved in the search for a spouse distinctly reveals the superiority of the groom's side to the bride's. The female's family had to take the first step, at least formally. The male's family often feigned indifference; seemingly casually, they spread the word that their son was "marrying this year." The female's family had to seek out and ask to be considered by the male's, or in any event, this had to be the appearance of things.

A preliminary assessment was made to see if the prospective mate was suitable. In castes that had exogamic restrictions beyond the *bhāuki,* inquiry was then made into the matter. At this point also the wealth and social standing of the families were assessed. The ages of the prospective spouses were considered; the male had to be older, or at worst the same age. Some status conflict could result from an older wife, for older members of the household, even females, were supposed to be superior to younger; yet husbands had to be unequivocally superior to wives. I was able to discover but one conflict of the two principles, the man being about 35 and the woman about 40.[9] As might be anticipated, the male was superior despite the age discrepancy.

After this initial assessment, the horoscopes of the couple were compared. If they were too disparate, the proceedings were usually stopped. Slightly conflicting horoscopes could be corrected by ceremonial precautions undertaken at the wedding. However, such a conflict could be used as a pretext to stop the match when there was a change of mind at this stage. Some delayed the horoscope until later, but this was thought unwise because it could result in disappointment where the arrangements had been extensive and satisfactory.

The next step was the examination of the prospective mates. A party of women from the male's family visited the girl's home, or she was brought to his home. In low voices the women asked her simple questions to see if she could hear well and speak clearly. They surreptitiously examined her skin color—light was preferred. They pretended to admire her bangles, the better to examine her hands for defects. The testing was usually thorough. For the male, however, it was usually less rigorous and was often omitted. His education and financial condition were most important.

If matters had been satisfactory up to this point, the

---

[9] There may have been other cases of the woman being older than the man, but none was reported. A few people in my census asserted that they and their wives were of the same age.

dowry or bride price was then arranged. In most castes, especially high castes, dowry—payment to the groom's father —was the rule. Bride price—payment to the bride's family— was most frequent among Harijans, but it could occur in any group if the male had highly undesirable characteristics and the female was considered an especially good mate. The amount was determined by the comparative qualities of the boy and girl and by the economic conditions of their families. It could be as low as fifty rupees and, in wealthy families, as high as 2,000 rupees. Throughout these proceedings the male's family often maintained the appearance of reluctance or indifference. Some were in fact so reluctant as to reject suitor after suitor, until further advances were discouraged.

The ceremonial formalities involved in marriage were numerous. Their number and intricacy, their expense—men were sometimes plunged into heavy debt by them—and the emotion invested in them is indicative of the importance of the husband-wife bond and the affinal tie that depended upon it. Weeks before the event invitations were sent out, sometimes to hundreds of people. Printed invitations were sent to affinal relatives and friends, while colored rice was given to *bhāuki* members. Two betrothal ceremonies were held before the regular wedding, one at the groom's village and one at the bride's village. If dowry was paid, the remaining ceremonies were usually held at the bride's village. The bride's family sent bullock carts to bring the groom's family and some of the groom's guests. Ten or more carts were often borrowed or hired for the occasion. On the evening of the arrival of the groom's party, all castes but the Brahmans performed the turmeric ceremony (*Hāḷḍi*), at which the bride and groom were purified by being rubbed with turmeric. On the next day there was a constant stream of ceremonies. Among the first was the worship of the groom by the bride's family—

he was an *avatār* of God on this occasion. The dowry was then publicly presented, and the mother of the bride ritually washed the feet of the groom and of the females of his family. There was a "confirmation" ceremony (*vān niścai*), at which it was publicly declared that "the great grandson of ————, grandson of ————, son of ————, is to be married to the great granddaughter of ————, granddaughter of ————, daughter of ————." There were further ceremonies, after which the parents of the groom visited the bride's house and presented her with a set of clothing. The groom, usually on horseback, proceeded to the Hanumān temple, where he publicly changed into a new set of clothing provided by the bride's family. In castes that had the *devak* symbol (see first section of Chapter 4), the symbols of both parties were carried to the Hanumān temple and there worshipped. Following this the groom went to the place at which the wedding paraphernalia had been constructed, a large canopy and a mud brick platform backed by a wall of the same composition. Several ceremonies took place under and around the canopy. In the central ceremony the bride and groom stood under the canopy, a white cloth stretched between them, while short poems (*mangalāṣṭakās*) were chanted by members of the audience, the first and last by the officiating Brahman. After each poem everyone threw colored rice at the couple. The poems were didactic; they advised the couple to be loyal, obedient, and so on. When the last of these was chanted, the guests presented their gifts, money or household articles. The name and gift of each donor were publicly announced. The bride and groom, standing on the mud platform, underwent a number of additional ceremonies. They remained on the platform while they and the guests were feasted. The bride and groom were supposed to take one bite of food from each other's hands, a symbol of their impending intimacy. They were often emotionally too disturbed to eat, let alone to swallow the morsel of food from the hands of another.

This is only a brief outline of the formation of the marriage bond, but it should give some idea of the importance of the affinal tie and some idea of the asymmetry that obtained between donors and recipients of women. This asymmetry can be further illustrated by an event that occurred at a Maratha wedding. The preliminaries to the wedding had been completed. The groom's family had made the trip to Gaon, and the actual ceremony was about to start. At this point someone in the groom's party discovered that the girl was older than the boy. The groom's party was indignant and wanted to return home at once. The bride's party, desperately searching for an alternative, came up with the would-be bride's younger sister, in defiance of the custom requiring that children be married in order of age. After some hesitation the groom's family accepted, and the wedding was held.

Two customs were at stake here. One was the necessity of having a husband older than his wife, the other that older siblings should marry before younger ones of the same sex. It is probable that in most cases the latter custom was more compelling than the former. Even where the ages of spouses were improper, as we have observed, the male remained superior, and no major difficulties occurred. But the marriage of a younger before an elder sister could create much difficulty in finding a spouse for the latter. A prospective groom's family would suspect that there was something wrong with a single girl whose younger sister had been married. Most people viewed the maintenance of an unmarried daughter for very long after puberty as socially highly undesirable. Hence the girl's parents in this case were in a trying position. That they gave way is simple testimony to the lack of value of women in the marriage market. It was very likely that they would continue to defer to their daughter's new family.

People who were poor and unpretentious could substitute a shortened form of marriage ceremony, called *mohotur,* for the full ceremony. This was most often done when a man or woman remarried, although one might and frequently did have a full ceremony under these circumstances. The relationship created by *mohotur* was not as sacred as the regular marriage, but it was a completely legal union, in which all children inherited in the normal manner. The status relations were the same as in a regular marriage.

The public face of the spouse relationship was aloof, formalized male superiority. The aloofness was especially marked in the presence of elders, particularly the husband's father. In conservative homes, if a man and wife were together when an elder entered the room, one or the other, usually the wife, left the vicinity "out of respect." A young couple could not speak to one another in public. In the presence of others men generally attempted to ignore their wives as much as possible. When guests were present, for example, a man would call out, apparently speaking to no one in particular, "I want tea," and tea silently appeared, the bearer inconspicuous and in this context clearly inconsequential.

The formality and sacred character of the relationship was symbolized by a taboo on uttering the name of one's spouse. Husband and wife never addressed one another by name. They used indirect means or a kinship term. One was not supposed even to refer to one's spouse by name in normal discourse. When men did this, disrespect was sometimes intended. To mention the name of one's spouse was called "taking the name of" the husband or wife. It was proper to do so only on specified occasions, usually ceremonial. The process of "name taking," especially among women, was always stylized; the woman "took" her husband's name in a short extemporaneous poem in which the husband's name was usually coupled with that of the deity Rām.

The husband was superior according to village norms, and usually his behavior reflected this. A wife was expected to be obedient and usually was. On important ceremonial occasions, it was through the husband that a woman worshipped the family deities. In village theory, she could attain religious blessings (*puṇya*) through his actions as well as her own. Men sometimes pointed out, in humor, that a woman had the religious advantage, for she did not suffer the effects of her husband's sins (*pāp*) while she assimilated his blessings.

There was talk among some young men of recent changes in attitude between husband and wife; women were said to have greater freedom of action. In fact, there was little evidence of this. The woman remained completely subservient even when her husband attempted to "modernize" the relationship. An instance of this occurred when a newly married young man and his wife visited me. Normally, when a woman accompanied her husband on a visit to a stranger (which was rare), she retired to the kitchen without greeting the male host, and she departed, when her husband gave the signal, in a similarly unobtrusive fashion. In this case the young man sternly ordered his wife to greet me. Embarrassed, she obeyed and then hurried into the kitchen. Later, as the couple left, she rushed away—not in time, however, to avoid his order, accompanied by a snap of the fingers, to "make *nāmaste*." The obedient though unwillingly "modern" wife returned and saluted. Such attempts nearly always missed the mark.

The distinction of rights and duties between spouses circumscribed male superiority to some extent. Most men preferred not to interfere in "women's affairs." For running the household, including discipline of the young children, women were expected to assume full responsibility. When men did interfere, they often found that they could not achieve their wishes. For example, a village leader, an unusually assertive man, vigorously protested to his wife that she was spoiling their son. He contended that she allowed the boy to stay home from school whenever the boy wished, and he wanted his son to be well disciplined and well educated. His protests to his wife, even beatings, were of no avail. She persisted in her permissiveness, and he was helpless.

It need hardly be mentioned that all of the rules regulating spouse relationships were not followed strictly. The public face of aloofness was not reflected in private, especially after family partitioning. Advice was exchanged on daily activities, the rearing of children, the running of the farm, and so on. One of the characteristics many young men said they wanted in a wife was some knowledge of agriculture. Moreover, personality differences in a few cases resulted in the female being dominant in the household, though the appearance of male superiority was still maintained.

Polygyny was permitted in all castes. The motive generally given was childlessness or lack of a son, though there was some prestige in being able to maintain two or more wives. It was rare in the village. There were but fourteen cases in a total of 212 marital alliances. Polygyny had become illegal by 1954, but it was still contracted in a few cases.

The death of his spouse did not change the position of the male or in any way require alterations in his behavior. But the nature of the woman's position following her husband's death varied. If she had children, she almost always remained with her deceased husband's family. If she was childless and had not been married for long, she often returned to her natal household. A widow suffered a number of disabilities, particularly ceremonial. For example, she could not prepare food for religious occasions, and she could not touch or worship a deity. She could not attend important ceremonies, especially weddings or thread ceremonies (see Chapter 6, note 2). She refrained from wearing a *kuṅku,* the cosmetic dot Indian women apply to their foreheads. A widow was supposed also to keep her hair cropped short, but this custom was no longer practiced. Only Brahmans were strict in these matters. They and the Marathas forbade widow remarriage. However, many villagers, including some Marathas, said that Maratha widows sometimes established *de facto* marital unions.

Marital ties were sometimes severed, especially among Rope Makers and Scavengers. I should estimate that about five per cent of the marriages were broken in these castes. It was often effected without formal procedures; the woman left or was forced to leave the man's household. Sometimes a formal notice, drafted by a village Brahman, was sent to one or the other party to announce that the relationship was terminated. Divorces were rarer in other castes, unheard of among Brahmans.

PARENT-CHILD RELATIONSHIPS

The father-son relationship was a formal one, especially in castes other than Scavengers and Rope Makers. In castes other than these, once a boy passed childhood there was a minimum of overt affection between him and his father. In all groups the son looked upon the father with some measure of fear and subservience. The father had little to do with his adolescent sons. The mother generally administered discipline for minor infractions; only major faults were reported to the father, and then not always. The father was usually very severe in punishing his sons. Fathers distrusted their sons' judgment. Even wealthy and generous fathers preferred not to give money to their sons, but instead gave actual articles on request. When a boy reached young manhood, the father yielded independence to him with reluctance, if at all.

Even adult sons with families of their own were almost invariably obedient to their fathers. Some men with grown children continued to wait on their fathers, obeying every whim. One such man remarked, with slightly bitter humor, that he was a servant in his own home. Men sometimes sacrificed their life ambitions in obedience to their father's wishes. For example, a Brahman wanted to study law, but he was an only son, and his father told him not to leave home. He obeyed, and hence remained a farmer. A similar case occurred with an ambitious young Scavenger. He had graduated from high school and very much wanted to go on to college. But he too was an only son, and at his father's insistence he remained in the village, performing *bālutā* duties and doing some farming.

Revolts against parental authority did occur, but very rarely. An effective weapon for someone in subordinate position was public exposure of private family affairs, and this could be used if the father resisted partitioning of the family wealth. As the data on family type shows, such incidents were unusual. Years after the event there was still talk of one young man who used public exposure of his quarrel with his father to precipitate partitioning of the property.

Relations of a father with his daughter were less formal than with the son, though his authority here, too, was unquestioned. Neither father nor mother felt it necessary to put much effort into training their daughter, for it was thought that most of her training should be left to her husband's family.

Mother-child relations were not expected to be restrained, and, in fact, they were quite informal. A child hailed its father by the formal *"āho,"* its mother often by the intimate *"e."* Often a mother even conspired against her husband for privileges for her son. The father recognized the mother-son intimacy and at times tried to influence his son through her.

SIBLINGS

In the system of kinship ideals nearly all statuses were merged in such a way as to point up the idea of rank. Ideally, brothers remained all their lives in an elder-younger hierarchy. In fact, however, the ranking persisted only so long as brothers were unmarried and their father lived; afterward they were rivals. They did not compete merely as brothers, but as brothers and *independent* household heads. Their independence could not be achieved while their father lived, for they were then still "children." As we have seen, a man's father was a distant, formalized authority figure to him from early childhood. The image a man had of himself vis-à-vis his father could not easily be altered while the latter was present. So long as his father lived, a man's status was partly assimilated to that of "child," irrespective of his or his father's age. Only when the father was completely senile did his authority wane. In the larger society outside the family "children" were not competitors. "Father" symbolized the position of the household as against other households; he could compete—usually, of course, with *his* brothers. Once he was gone, if the brothers had married, or if they later married, they became not only "brothers" but also potential household heads —"husbands." As such, their total social status approached equality. They were in constant contact with one another. They shared the same goals and the means of attaining their goals and so validated status in the same way; they could not help but measure their worth against one another. They were rivals and, furthermore, rivals in a society that emphasized differences in rank. Hence petty bickering and major disputes were frequent. Under the circumstances they could rarely live together, let alone maintain common property, for property was one of the most important means by which one attained social honor. As might be expected, the high incidence of conflict resulted in a frequent reminder of the ideal regarding brothers; the elder "should be treated like" a father, the younger like a son.

Brother-sister conflict was very rare; sex role differentiation made for different ways of assessing one's worth. Shared goals, the grounds for competition among brothers, were not present in this relationship. The ideal was not infrequently attained. A man often acted toward his younger sister as toward a daughter, although a sister assumed a mother role toward her brother only if she was much older than he.

Conflicts occurred in a few cases after marriage, especially when a man was reluctant to give his daughter in marriage to his sister's son. The sister, protesting that she herself had been given to this family, demanded, "Now you do not give your daughter here? Why is that?" Such quarrels were most frequent among Harijans (Untouchables), where there was a high incidence of mother's brother's daughter marriage, but even there they were rare. Indeed, the brother-sister tie was very strong. The affection involved in the relationship was recognized symbolically in the yearly ceremony of Bhāu Bīj, when he gave her a gift, and she gave him a ceremonial oil bath.

Relations among sisters did not usually approximate the mother-daughter ideal unless the age discrepancy was very great. The ideal was rarely mentioned. Conflict was infrequent. There was little reason for rivalry between sisters. They knew they were to be married in order of age, and they knew they would probably go to different places after marriage. After marriage a woman's status was determined by that of her husband, and his status was assessed relative to his

fellow villagers. Any conflicts she participated in were more
likely to be in his sphere of activities, for example, with his
brothers and their wives.

AFFINALS WITHIN THE HOUSEHOLD

A new bride had, by far, the lowest position in the household. The ideal "daughter" status that she should have held
vis-à-vis her husband's parents was sometimes maintained at
the start, especially if she was very young; but this did not
usually last long. She was soon given the most work of the
most disagreeable sort and sometimes the least adequate
food. Her gruff treatment, entirely contrary to the ideal
"daughter" status is, perhaps, ascribable to the fact that her
husband's group had accepted her, as it were, as a favor; she
was the cause of the subservience of her natal family.[10] Furthermore, she was still associated with it. In this region, as in
most of India, a woman never quite lost her ties to her original household, yet she was conceived as properly incorporated into her husband's family. Her loyalty was thought to
reside, in part at least, with the other group, a subservient
group. Hence, however often the ideal was set forth—and it
was repeatedly articulated—her treatment was far from
approximating it. Nevertheless, after the passage of time, and
especially after the birth of children, she was accepted as
more fully a member of her husband's family, and her position improved.

The relationship between a woman and her brother's wife

[10] This gives an odd situation in the lower castes, where bride price
was often practiced. The payment is, I believe, a case of "lag," for my
evidence indicates that, despite bride price, the woman's family was
often treated more overbearingly in these than in higher castes. I conjecture that bride price had been associated with a past condition,
wherein the woman's family was equal or superior to the man's; in time
the behavior of the low castes became more like that of high castes, but
the custom of bride price had not, as yet, been abandoned.

was usually smooth. After a woman's marriage she met her brothers' wives only infrequently. If she was widowed and returned to her natal home, it was thought proper for her to act as a guest and to defer to her brothers' wives' wishes. Where she attempted to assert her status as sister, conflict was always forthcoming.

A woman and her husband's brother's wife rarely, if ever, achieved the sisterly or motherly ideal. Conflict was frequent, and this is comprehensible. A woman's status was determined by that of her husband, who was frequently in conflict situations with his brothers. Again and again it was said that the elder brother's wife should act like "mother" in the absence of the mother-in-law. In fact, the older brother's wife's behavior was more often like the norm than the ideal. She was gruff and harsh with the other women rather than motherly. "She becomes the mother-in-law."

Men and their brother's wives were in a conflict- and tension-laden relationship. The brother's wife was the cause of brother conflict, for it was she who defined the brothers as more nearly equal in total social status. Another tension-producing aspect of the relationship was that, in some cases, brother's wife had been a direct or indirect cross cousin, a *"mehuṇi,"* prior to marriage. There was a joking relationship with one's *mehuṇi,* often one that assumed sexual overtones, at least in language. Sometimes actual sexual intercourse occurred. A joking relationship also obtained with brother's wife, but it was a much more guarded one. Sexual allusions were completely forbidden, the idea of sexual intercourse thoroughly shocking. Sexual relations of this kind were sometimes spoken of as incestuous. So a man now had to be very careful with a woman with whom he had formerly been on casual terms sexually. It makes sense, then, that brother's wife was very often said to be "like a sister."

4

The *Khari Bhāuki*

THERE were some exogamous groups represented in the village having little or no significance in social relations apart from marriage regulation. These were the *gotra,* the *kūli,* the *devak,* the moiety, and the *bhāuki.* The *bhāuki* will be discussed later.

The Basket Maker caste was divided into moieties. All Basket Makers were surnamed either Jādho or Māne, and surname exogamy was practiced. The moiety divisions had no unity and, apart from the regulation of marriage, no functions. These divisions existed only among Basket Makers.

The Brahmans, Temple Priests, and Goldsmiths conceived themselves as grouped into *gotras,* the Rajputs into *kūlis.* *Kūlis* and *gotras* were, as social entities, identical in all but name. Each *gotra* and *kūli* subsumed a number of surnames which were believed to have had a common ancestor. Although there are some problems on the historical development of the *gotra,* it is plain that in recent times they and the *kūlis* have been no more than exogamous patrilineal descent groups without common residence and without cohesion or intragroup cooperation. Sometimes individuals did not even know their *gotras,* and the matter had to be investigated before a marriage was arranged.

The *devak* was a symbol, such as a sea shell or a flower, that was worshipped at marriage ceremonies. Its significance in the Maratha caste has been discussed by Irawati Karve. Referring first to "clan-names," probably the shared surname that I will take up later, Karve continues: "The rule of exogamy is however not dependent on the clan-name but on the

symbol connected with the clan. This symbol is called the
'Devaka.' . . . They seem to have very little significance in
ordinary life but each family worships its 'Devaka' at the time
of marriage and no two people having the same 'Devaka' can
marry. . . . The 'Devaka' is not known to many people; it
is however known to the elders who look into these matters
at the time of marriage." [1] This description applies completely
to the Marathas and Watchmen in Gaon. In these castes the
same *devak* was employed by some individuals bearing different surnames, thus prohibiting marriage between them. In
two other castes, Water Carriers and Scavengers, only individuals having the same surname shared *devaks,* and as surname exogamy obtained, it was but an additional means of
indicating the exogamic barrier. The remaining castes either
did not profess to have *devaks,* or they had simply borrowed
the idea, probably from the Marathas, and adopted a symbol
without associating it with exogamic restrictions. The Goldsmiths, for example, had both *gotras* and *devaks,* but their
devaks played no part in the regulation of marriage. However, even in the castes in which it did restrict marriage, the
devak was like the *gotra* concept in that it affected interpersonal relations in this regard only.

The *gotra* and *devak* groups differed in significance from
the Basket Maker moieties, for they were involved in caste
rank and in the vertical diffusion of culture. The copying of
the *gotra* concept was a part of the process of sanskritization,
whereby lower castes absorbed Brahman customs. The spread
of the *devak* concept was part of a similar process by which
all castes, possibly excepting Brahmans, copied the ways of
the dominant caste of a region, in this case the Marathas.

[1] Irawati Karve, *Kinship Organization in India* (Deccan College
Monograph Series: 11), Poona, 1953, p. 157.

THE KHARI BHĀUKI

In most castes a number of patrilineally related households formed a distinct, largely localized exogamic group. As I mentioned, villagers sometimes used the term *"kutumb"* for it. Usually, however, they called it a *"bhāuki"* or *"bhāuband,"* although these terms were also used to refer to a more wide-spread group which subsumed a number of localized groups sharing one surname. In a few cases villagers used the term *"khari bhāuki"*—"real" *bhāuki*—to distinguish the localized group from the broader one. In the anthropological literature on rural India, groups similar to this are frequently called lineages, but in point of fact, as we shall see, those in this region, and possibly elsewhere, differ from a lineage as ordinarily defined. I will use the native terms. Where the distinction is necessary, I will use *"khari bhāuki"* to refer to the localized group and *"bhāuki"* for the more widespread one. This gives more precision than existed in the minds of the villagers, and I would emphasize that most people used the term *"bhāuki"* alone, usually meaning the localized group, but in context sometimes referring to the widespread one.

The only castes in which the *bhāuki* concept was not found were the Basket Makers and possibly the Goldsmiths. I have already mentioned the former. As for the latter, I interviewed, in addition to Gaon's Goldsmith, a number of others from Mot and from another village; most were completely unfamiliar with the concept. Some denied they had groups like this, and others were confused in their descriptions when they attempted to employ the term. I think it probable that in this region Goldsmiths rarely, if ever, held the notion of *bhāuki*. This is understandable. The caste was largely urban, and village Goldsmiths were usually much dispersed. Many villages in the *tālukā* had no Goldsmiths, and others usually had no more than one or two isolated households. The long-term dispersion of kinsmen is a probable explanation for the absence of the idea of the *bhāuki* in this caste, for the unity of the *khari bhāuki,* as will be shown, was based on contiguity, especially common village residence.

Within this village and in others of the region there was a tendency to have but one *khari bhāuki* of each caste. The tendency was not usually fully realized, but most castes had one *khari bhāuki* that monopolized traditional village duties and was dominant in population. Where it is necessary to distinguish this *khari bhāuki* from others in the village, I will call it the "traditional" or "main" *bhāuki*. People thought of the main *bhāuki* as being the sole one of its caste in the village. The village was not exogamous, yet when giving the rule of exogamy, informants often referred to the village rather than to the *bhāuki*. Fellow villagers not in the main *bhāuki* were sometimes said to be "outsiders," despite the fact that their families had been living in the village for many generations.

The castes that deviated most sharply from this tendency were the Scavengers and Marathas. The Scavengers had two main *bhāukis,* each with its own surname. Their coexistence was explained by the villagers as due to a conflict over *bālutā* a few generations back, in the course of which village leaders brought an additional Scavenger *bhāuki* to the community (discussed later in this chapter). Official records pertaining to traditional village rights (*vatan*) confirm this. There is but one *bhāuki* listed for 1874, two for 1884.

The Scavenger *bhāuki* situation was further complicated by the fact that one household of the immigrant group claimed to be a separate *khari bhāuki*. The members of this household asserted that they were the original immigrants invited to the village, but that remote relatives assumed their name and usurped their rights. However, they behaved as if they were in the same *khari bhāuki* as their kinsmen. I will count the entire immigrant group as one *khari bhāuki*.

In fact, there were some respects in which the two traditional Scavenger *bhāukis,* the original one and the immigrant one, acted like one *khari bhāuki*. Their long-term traditional ties to the village had given rise to a notion of fictive kinship. In inviting one's *bhāuki* members to weddings, it was customary to give them colored rice and to give other guests invitation cards. The two Scavenger *khari bhāukis* gave rice to one another. In seeking a spouse for one's child, one had to take along some *bhāuki* members. The Scavengers took representatives of both *bhāukis*. Intermarriage was forbidden between the two groups. As one Scavenger put it (in English): "We suppose them as [in our] *bhāuki*."

The Marathas were represented by fifteen *bhāukis*. The household composition was as follows:

No. of Households in a *Bhāuki*	1–2	3–4	5–6	7–8
No. of *Bhāukis*	7	4	3	1

None of them was considered a traditional *bhāuki*. Villagers explained this by saying that the caste was not originally from Gaon.

Apart from these two castes, the other exceptions to the norm of one *bhāuki* for each caste was broken only by isolated households, almost all of which were affinally related to households in main *bhāukis*. In Table 6 I give those castes in which there were households outside the main *bhāuki,* omitting Marathas and Basket Makers.

The two main *bhāukis* given for Scavengers has been explained. The immigrant *bhāuki* was the larger of the two. It had close ties to Scavengers in another village; indeed, they were of the same *khari bhāuki*. This will be discussed later. The figure includes only those from Gaon. In the remaining

castes of the village non-traditional *bhāukis* were absent.
However, in most of these there were but one or two households. Those with more than two were the Leather Workers,
who had thirteen households, and the Brahmans and Temple
Priests, with five and four respectively.

TABLE 6

Household Composition of *Bhāukis* by Caste

	Potter	Rajput	Watchman	Scavenger	Rope Maker
Households in Main *Bhāukis*	6	43	1	16;4	20
Additional *Bhāukis*	1	3	1	2	1
Households in Additional *Bhāukis*	3	3	1	5	2

One *bhāuki* per caste in the village was a norm in the sense
of an expectation and in the sense of a statistical tendency.
But there is no reason to believe that it had ever been completely so in fact. Other villages I surveyed were similar to
Gaon in having some non-traditional *bhāukis,* and some of
these were known as very conservative villages. In Gaon the
surnames listed in the 1881 land records (the earliest available) indicate that Rajputs had, in addition to their main
bhāuki, four *bhāukis* containing five households, while Brahmans had two such *bhāukis* containing four households.
Apart from Marathas, all other landowners are listed by caste
name instead of surname, so the number of *bhāukis* could
not be counted. Of course, the record tells us nothing about
landless groups.

There was a tendency toward marriage outside of the village, because a considerable number of people in each caste
were of the same *bhāuki*. A few intravillage marriages did
occur. Among Marathas, where there were many *bhāukis* in

the village, several marriages took place. Although a complete count was not made, in the course of my census I came upon four intravillage marriages occurring within the recent past. In the remainder of the village there were within the memory of informants but eleven cases, all among Scavengers and Rope Makers.[2] Ten instances were in the former group, one in the latter. The Scavengers had at different times a number of "outsider" *bhāukis* represented in the village, some of which had since left. A few people in these castes expressed a preference for such marriages. As one Scavenger put it: "We are better acquainted with them than with others. Without going anywhere, we choose a girl from [them] and they do the same thing." The informant added that there were some who disliked this practice. Indeed, a number of people objected. Some said the girl would be too close to her natal home and would never completely wean herself from it. She would be subject to suspicion of favoring her father's household, even of giving her husband's produce to her father. Thus, one of those opposed: "I gave my daughter to [a resident of Gaon] because his wife is my sister, and you know very well that a sister has the right to ask a daughter of her brother [for her son]. But I dislike this system, because we both live in Gaon. My daughter comes again and again to my house, so my sister suspects that she is giving things to me. And in this way there came to be a quarrel between us. So I think it is a hundred times better to give a daughter to

[2] This difference among the castes, as well as others, indicates the utility of Srinivas' notion of sanskritization. "Sanskritic" culture moves from north to south and, by and large, from high to low caste. The Harijans in Gaon were, it seems, more like the peoples of southern India than were the higher castes. Gaon as a whole, situated in central India, was intermediate between northern and southern India in social organization in that, for example, mother's brother's daughter marriage was preferred and that there was a prejudice but no prohibition against father's sister's daughter marriage.

a distant place than to give her to a relative [who lives close by]." Apart from Marathas, Scavengers, and Rope Makers, there were no cases of intravillage marriage, and everyone expressed some prejudice against it, although all agreed that it could take place. In any event, when seeking a mate one rarely could find a suitable one within the village.

One of the features of *bhāuki* membership was a common surname. This was not invariable, for an individual remained in his *bhāuki* even if he changed his name. Name changes could be intentional, as in the case of one Brahman who assumed the name of an affinal relative in order to take advantage of resident's rights in a distant city. Changes could also be gradual uncalculated processes, as where an occupational title or a caste name gradually displaced a surname. For example, instead of being called by their regular surname, Brahmans in the village were often called *"kulkarni,"* the word for "accountant" in the traditional village economy. Such things occurred in all castes. Where the caste name or occupational title completely displaced a surname, one of the distinguishing features of a *bhāuki* was obliterated. This happened to only one caste in Gaon, the Potters. Their caste name (Kumbhār), also the name of their occupation, was used in place of surnames. Potters asserted that they once had surnames, and a few in the region still recalled their surnames, but none used them; hence their *bhāukis* were not distinguishable by this means.

The term *"bhāuki"* was usually used to refer to what I call the *khari bhāuki,* as well as to a larger group, the members of which bore the same surname and believed themselves descended from one ancestor. This group extended well beyond the borders of the village, but in most castes the interacting group, the *khari bhāuki,* was defined by contiguity, usually common village residence. Beyond this the *bhāuki* tie was

feeble. Like the *gotra* and other such aggregations, it was of
significance only in the regulation of marriage. Many people
did not know where *bhāuki* members lived who were not in
their *khari bhāuki;* others who knew some such villages had
no relations with them. Relations were maintained over distances when the generation separation was not great. If an
individual moved to a distant place, he often kept some ties
to his original *khari bhāuki,* and his children did so too, to
some extent, but the third or fourth generation was likely to
keep few if any affiliations. The father of a now deceased
Leather Worker had moved to Bombay. The emigrant died,
and his son, who was wealthy, gave financial aid to some
khari bhāuki members in the village. But members of the
immigrant Scavenger *bhāuki* said they had a branch some
four or five generations removed in another district, yet they
knew practically nothing of the people there. When they went
to that locality, they did not even trouble to visit their fellow
bhāuki members. As was mentioned, official records indicate
that the group arrived between 1874 and 1884, probably a
separation of about four generations from 1954.[3]

The nature of the *bhāuki* tie is clearly seen from the distribution of wedding invitations. Weddings, it should be mentioned, were among the most important occasions on which
people met. In some castes this was the only occasion on
which decisions were taken in caste matters. If good relations were to be kept, it was vital that all *khari bhāuki* members be invited. Hostility had to be very severe within a *khari
bhāuki* to prevent the tendering of invitations, more severe
than it usually was among close agnates even soon after partition. It was sufficiently severe in a feud between two groups

[3] The only groups in which I could assess the length of a generation
were Brahmans and Rajputs, where a generation gap for family heads
between 1881 and 1954 was a maximum of four, a minimum of one.

in the main Rajput *bhāuki*. Apart from this instance and rare severe hostility in individual cases, all *khari bhāuki* members were invited. They were invited, however, along with many other relatives, as well as friends and important villagers from other *bhāukis* and castes.

Invitations were given to large numbers of affinal relatives, even at considerable distances from the village, but they were rarely extended to *bhāuki* members outside the village. I examined six lists of people invited to weddings in the recent past among Rope Makers and Scavengers. Excluding members of the *khari bhāukis* concerned, there were sixty-five relatives invited, of whom only four were *bhāuki* members. The four were, in fact, affinally related to some members of the inviter's *khari bhāuki,* three being wives' sisters and one being the groom's brother's wife's sister's husband.

Among members of the main Rajput *bhāuki,* whom I will call the Kokes, invitations were extended by most people to groups of households that were closely related in the patrilineal line—*takśimās*—hence people did not always remember all individuals or households they habitually invited. The number of *takśimās* invited was usually about fifty or sixty, assuming adequate finances. This takes in a considerable number of households, and attendance at weddings was often quite high; 300 guests, excluding residents of Gaon, was a good sized but not an extraordinary wedding. The largest number of Koke households (not *takśimās*) invited from outside Gaon was fifteen; most people invited but two or three. Some of these were closely related agnates. Others were affinally related to affines usually invited and living in the same village as the latter. A few were acquaintances, acquired through economic activities or chance contacts.

It was similar in most other castes. The village Blacksmith, for example, invited four of his *bhāuki* members, none of whom were from the village, but all of whom were sufficiently closely related to him for common ancestry to be readily traceable. The village Washerman invited only one *bhāuki* member from outside, a father's brother's son.

Three castes were exceptions to the general rule, in that the interacting *bhāuki* consisted of distantly related individuals in more than one village. Unlike other castes, the Brahman main *bhāuki* had a written genealogy extending back to a single founder and including all members, wherever they lived. All lived in Gaon and in a town about thirty-five miles away. The two branches of the *bhāuki* communicated with one another by mail and occasionally visited. Wedding invitations were exchanged, and the method used was as between members of a *khari bhāuki,* by giving colored rice. However, those not residing in Gaon were excluded from the *khari bhāuki* in death pollution (described later in the chapter). I will refer to the localized Brahman group as the *khari bhāuki.* The Potters were another exception. They said they originally came from Mot and considered themselves in the same *khari bhāuki* as the Mot Potters, although no genealogy existed and relations were too distant to trace. The situation was similar regarding the immigrant Scavenger *bhāuki.* They considered themselves in the same *khari bhāuki* as those in a contiguous village and said that the two villages were settled by brothers. A number of them had traditional land rights (*īnām* land) in the neighboring village. In both of these cases, the Potter and the Scavenger, wedding invitations were exchanged by giving rice. Members of the *bhāuki* not in the *khari bhāuki* were treated as in other castes.

Apart from these three instances, geographic separation need not have been great for the *bhāuki* tie to lose its hold. Even where a *bhāuki* was found in a nearby village, even a contiguous one, relations were usually restricted to people

within the same village. Members of the main *bhāuki* of Rope
Makers claimed that individuals of their surname were traditional Rope Makers in "seven villages" (probably a traditional number) in the immediate vicinity, yet no one could
name more than two or three of these. Those in Gaon had no
more, possibly less, to do with *bhāuki* members from without
the village than they did with other Rope Makers of the region. The Kokes, the main Rajput *bhāuki,* offer another example. They said that their ancestors had originally settled
two villages, one of which was Gaon. From these two, they
said, they spread as population increased, until they became
headmen in "fourteen villages" in the vicinity. (The number
fourteen was traditional; there were, in fact, more.) One of
these villages was less than a mile from the main settlement of
Gaon, yet the Kokes of these two villages had little to do with
one another. There was no occasion on which all Kokes met
to the exclusion of other Rajputs and none on which they believed they should meet. Although there were no formal meetings of Kokes within the village, communication both direct
and indirect was frequent, despite the fact that some lived
miles apart on their farms. Aside from exogamy, the only tie
among all Kokes was the common worship of the deity Datta,
whose temple was situated within the borders of Gaon, outside the main settlement. This was the only *bhāuki* represented in the village that had a particular temple with which
it was associated.

The *bhāuki* differed from a lineage as ordinarily defined in
that a woman was considered a member of her husband's
group, both his household and his *bhāuki*. When she married,
the alteration in her group membership was signified by a
complete change of name, both given and surname. A tenuous affiliation with her natal household was maintained
through frequent visits, usually undertaken in the early stages

of the marriage, and through the belief, rarely acted upon, that she could permanently return to it in case of widowhood or, among non-Brahmans, divorce. Her double membership extended to the *bhāuki,* where it was seen in exogamic restrictions; in castes that permitted widow remarriage (all but Brahmans and Marathas), the widow was prohibited from marrying into either her deceased husband's or her natal *bhāuki.* Her inclusion in her husband's *bhāuki* was also seen in the use of the kinship classification *"soyare."* This will be more fully explained later, but for the present we may define it roughly. The *soyare* of any given individual consisted of all individuals in the *takśimās,* small groups of patrilineally related households, with which his *khari bhāuki* had marital ties. A married woman referred to members of her natal *takśimā,* including her natal household, as *soyare,* thus completely identifying herself with the *bhāuki* and household of her husband. Another difference between the *khari bhāuki* and a lineage is that descent from a common ancestor could not be traced in most of the *khari bhāukis.* This will be discussed subsequently.

The boundaries of a *khari bhāuki* were partly defined by exclusive participation in traditional village work. This work included the jobs of village headmen, as well as those duties associated with the *bālutā* system. It was only the main *bhāuki* that served the village; "outsiders," no matter how long resident in the village and no matter what their relationship to the main *bhāuki,* had no right to work at traditional tasks unless they were given permission by members of the main *bhāuki* or had been specifically brought in to do so. The right to work and its remunerations could be temporarily alienated, as by mortgage, but it was not allowed to be permanently sold or given away to people not in the main *bhāuki.*

The boundaries of the group were also defined, in some cases, by traditional caste offices. In those castes that had traditional officers (see Chapter 7), each post was inherited by one whole *bhāuki,* actually one *khari bhāuki,* allegedly the original one. For example, all members of the main *bhāuki* of Rope Makers in Gaon were *"pāṭīls,"* all those of Mot were *"mhetres"* (see Chapter 7 for descriptions of these offices). Those in the *khari bhāuki* selected one of their members to carry out the actual duties of the office, but all members of the main *bhāuki* were called by the appropriate title during caste meetings.

The nature of the *khari bhāuki* is seen in birth and death taboos and, in part also, in some *śrāddha* (ancestor propitiation) ceremonies. The death, generally only that of a married person, defiled his kinsmen for a stipulated period of time during which taboos and austerities were required. The condition was called *"sutak."* Eating sweets was prohibited. In taking meals one sat on the ground instead of on the regular low wooden seat (*pāṭ*), and one could not sleep on the woolen or cotton rug normally used for the purpose. Happy occasions, such as sacred thread rites (Chapter 6, note 2), could not be celebrated. No deities could be worshipped or contacted in any way. Touching someone not in *sutak* polluted him, and he had to undergo ritual purification. Cooking food for others was, of course, prohibited.

By and large, high castes observed a ten-day *sutak,* low castes twelve or thirteen days. Scavengers, Rope Makers, Leather Workers, and Watchmen kept *sutak* for twelve or thirteen days. Washermen and Rajputs were in *sutak* for thirteen days in case of a death in the household, for ten days when in the *khari bhāuki.* The remainder held a ten-day *sutak.*

A death generally entailed *sutak* for all members of a *khari*

bhāuki and, in abbreviated form, for some kinsmen outside
it. A ten- to thirteen-day period was observed in case of
death within the *khari bhāuki*. Among the Kokes, this included the two feuding groups previously mentioned. The
only exception to this—really an exception in theory rather
than in fact—was among the Brahmans. They said they practiced a ten-day *sutak* only for deceased *bhāuki* members separated from them by five generations or less. They believed
this to be coincident with those of their *bhāuki* living within
the village. They did not consult the genealogy in their possession—they kept it in a way that made it extremely difficult
to read—but their assessment was not very far wrong, for the
Brahman *bhāuki* in the village had a common ancestor four
generations removed. At the demise of a *bhāuki* member
from the branch living in another town, they underwent *sutak*
for three days. The five-generation rule employed by Brahmans approximated, although inexactly, the Sanskritic
sapiṇḍa rules.[4] In any case, according to Brahman theory,
the entire *khari bhāuki* was not necessarily involved in a
regular ten-day *sutak*. Despite the tie to the branch *bhāuki,*
the entire group was not fully equivalent to the *khari bhāuki*
of other castes; the localized group was completely equivalent, however.

Bhāukis in all castes held a regular ten- to thirteen-day
sutak at the death of a man's wife or mother, and these, themselves, were in pollution if any member of the *khari bhāuki*
died. The death of any non-*bhāuki* kinsmen involved no *sutak*
among Scavengers and a *sutak* of but three days in all other
castes. This included relatives such as wife's mother, father's

---

[4] "*Sapiṇḍa*" refers to an exogamic kin group important in Hindu
sacred literature but not actually extant in India. Roughly we may say
that it comprises all those related within seven degrees in the paternal
line, five degrees in the maternal line. For a more precise description,
see I. Karve, *Kinship Organization* . . . , pp. 54–57.

sister, and daughters and their offspring. Married women underwent a three-day *sutak* for their own parents.

A full *sutak* was undergone only for those within the *khari bhāuki*. Among Potters and ·in one Scavenger *bhāuki* this included *bhāuki* members from two different communities, but in the rest this was almost always restricted to the village. Brahmans and Potters said they performed a three-day *sutak* for *bhāuki* members outside the *khari bhāuki*. However, the Potters, unlike the Brahmans, had no communication with other *khari bhāukis,* so the three-day rule was purely theoretical. Leather Workers said they did not perform *sutak* for any *bhāuki* member outside the *khari bhāuki*. All other castes said they should perform a full *sutak* for all *bhāuki* members, whether *khari bhāuki* or not, "if we hear of the death in time." *Sutak* was counted from the time of death, not from the date at which one first heard of it. People said that if they found out about the death of a *bhāuki* member not of their *khari bhāuki,* they would probably hear of it late, and would need only do *sutak* for the remaining time. However, no one in the village knew of a case in which news of such deaths had been communicated.

There were two cases of *bhāuki* members outside the *khari bhāuki* who had recently moved to Gaon, one of the main Rajput *bhāuki* and one of the immigrant Scavenger *bhāuki*. (Both of these were new residents.) However, the Scavenger lived out on the farms, and many Scavengers did not know of his existence. When I brought up his case, they said that the regular *sutak* rule should hold for him. Opinions differed among Rajputs. Most held that the outsider could do *sutak* if he wished, but that it was not mandatory, as in the *khari bhāuki*. Others, including the outsider himself, insisted that the full period of *sutak* must be undergone.

The condition of pollution following birth was called

"soher" by a few castes, but most used the term *"vitāl,"* which signified ritual pollution in general. The woman giving birth was taken to be highly polluted and polluting, and she was subject to many taboos. Other kinsmen were mildly defiled and had only to abstain from contacting or worshipping deities. The rules as to who was involved in this pollution were identical with those for *sutak,* although they were more loosely held. A few people said that only the particular household was subject to pollution, not the whole *khari bhāuki.*

In some cases the *khari bhāuki* was partly defined by ancestor propitiation rites. There were two of these regularly performed in the course of an individual's lifetime, the *varśa śrāddha* and the *pakṣa śrāddha,* or *pakṣa.*[5] Most households performed only the *pakṣa,* but all Brahmans and Temple Priests and a few households of other castes did both. Although both ceremonies emphasized the deceased father's spirit, a number of other deceased relatives were also propitiated. Among Brahmans the *pakṣa* subsumed all deceased individuals within the bilateral kindred who were no more than three generations removed from the celebrant. The *varśa śrāddha* was more restricted. It subsumed only members of the *khari bhāuki,* and of these no more than three ascending generations. It extended from mother and father through father's father's father and father's father's mother; but it specifically excluded, for example, mother's father.

For members of the Temple Priest caste, who sometimes dispensed with Brahmans in favor of their own priests, the *varśa śrāddha* was the same as among Brahmans. Their *pakṣa,* however, involved greater generation depth; it included all known deceased members of the *khari bhāuki.* All others were excluded. Thus, father's mother was included,

---

[5] One *śrāddha* ceremony, called *bharṇi śrāddha,* was celebrated only once, soon after the death of the father.

but sister, father's sister, and mother's father, for example, were excluded.

Brahman priests did not serve at the *pakṣas* of a number of other households—Harijans (Untouchables), whom they would not serve on this occasion, and others, who preferred not to use their services. Among these there were variations from household to household, but far the largest number were like the Temple Priests in including all the *khari bhāuki* and excluding all others.

The *pakṣa* of the village Goldsmith included only one ascending generation from ego—his parents, their siblings, and their siblings' spouses. Some other Goldsmiths in the area, however, included three generations in the patrilineal line, much like the Brahman's *varśa śrāddha,* but excluded ego's mother. It should be recalled that the *bhāuki* concept was probably not employed in this caste.

The localized nature of the *khari bhāuki* was related to ignorance of genealogy. As noted, there was but one case, that of the Brahmans, in which members of a large *khari bhāuki* could literally trace their relationship to a common ancestor. The Rajput Kokes had a written genealogy, but this included only residents of the village. It excluded a group of seven Koke households of the village who were thought to be of lower status and who were involved in a feud. The members of the remaining large *bhāukis,* Scavenger, Rope Maker, Leather Worker and some Maratha *bhāukis,* assumed they had a common ancestor, but they could not trace their ancestry to a single man, they did not have fictitious genealogies purporting to do so, and they did not claim to know with any precision the genealogical depth of the whole group. Knowledge of common ancestry was in most cases limited to a maximum of four generations, hence particular groups of households within large *khari bhāukis* could establish common ancestry, but the whole *khari bhāuki* could not do so. We may take as an example the genealogies of members of the immigrant *khari bhāuki* of Scavengers, so far as known to them, shown in Chart I.

The lines connecting the genealogies indicate households that were considered to be closely related, although ancestry could not be traced, and genealogical depth was not known. The solid lines indicate major divisions of the *khari bhāuki,* the dotted lines subdivisions of these.

Two different terms were used for the major subdivisions, *"ilānā"* and *"takśimā." "Takśimā"* was more rarely used in this connection and was also used for a smaller group of kinsmen, while *"ilānā"* was not. I will use *"ilānā"* for a major subdivision. The *ilānā* and its subdivisions were significant in the allocation of traditional village work. In this region, as apparently elsewhere, work was inherited as land was, hence subdivisions of the *bhāuki* are revealed in the context of the traditional economy. The Scavenger *khari bhāuki* in Chart I served in the *bālutā* system six months of the year, with the remaining time going to the other Scavenger *khari bhāuki.* Each *ilānā* worked two months, each of its subdivisions one month. Each month was divided equally by households or minimal segments (solidary groups, further described below) of each *ilānā* subdivision. Within the household or minimal segment work was divided informally, as convenience dictated. The only qualification (or, rather, possible qualification) to the work-group–kin-group nexus was in *ilānā* II, where the households in subdivision A assumed their position because one of their ancestors had been adopted by an ancestor of group B. The fact of their incorporation was recognized by their inclusion in *ilānā* II, and the absence of "real" close consanguinity was recognized by the separate subdivision. Their position in the system prior to adoption was not known

CHART I

Scavenger Genealogies

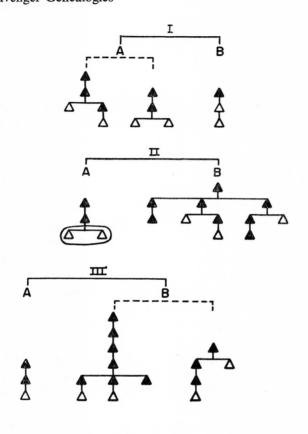

△   Household Head
▲   Deceased
⬭   Minimal Segment
⌐ ¬   *Ilānā*
⌐---¬   *Ilānā* Subdivision

with certainty. Informants believed that the adopter was the father's brother of the ancestor of B, which was, I might add, consistent with most adoption practices.

Systems similar to this were found in other *bhāukis* wherever they held traditional village duties and found it necessary to allocate work—in the Brahman, Temple Priest, Potter, Leather Worker, and Rope Maker castes. The allocation of the headmen's positions within the Koke *bhāuki* of Rajputs was different in some respects. The traditional way in which it operated, about thirty years prior to this study, was similar to inheritance by the method of tanistry, especially as described by Henry Maine.[6] There were two headmen on duty at the same time, each with different tasks. The two positions were rotated every ten years among the four *ilānās* into which the Kokes were divided. Each of the *ilānās* had a name, allegedly based upon the nickname of an important ancestor, and each had an equal share of the *īnām* land traditionally associated with the position of headman. The *ilānās* were not subdivided into groups of households for the purpose of allocating work, as in other castes. They were traceable to four sons of the ancestor of the *khari bhāuki*. There was one household in each that was directly descended from one of the original sons, and the oldest male in this household was head of the *ilānā*. He took one of the headmen's positions for himself or gave it to his eldest son when it was his *ilānā*'s turn to serve. The remaining post was traditionally given to the oldest male in the *ilānā*, irrespective of the household to which he belonged and however remote his kinship to the

---

[6] Sir Henry S. Maine, *Dissertations on Early Law and Custom*, London, 1883, pp. 136–138. This change was not necessarily a result of recent innovations. It was a shift from tanistry to primogeniture, which Maine believed to be a part of a long-term process of evolution. I think it likely that such shifts take place whenever a group expands in size so much as to lose all resemblance to an extended family.

ilānā head. Thus, in allocating one of the two positions, the entire *ilānā* was considered as if it were not divided into separate households. By 1954 the system had changed, and the *ilānā* head had the right to give the second post to anyone he chose. This was always a close kinsman, usually his eldest son. In the traditional system, as among non-Rajputs in 1954, it is clear that the relevant units were *ilānās* or *ilānā* subdivisions, not individuals. However, among Rajputs and in all other castes *ilānās* and their subdivisions were usually unimportant outside the system of traditional job allocation.

Individual households aside, the smallest subdivision of a *bhāuki* consisted of a few, about two to four, households, often called "*takśimā*" by the villagers. It was vaguely defined and variable in size, but usually comprised brothers, fathers' brother's sons, or men and their brothers' sons. In extending and receiving wedding invitations the *takśimā* almost always invited the identical people and was always invited by the same people. The group varied in solidarity. In a few cases it was well knit; traditional village duties, then, were allocated informally instead of by rule, and land was sometimes owned in common. I would estimate that there were about twenty such solidary groups in the village. I will refer to the solidary groups as minimal segments.

As one might expect from the data on "*bhāu bandaki*" (brothers' quarrels), there were often tension and overt quarreling in the *takśimā*. This could reach severe proportions in some instances, so that men sometimes did everything they could to avoid benefiting members of their *takśimā* and even attempted to harm them. When a man had to sell his land, he sometimes went out of his way to avoid selling it to *takśimā* members, although (perhaps because) their land was often contiguous with his and made a convenient addition. In order to make such a purchase, a *takśimā* member, in some cases, had to have someone else buy it for him. This indirect form of purchase was sufficiently frequent and long standing as to have been given a name, *"dalali."* Most *takśimās* varied between these two extremes of solidarity and intense conflict; there were usually tension and cohesion. Tension was accompanied by the belief that the members of the group should defend and help one another. Financial assistance was sometimes given, especially when one member was far wealthier than others. It occurred thus in the case of a Leather Worker who left the village, had considerable economic success, and then lent money to some of his kinsmen in the village. But such a thing was rare. It occurred in this case because the great difference in wealth created marked inequality within the group; the poor kinsmen, literally debtors, deferred to the wealthy, and the latter gave assistance. In most *takśimās* obligations were indeed felt, but they were felt as pressing. The group itself was formed of, or inherited, brothers' tensions and brothers' ties.

In the *khari bhāuki* as a whole, two of the most important areas of obligation and cooperation were in marriage and death. It was considered absolutely necessary at the time of death to have *khari bhāuki* members assist in removing the dead body from the house. They were required to be among the "pall bearers" who carried the deceased to the place of cremation or burial. In deciding on a spouse for one's child, it was thought highly desirable to have some mature members of the *bhāuki* participate, at least nominally, in the decision. Five was usually said to be the proper number, but this was a traditional figure; there were sometimes more and sometimes necessarily less. A man could make marriage contacts himself, although he often did so with the assistance of *khari bhāuki* members or other kin, but after making a contact, he discussed the matter within his *khari bhāuki*. He usu-

ally visited the village of the prospective spouse along with
some mature men of his *khari bhāuki,* about four or five. In
part, at least, this was intended to testify to his bona fides. "If
someone goes to the other village to choose a girl without
people of his *bhāuki,* no one will give him respect or value.
They will think there is something wrong with him. . . . His
family must not be a pure one." In some castes, especially
Harijans, *khari bhāuki* participation was considered not
merely preferred, but mandatory. "If we do not call them at
such a time, and after some days someone dies, nobody will
come to remove the dead body from the house. So at the
time of marriage or death it is necessary to ask help of [one's]
bhāuki."

Yet, the *khari bhāuki* was not an unambiguously solidary
group; as in the *takṣimā,* there was ambivalence. In a few
cases, especially among Marathas and Rajputs, there were
pride in one's *bhāuki* and boasting of its past. The identity of
the *khari bhāuki* was clearly marked in the minds of members by the obligations prescribed for marriage arrangements
and death ceremonies. The *bhāuki* relationship was a significant route along which cooperation could be, and not infrequently was, channeled. Thus, as I will show later, the Maratha caste was the most populous and one of the wealthiest in
the village, yet it had few village leaders. One of the most
important reasons for this was that the caste did not have
large numbers of people in any *bhāuki* within the village to
which a potential leader might turn for support. Nevertheless,
persistent and intensive cooperation was not a distinguishing
mark of the *bhāuki* or its subdivisions. The affinal bond was
at least as important in this regard. Cooperation was not usually more intense as one descended to less inclusive subdivisions. Much mutual aid was given in some *takṣimās,* and the
Koke feud, which divided one *ilānā* in half, helped to produce

cooperation, in relevant contexts, within the two *ilānā* subdivisions. But there was often muted hostility pervading the group, in both the larger *bhāuki* and the *khari bhāuki*. Some of the evidence for this appeared in subtle form. In the course of visiting other villages, if I came upon a surname held by a main *bhāuki* in Gaon, I sometimes made mention of it; the response was in a number of cases silence, followed by a change of subject. People were at times overly hasty in denying the existence of hostility within their *bhāukis*. When asked whether any ties existed with *bhāuki* members outside the village, some answered rather hastily that there was no enmity.

There were also allusions to past misdeeds perpetrated by *khari bhāuki* members on the ancestors of the speaker, especially land theft and poisoning. The fear of being poisoned by a *bhāuki* member was fairly widespread. People were frequently required to take food from members of their *khari bhāuki*. If they then became ill, and especially if there was a stomach disorder (a frequent enough occurrence), there was often suspicion of poisoning. The poisons used were said to be the stools of rats and mice, as well as ground glass, and, rather implausibly, tiger moustaches. The motive attributed to such alleged activity was vaguely thought to involve property —with little good reason, however, for the relationship was often too distant to allow for inheritance.

The existence of hostility within the *bhāuki* was overtly recognized and attested to by the villagers. Enquiry about the matter or even about matters not directly on the subject, often elicited statements such as, in the words of one man, "Brothers always fight . . . there is always fighting among *bhāuki* members."

In fact, actual conflict was rare among distantly related members of a *khari bhāuki,* but there was tension. This might be anticipated. Quarreling was frequent and often bitter within the *takśimā,* especially among brothers; it was generated by intimacy, mutual obligation, and by approximate equality of total status. The frequent bitter quarrels and constant hostility among *takśimā* members were bound to have an effect on the *khari bhāuki* as a whole. In composition it was an expanded version of the household, but with less intimate contact and less pressing mutual obligation. Many of the statuses within it were difficult to rank, hence the originating tension was sustained. But because mutual obligation and intimacy were less marked than in the *takśimā,* open conflict was less frequent than vague tension and distrust.

Open conflict resulting in a sharp division within a *khari bhāuki* existed only in the Koke group, the main *bhāuki* of Rajputs. The feud included many but not all Kokes. Seventeen households were involved. Conflict between the two groups was intense. Physical violence occurred at times, and on some occasions, especially ceremonial, even pitched battles. All villagers, including members of the two groups, testified that the antagonism dated back many generations.

The members of one of the groups, which included nine households of Kokes, lived in a hamlet about one and one-half miles from the main settlement. I will refer to them as the "Annas." (The most specific meaning of *"ānnā"* is "elder brother." I omit the diacritics.) The Annas were all wealthy and had six well-to-do allies, four Koke and two Maratha households, as well as the sympathies of most of the "respectable" people of the village. The other group, which I will call "Bal" (pronounced *"bāḷ,"* meaning "baby"), after the (fictitious) nickname of its leader, resided in or near the main settlement. It included eight households of Kokes. While not poor, the Bals were less well off than the Annas, and apart from one affinal kinsman, all of their allies were poor Harijans.

The allies of the groups openly took sides but were not central in the dispute. The Annas' allies helped them, but only in major difficulties. The Bal group attacked the Annas on some occasions, but never their allies, unless they came to the Annas' aid. The most active of the Bals' allies were Harijans, whose role in the affair will be described later.

All of the Annas' allies lived on their farms, which were situated on the same side of the village as the Anna hamlet. Most were in the general vicinity of the hamlet. Almost all villagers in or near the main settlement, out of deference to the power of the Bals, were careful to maintain cordial relations with them. As a result, some people conceived the village as divided into two "parties," the "main settlement party" and the "Anna party." In fact the split was not so sharp or all-embracing as they seemed to think. Many important villagers lived outside the main settlement, nowhere near the Anna hamlet, and though these sympathized with the Annas, they did not openly side with them, but remained neutral. Most of those who lived in or near the main settlement also sympathized with the Annas but continued to maintain a façade of friendliness with the Bals. Thus the feuding groups did not have the clear-cut boundaries or all-inclusiveness of the "factions" reported from other parts of India. Despite this, I will, for convenience, refer to them as factions.

All of the Bals except one household, a Koke from the main settlement, were of one subdivision of one Koke *ilānā,* and the Anna households comprised the remainder of the same *ilānā.* The seven-household core group of Bals comprising an *ilānā* subdivision were considered by other Kokes to be of lower status. They were alleged to have had an inter-caste marital relationship in their background. The Bals, like all other Kokes in the village, were sometimes referred to as *"pāṭīl,"* and they held some of the *īnām* land associated with the position of headman; but other Kokes asserted that the seven households were ineligible actually to assume the position of headman. The seven households were omitted from the Koke genealogy, which was kept by one of the Anna households. As a result of the feud and the allegations of inferiority, the two subdivisions of the *ilānā* were sharply defined, much more so than other such groups. However, outside the context of the feud, there was no more cooperation in these *ilānā* subdivisions and no less tension in them than existed in others. For example, it had been rumored that Bal's father's brother's son had attempted to murder him, allegedly to take over leadership of the group. In fact, the rumor was based upon little more than a violent quarrel. Despite this, at most times the two men and others in the group maintained an appearance of harmony and acted together against the Annas.

The existence of these factions is understandable when we consider the tension generally found within *bhāukis*. That it existed among Kokes is even more comprehensible. They were dominant in the village and were prone to think of themselves as dominators by right and by nature. But dominance resided in the group; all Kokes were *"pāṭīls."* The particular man who was to hold the position of *pāṭīl* was designated by rule, but, as I will show later, his legal position did not in itself give much power. There was no prior stipulation as to the individual Kokes who were, in fact, to exercise domination. As a result, Kokes were more likely than others to make the effort to assert superiority. More than any others they were given to status competition and to sensitivity over matters of rank. An allegation of inferiority among them was, therefore, very likely to lead to open antagonism. Among Marathas, who did not have a main *bhāuki* in the village, there were allegations of inferiority among *bhāukis;* these were resented, but they did not lead to open conflict or even severe hostility. This was in part because of the absence of unity and mutual identification that goes with membership in one *khari bhāuki;* but it probably was also because Marathas did not consider themselves dominant in this village and so did not compete so much with one another in order to exercise domination.

 5

The Bilateral Kindred[1]

VILLAGERS used the term *"nātlāg,"* similar to the English "relative," to refer to *bhāuki* members and *soyare*. The term *"soyare"* was defined in terms of membership in groups of people with histories of marital connections. It was not the same, however, as the English concept of "in-law." The term was used to designate individuals, but it did not connote marriageable as against interdicted individuals. For example, ego's father's brother's unmarried daughter was not his *soyare;* she was unambiguously in his *bhāuki,* and marriage within this group was prohibited. But once she married into an appropriate group, that group, including herself, was considered to be *soyare,* by virtue, at least, of her marriage into it. I will employ the term without modification for both singular and plural.

The term *"soyare"* was intended for all members of *khari bhāukis* with which anyone in one's *khari bhāuki* had a history of marital ties. There was one major exception to this, the seven households of Bals who were said to be "lower" Rajputs. Despite the fact that these Bals were, by and large, treated as full members of the *khari bhāuki—sutak* was performed for them, for example—they were said to have different *soyare* than other Kokes. Investigation revealed this to be true.

Concept and practice tended to coincide. Interaction was fairly frequent among people who referred to one another as

---

[1] I use the term "bilateral kindred" in a slightly different, more general, sense than is often intended in anthropology. I mean the term simply to refer to a non-residential, bilateral kinship group, not necessarily the exact kind of kinship group found in the West.

"soyare," and most people in a *khari bhāuki* did, in fact, have the same *soyare*. However, most extended wedding invitations not to whole *khari bhāukis* but to *takśimās*. Where one household in Gaon extended an invitation to a *takśimā,* most households in its *khari bhāuki* did the same. Examination of wedding invitation lists kept by four Koke households revealed a total of forty-eight *takśimās* to which invitations were regularly extended; thirty-two of these were shared by all four. Some of those not shared by all involved recent marriages. As regards others not shared, further enquiry revealed that a considerable number of Gaon's Kokes invited them. In these instances, there had been some history of marital ties with Gaon's Kokes, but not so many ties, and not so long a history as in cases of *takśimās* invited by all. A few cases involved households which had emigrated from their traditional village; they were invited only by the particular *takśimā* in Gaon with whom they had affinal ties.

In a few instances people from Gaon invited not just *takśimās* but whole *khari bhāukis*. This was done when a large number of ties existed between the *khari bhāuki* in Gaon and that in the invitees' village. Some particular individuals who were both wealthy and ostentatious always invited all of the *khari bhāukis* with whom their *khari bhāuki* had affinal ties. This took in nearly all of the people whom they, in fact, called *soyare*. But specific questioning revealed that there were always a few *khari bhāukis* considered to be *soyare* who were not invited. That is, there were some villages containing people called *soyare,* with whom little interaction took place. In such cases the relationship was remote, usually involving a gap in marital ties extending over three or more generations. If someone resumed ties with households in these groups, he and his fellow *takśimā* members invited them to weddings, but their entire *khari bhāuki* did not do so at the start. If a few more marital ties were formed, which was not unusual, then the new group would be invited to most wedding ceremonies within Gaon's *khari bhāuki.*

Thus, a particular household's bilateral kindred included its *khari bhāuki,* a few *bhāuki* members not in the *khari bhāuki,* plus a large number of affinals shared with most, not all, of its *khari bhāuki.* From the perspective of the *khari bhāuki,* we may say that there existed a core of relatives with whom it had a fairly constant relationship. As we move out from the core, we encounter a gradual lessening in the number of ties, until we get to *soyare* who constituted potentially rather than actually interacting kinsmen.

Where the *khari bhāuki* was fairly small, this gradation did not occur. The entire *khari bhāuki* shared all *soyare;* if anyone invited a *takṣimā* to a wedding, then all did so. This was the case not only in the very small groups, like the Washermen and Blacksmiths, but also among Temple Priests and Brahmans, where four and five households comprised the *khari bhāukis.* These groups had clearly defined bilateral kindreds shared by all members.

The relationship that has been suggested between the bilateral kindred and wedding invitations did not obtain in all cases. Where individuals were too poor, they could not invite their entire bilateral kindred, for there was not only the expense of having invitation cards printed and mailed, but also the fear that too many would accept, thus making for large expenditures for feeding. This occurred in individual cases in many castes, but especially among Rope Makers and Scavengers.

The relatively constant composition of the bilateral kindred was related to preferential marriage rules. There was a preference for marriage with families with whom one had a history of marriage ties, direct or indirect. For example, if a man could not find a suitable wife for his son in a family with whom there existed a close affinal bond, he tried another household with whom they, the latter, had such ties. Some link of this kind, no matter how indirect, was considered highly desirable, although not mandatory.[2] As a result of this preference, the *soyare* of any *khari bhāuki* tended to be constant in composition through time. Shifts in membership took place at the periphery of the group, but the core changed only very slowly.

Preferential cross-cousin marriage heightened this tendency and gave it a degree of direction. Excepting Brahmans, all castes employed one kinship term for cross cousins, along with wife's sister and some others; for males, *"mehuṇā,"* for females, *"mehuṇi."* [3] Actually these terms covered a number of kinsmen, since indirect cross cousins were also included, such as mother's father's brother's son's daughter. However, direct relationships were preferred in seeking mates. Mother's brother's daughter was much preferred to father's sister's daughter. Most expressed some prejudice against the latter form of marriage, and ceremonial precautions were required if it was undertaken.[4] Most people asserted that father's sister's daughter marriage had been considered desirable in the past. The kinship terminology obviously reflected this. Brahmans, however, said that this form of cousin marriage had not been practiced by them in this region. The highest incidence of father's sister's daughter marriage took place among Scavengers and Rope Makers. These Harijans seemed to prefer both types of cross-cousin marriage more than other castes. Table 7 gives the incidence of cross-cousin marriage by caste. It includes both direct and indirect cross cousins, but the lat-

[2] See Irawati Karve, *Kinship Organization in India* (Deccan College Monograph Series: 11), Poona, 1953, p. 159.

[3] See Appendix A for a list of kinship terms.

[4] See I. Karve, *Kinship Organization . . .* , p. 160.

ter were few. Eight are included in the mother's brother's daughter column, three in the father's sister's daughter column.

TABLE 7

Incidence of Cross-Cousin Marriage by Caste [5]

	MOTHER'S BROTHER'S DAUGHTER		FATHER'S SISTER'S DAUGHTER		Total Marriages
	No.	Per Cent	No.	Per Cent	
Brahman	3	16	0	—	19
High Castes	36	13	9	3	273
Low Castes	4	29	1	7	14
Harijans	47	32	13	9	145

Among Harijans, the Leather Workers had but one case of father's sister's daughter marriage, while the other two castes had six each. The exchange of women between two families may once have been considered desirable, if we may judge from the kinship terminology. Some villagers expressed a partiality for it, but most asserted that it had little prestige, that it was done only by the poor in order to avoid dowry. There were but four cases out of the 450 collected.

Soyare were of considerable importance in mutual aid, especially close *soyare*. One often depended upon them to help discover a potential spouse for one's child; this follows from what has been said regarding preferential marriage rules. Furthermore, wherever possible, enquiries were made with one's *soyare* regarding the character, family respectability, and "purity" of a potential spouse.

Mutual aid among *soyare* can be seen in patterns of immigration. Excluding Marathas, there were forty-one house-

[5] The small number of instances, especially among Brahmans and in low castes, keeps us from generalizing, but these data, if they are shown to hold for a larger area, would give further evidence of the utility of the concept of sanskritization. See Chapter 4, note two.

holds, new and old residents, not in main *bhāukis* among long-standing castes of the village. Thirty-seven of these were affinally related to main *bhāukis*. Two were distant *bhāuki* members, but these were affinally related to affines of members of main *bhāukis*. The Marathas' ties were very complex, and information is incomplete, but each *bhāuki* had affinal ties to at least one other *bhāuki,* many to several others. It seems probable that Maratha immigration, by and large, took place much as in other castes, through affinal connections, though some immigrants were probably closely related *bhāuki* members of Gaon residents. All of the affinal connections would no longer be traceable, for though affinal bonds were strong, they were not persistent, and there were no strong ties to the *soyare* of one's *soyare,* even where contiguity existed.

Asymmetry between *soyare* was an important determinant of the direction of migration. When a man wanted to move to another village, either to buy land or to find employment, in most cases he moved to a place from which his family had taken a woman, that is, where his kinsmen were his "debtors," inferiors. I have relevant data on fifty-four immigrants, new and old residents. Thirty-nine of these had been recipients of females from Gaon, twelve had been donors. The remaining three had multiple ties to households of the village, which involved both superiority and inferiority relationships.

The bond among *soyare* existed even when considerable distances were involved. With the assistance of affinal relatives living in Gaon, people from unirrigated areas came to the village for work in the sugar-cane crushing season. Sometimes *soyare* who herded sheep came to the village for a month or so to graze their animals. Whenever these trips were made, people counted on their kin for a place to stay. Visits were often made with no apparent economic motive. One of the most popular occasions for meeting close *soyare* was the village fair. Unless villages were contiguous, people did not travel to attend the fairs of villages in which they did not have relatives, but they frequently attended those where *soyare* lived.

Visiting was especially frequent between close and newly acquired *soyare*. They usually visited one another two or three times a year, more often than any other kinsmen. But the relationship was brittle; visiting was very rare when the connecting relative, the wife, child, or child's spouse, had died.

The most immediate, clearly defined, and formalized hierarchy was between donors and recipients of women. We have described the superior position of the groom's family during marriage negotiations; after marriage this was manifested repeatedly in the good treatment and deference given them. Thus one man, generally said to be misanthropic, complained: "No one treats me well, not even my relatives. No one treats me really well but my wife's family. Only they value me."

This ranking continued, although to a lesser extent, through the second generation. Relations between a man and his mother's siblings, especially his mother's brother, were generally close and persistent. Visiting was frequent and did not much decrease on the demise of the mother. The age or generation difference in this case established the superiority of the uncle or aunt, but their ranking as donors of a woman vis-à-vis one's own family "softened" the relationship.

Antagonism and even open conflict did obtain between *soyare* at times, but it was rare. It was most infrequent between a man and his wife's family or a man and his children's spouses' families. The only cases I found of such quarrels were where cross-cousin marriage had taken place, which could generate disputes (see last section of Chapter 3). It was more frequent, although still quite rare, between men and their mothers' siblings. All instances of such quarrels that I heard of involved some form of aid given by a man to his mother's siblings, lending money or giving some other kind of material assistance, over a considerable period of time.

The significance of interaction between *soyare* is best seen against the background of *khari bhāuki* relationships. The latter "inherited" the tensions of brother rivalry; thus the individual was forced to depend upon relationships with *soyare,* especially close *soyare.* In these relationships he was clearly either superior or inferior, hence could interact smoothly.

There was relatively little lending of money among kinsmen, either *soyare* or *khari bhāuki,* although it did occur in a few instances. Requesting a loan from a kinsman placed the borrower in the position of a "beggar," the lender in that of "gift giver." Hence people rarely borrowed from their wives' families; that would have been "begging" from an inferior. One borrowed from one's sister's or daughter's husband with hesitation, for the inferior preferred not to aggravate his inferiority and thus expose himself to taunts. So long as cross-cousin marriage had not taken place, one's mother's brother offered fewest difficulties in this matter, and borrowing of money, to the extent that kinsmen were involved, was most frequent here. This was not the case among Harijans, it should be mentioned, for there was a marked tendency to think of mother's brother as wife's father, even when cross-cousin marriage had not taken place. If money was needed, most villagers preferred to turn to money lenders in Mot or, very recently, to the village Cooperative Credit Society. For small loans, in rare cases even fairly large ones, some turned to friends or acquaintances in castes distant in rank from themselves. There were two cases in which Rajputs borrowed

from a well-off Leather Worker. However, as might be anticipated, it was much more frequent for low castes to borrow
small sums from higher ones.

Considering the bilateral kindred as a whole, there were,
apart from actual cash loans, considerable interaction and
cooperation. This, of course, included the *khari bhāuki,* for
the hostility did not preclude mutual assistance in a considerable number of individual cases. For example, if a man's land
was put up for public auction, due perhaps to default on tax
payments, it was thought proper for a kinsman to come to his
aid. A relative bought the land, then later resold it to him at
the original purchase price. Several such cases occurred.
This was not thought of as a money loan, but simply as helping one's kin against "outsiders." The assistance could come
from any kinsman, either *soyare* or, if special hostility did not
obtain, from a *khari bhāuki* member. If a man's wife died, or
if for any reason he found himself without a woman in the
house to prepare food and perform household chores, a
female relative, *soyare* or *bhāuki,* often helped out. In some
cases, especially if the man had no children, he joined the
household of his brother, his mother's sister, or of some other
kinsman; in other cases, the female entered his household. In
any circumstances where individuals were left alone or required care, because, for example, they were very old or
young or very poor, they were able to find a kinsman on
whom they could depend. About nine per cent of the households, new and old residents, included as permanent residents
one or more such relatives.

When a child had to live at a distance from its home, as
was sometimes necessary for educational purposes, it was
almost always sent to live with a kinsman. This was rarely, if
ever, the home of a *bhāuki* member outside the *khari bhāuki;*
but apart from this, and so long as no overt quarrel existed

between households, the nature of the relationship was of little significance. When responsibility for orphans was assumed, the alternative was often between a close *bhāuki* member, such as a father's brother, and a close matrilineal relative, such as a mother's sister (who could have been in one's *bhāuki*). In cases of adoption, the complexion of the choice changed. These cases were always undertaken within the *khari bhāuki;* the closer the relationship within the *khari bhāuki* the better; but the *khari bhāuki* was preferred, no matter how distantly related, to other kinsmen, no matter how closely related.

This kind of mutual aid was available within a *khari bhāuki* and among close *soyare*. With distant *soyare,* for example, beyond one's son's wife's parallel cousin, such assistance was not expected, except in some cases involving migration and prolonged contiguity. Even with prolonged contiguity distant *soyare* ties were usually brittle. The Marathas were an example; the *soyare* bonds among them were indirect and most had long been forgotten. Marathas showed less unity and, one might add, despite allegations of inferiority, less intragroup hostility than any other caste. Not having a main *bhāuki* as a base, they were the least conscious of themselves as a group bounded by the village.

But even fairly distant *soyare* comprised a group. People invited almost all of their bilateral kindred to all important life-cycle rites, especially weddings. Attendance at weddings was often very high; while it was not mandatory, some people travelled over much of India to attend. It was on such occasions, as will be brought out later, that important caste decisions were often made.

Smooth relations within the bilateral kindred were facilitated by the customary use of address terms among kinsmen in accordance with fairly precise, though not consciously formulated, rules. If a term of address was used in speaking to someone, this was, with few exceptions, recognition of superiority and/or formality.

Some address terms were intended for specific kinsmen or groups of kinsmen. For example, *"bhāuje"* was used for brother's wife and a few other relatives. However, such terms were sometimes also used for different (often more distant) kin or even for unrelated persons in order to indicate respect. Other terms were used to address people without any specific kinship link, sometimes without any kin tie whatever; thus *"bāī"* was used in addressing mature women. Some terms implied more respect than others; for example, *"dāji,"* used for male kinsmen, was more respectful than *"āṇṇā."* Mild respect was indicated by the addition of an affix, most frequently a suffix, to the person's name, such as *"-ji"* or *"-rāv."* To address a relative by name without qualification indicated informality, usually associated with the superiority of the speaker. Also used generally were terms for calling people; *"āho"* showed formality and respect, *"e"* informality. The use of *"e"* often indicated the inferiority of the person addressed, but not necessarily, for it was also a sign of intimacy. For example, men often called their mothers by *"e"* but very rarely addressed them by name.

Brahmans, especially conservative Brahmans, used a different system in regard to address terms. They employed a term of respect for all persons in the generation above the speaker. For example, they gave respect to a mother's sister's husband or a mother's brother's wife regardless of his or her age relative to ego. On the other hand, in addressing a member of the first descending generation, the speaker used an individual's own name, although he might (and often did) use a respect affix if the difference in age was great. In ego's own generation the speaker addressed kinsmen older than himself by a respect term, those younger by name. In other castes age was the main criterion; seniors were addressed by a term, juniors by name, irrespective of the generation to which they belonged. The system was qualified in all castes in respect to married women; if a term was used to address a male kinsman, it was also used for his wife, even if younger than ego.

The system was further qualified where the affinal bond was involved. A woman always addressed her husband's siblings by an appropriate term, even if they were younger than she. Donors and recipients of women in marriage were sharply marked off from other relatives by those who behaved most properly—ideally. All relatives to whom one had given a woman were supposed to be addressed by a term of respect or, at least, by a respect affix, irrespective of their age relative to the speaker. Thus some respect had to be given to sister's husband, "classificatory" sister's husband, husband's sister's husband, daughter's husband, and sibling's daughter's husband. With regard to the donors of women the ideal was less clear. Wife's siblings, for example, were supposed to be addressed by a respect term if older than ego, but if younger they could be addressed by name or by name plus an affix. In any case they were supposed to be hailed with *"āho"* rather than *"e"*. One's eldest son's wife was supposed to be addressed by a term—according to one informant, because she might become the household head's wife one day. But no term was used for other sons' wives or for siblings' sons' wives. Daughter's husband's parents and son's wife's parents were supposed to address one another by respect terms irrespective of relative age. There was thus some reciprocity, ideally, between donors and recipients of women.

"Distant" relatives were treated differently. They were not infrequently contacted, for, as was mentioned, the *khari bhāuki* tended to invite the same people to weddings, and

one almost always went to the weddings of one's *khari bhāuki.*
There were no terms of reference for such; they were "just
soyare," and they were treated, not in accordance with the
rules given, but as "guests." All "guests" had to be honored;
all, except very young children, were addressed with some
form of respect.

There were exceptions to the rules. Some people were
called by name or by a particular kinship term so often that
others, no matter how related, even if unrelated, came to call
them so. For example, in one case children addressed their
mother by name, in another a kinsman younger than the
speaker was called by the term for mother's brother (*māmā*),
although no such relationship existed. Individual variation
also obtained in the application of the rules, largely in degree
of respect given. For example, some speakers used a title for
sister's husband younger than themselves, some used a respect
affix. Variation was greatest regarding recipients of women,
in that some gave them less respect than was ideally required.
A few were even haughty and disrespectful to them.

The use of terms between donors and recipients of women
symbolized the formality of the relationship and served as a
reminder of an ideal (not always held to) of mutual respect.
The asymmetry in the use of terms, although slight, reflected
the inferiority of one side to the other. In fact, the inferiority
of donors of women was so well established as not to require
reinforcement. But the opposite was necessary: to help instill
in the recipient of a woman some respect for her kinsmen. In
other cases the use of terms evidently symbolized ideal differences in rank. Accordingly, people were stimulated to
think of one another in terms of hierarchy and to interact
more easily in terms of it.

The phenomenon of merging, whereby one's relationship to
a more distant kinsman was said to be "that of" or "like" a

closer one, was discussed in connection with the family. It indicated, as was mentioned, the ideal distribution of dominance and submissiveness. This also occurred with respect to "close" relatives outside the family, who were frequently merged with statuses involved in a joint family, or, in any event, with statuses closer to ego than they were in fact. Everyone merged close relatives, but the manner and extent of it varied.

Variation in merging was due to a number of factors. One of these was differences in kinship terminology between Brahmans and others. For example, despite preferential mother's brother's daughter marriage, kin terminology among Brahmans grouped all cousins with siblings, distinguishing them by descriptive prefixes. Among Brahmans, all cousins were, therefore, merged with siblings, and aunts and uncles with parents. Other castes' terminology classified parallel cousins with siblings, but not cross cousins; and merging was influenced by this. Cross cousins were not so frequently merged with siblings as with siblings' spouses. The incidence of types of marriages was not relevant, only the terminology. For example, a Maratha woman, speaking of her daughter's husband's father, said that despite the separate term used for him "the relationship is that of brother, because he probably will be a brother." Yet the same informant on another occasion expressed a distaste for father's sister's daughter marriage and insisted (correctly) that such matches were rare. This informant was no isolated case; many people merged cross cousins' spouses with siblings, despite the low incidence of appropriate unions.

Conflict of norms also affected the extent to which merging occurred. In some contexts even non-Brahmans merged female cross cousins and wives' sisters, that is, *mehuṇi,* with siblings. A joking relationship obtained between a man and his *mehuṇi,* and the jokes were not infrequently of a sexual nature. Less "respectable" men would, at times, refer to such women as "half-wives," and sometimes extra-marital sexual relationships occurred. At the same time, all extra-marital sex relationships were, ideally, undesirable. In condemning such behavior, "respectable" people called upon the idea of the sibling tie. "Your wife's sister is like your sister. People who call them 'half-wife' are bad. They are like animals." Thus, a norm of permissiveness clashed with one of restraint, reinforcing the assimilation of a more distant kinsman to a closer one. A similar process occurred in regard to a man and his brother's wife, as noted earlier.

Interpersonal conflict also affected the amount of merging. The high incidence of conflict among brothers resulted in their frequently being merged as "father" and "son." Father's brother's sons were less intimate, the obligations were less pressing, and conflict, although not infrequent, was less than among brothers; they were often said to be "like brothers," more rarely like parent and child. However, with kinsmen not close enough to live in one joint family this factor was usually not relevant.

In contrast to this, interaction between a man and his *mehuṇā* involved little tension or conflict. There was a joking relationship, especially between a man and his wife's brother, who, following the general pattern regarding donors of women, was unambiguously subordinate. Joking was reciprocal, but the wife's brother was almost invariably more passive, more frequently "teased." Wife's brother was rarely merged with brother.

Other factors influenced merging. Where relatives rarely contacted one another, for example, merging was less frequent. People who emphasized ideal behavior merged kinsmen more than those who were "realistic." Merging was rarely carried all the way, as in a joint family, where almost all relationships could be merged to those of "parent" and "child." But everyone merged kinsmen to some extent. This "condensing" of relatives helped to symbolize the unity of the bilateral kindred, to bring kinsmen closer together, as it were. It also helped to order status in terms of rank. Father's brother's son was not, as such, ranked relative to ego, but when merged as "brother" his age relative to ego resulted in an elder-brother–younger-brother, or even a parent-child ranking. Thus, we may view merging, figuratively, as an effort to organize kinship so as to minimize equality and hence rivalry, and to maximize unity among kinsmen.

6

The Castes and
Their Place in Village Life

BEFORE turning to a general consideration of the nature of caste, I will describe briefly the old-resident castes of the village, giving for each in turn something about their occupation, their relationship to the *bālutā* system, and some of their ritual duties.

The five old-resident households of Brahmans in the village were of the Deśastha subcaste and the Bhāgvat sect. Bhāgvats are more generally referred to in the literature as Vaiṣṇavites, followers of Viṣṇu. Brahmans asserted that sectarian differences were of little importance. Intermarriage and interdining took place freely with Brahmans of the Smārtha (Śaivite) sect. The differences between the two sects were only in ritual detail, and even in this regard they were not strictly followed. Village Brahmans wore horizontal forehead markings during rituals, though they recognized that this was a Smārtha practice. Similarly, they used black powder (*bhasma*) in some rituals, which, they said, was a Smārtha practice. They explained that these were family customs arising out of the fact that one of their main household deities was Khaṇḍobā, a manifestation of Śiva. They said that most of their rituals were, in fact, in accordance with Bhāgvat rules, despite these deviations. They employed *"paṇḍits,"* other Brahmans who were full-time specialists in ritual, to officiate at their ceremonies; a Bhāgvat was preferred, but not mandatory. (In 1954 they employed a Bhāgvat.) Village Brahmans asserted that all the other castes in the village were Bhāgvats and that they were not divided into sects. Few other villagers knew anything of sectarian distinctions.

Full-time specialists were not employed by castes other than Brahman. With some exceptions, the other castes used village Brahmans for household rites, such as weddings, *śrāddhas* (ancestor propitiation ceremonies), and Satyanārāyaṇa Pujās ("good luck" ceremonies). Village Brahmans also officiated at some of the village communal ceremonies; for example, a Brahman read the horoscope for village prospects on Makar Saṅkrānt (celebration of the winter solstice, when the sun enters the sign of Makara or Capricorn). When a Brahman served in the capacity of priest, he was referred to by the term *"jośi."* Village Brahmans also served as *"kuḷkarṇis"* (accountants), allegedly but not actually subordinate to the village headman. For their services to the village they received *bālutā* payments annually. Agriculture was their main source of income.

Temple Priests (Guravs) of Poona District have been reported in an early ethnographic account as serving only in Śiva temples and as having the additional occupations of beggar and musician.[1] The Temple Priests in this *tālukā* did not beg and, apart from performing *bhajan* (religious chanting), they did not play music; they claimed never to have done so. In Gaon they tended the temples of Śiva, Hanumān, and Bhavāni Devi. They were not responsible for the Mariai temple, cared for by Scavengers, the Vetāḷa temple, kept up by the Watchman, or the Viṭhobā temple. The Viṭhobā temple was looked after by a Brahman whose house was contiguous to it; this was by mutual agreement with the Temple Priests, with whom the rights to the temple were understood to reside.

The priests kept the temples clean, worshipped the deities

[1] James M. Campbell, *Gazetteer of the Bombay Presidency,* Vol. XVIII, Pt. I, *Poona,* Bombay, 1885, p. 379.

every morning, and at night lit lamps in the temples. The caste also supplied some of the materials used in important ceremonies, especially leaf plates and cups. These were most frequently given to Brahmans, but also to other castes when requested, usually for wedding feasts. They had a few other village duties—for example, carrying the palanquin on the day of the village fair and applying dung to the ground around the village sugar-cane crushers. They held *inām* land for tending the temples—officially really only for the Bhavāni Devi temple—and they received *bālutā* from landowners. They were themselves farmers, though not on a large scale. One household earned additional income by selling dairy products, and one man worked in a shop in Mot.

The caste of Temple Priests had their own priests to officiate at household rituals, but in fact these were often not available, and village Brahmans were usually used.

The one household of Goldsmith caste (Sonār) in the village worked in gold, silver, and copper. (Most villages of the *tālukā* had few, if any, Goldsmiths.) Before the introduction of paper money the primary village duty of the caste was to inspect coins given for taxes; for this, *bālutā* was given. When paper money was introduced, a small *bālutā* payment was given for minor manufacture and repair of jewelry and for polishing images of deities (*ṭāks*) for ceremonial occasions. Ceremonial duties included, for example, piercing the ears of babies and, in the case of girls, piercing the nose for nose rings. (A gold wire was used for this work.) Major repairs and manufacture of jewelry and *ṭāks* were done for cash payment. Additional income was earned by a small amount of farming. The son of the household head worked in a goldsmith's shop in Mot.

Members of this caste considered themselves to be "Pāncāl Sonārs," and as such conceived themselves to be associated

with four other castes, not goldworkers, who also called
themselves "Pāncāl." They will be mentioned subsequently.
Pāncāls had their own priests, always of Goldsmith caste. The
Goldsmith in Gaon used his caste priest on some occasions,
the village Brahmans on others.

As has been mentioned, Marathas were not original residents of the village, but they had lived in the village for some
years and many were well integrated into village life. However, the two oldest Maratha hamlets (I and II) had little to do
with village affairs. They interacted with some particular members of Gaon, usually people who served in the *balutā* system,
most often Brahmans, but also with people living or working
on nearby farms. These hamlet Marathas made financial contributions for village ceremonies if someone came around and
requested them, but in general they were rarely subject to pressures—social, economic, or political—to the extent that other
villagers were. They identified with the village much less than
did others. Neither those Marathas who participated in village
affairs nor any other villagers had sharp conflicts with the
Marathas on hamlets I and II. Some of these hamlet Marathas
expressed mild irritation regarding the Marathas who were
involved in village affairs, but there was no antagonism, only
rejection.

The traditional occupations of the caste were those of soldier and of landowner, and almost all Marathas were farmers.
In addition to farming, one operated a small shop in the main
settlement. Two Marathas were tailors; most of their trade
was in Mot. Most Maratha landholders, even including those
on the two original hamlets, gave *balutā* to service castes.

The Sagar Rajput caste was dominant in the village. It included the largest number of active participants in village life.
The caste was among the wealthiest and contained the largest
number of village leaders. The office of headman (*pāṭīl*) was

inherited in the main *bhāuki* of Rajputs, the Kokes. They held *īnām* land associated with the position of headman.

This caste's name had been Śegar Dhangar earlier in the century; the change of name had been associated with an effort to move up in caste rank. Kokes had been dominant in Gaon at least since 1881, as revealed in the land records. Yet the census of India for 1901 gives the entire population of Rajputs in Mot *tālukā* as under forty people, while the population of Dhangars is given at over 10,000. Dhangars were shepherds by traditional occupation, but in 1954 almost none of the Rajputs kept sheep, and very few kept goats in large numbers. Like Marathas, they considered their traditional occupations to be those of soldier and cultivator. All were cultivators, though two men, in addition, owned small village shops.

Of the nine households of Potters (Kumbhārs), five had ceased to practice their traditional occupation. The other four supplied clay vessels and "stoves" to villagers for *balutā* payments and sold some of their wares in Mot. (The stove was a small three-sided square without top or bottom; a fire was made inside and the pot placed on top.) Water storage pots, having a diameter of about two feet, were made, as well as smaller pots for grain storage and other purposes. A few very small pots, about two inches in diameter, were regularly distributed to villagers for use in ceremonies. Small clay dishes were sold on Divāḷi (the "festival of lights"); these were placed about the outside of the house and used as lamps.

All Potters did some agriculture, and one worked in Mot in a cloth shop.

One of the two Water Carrier (Koḷi) households regularly practiced the traditional occupation of the caste; the other did so infrequently. Their traditional occupation included fishing, of which the women did a little, as well as delivering water. Water was brought from a nearby stream to individual households. Many of the households did not use this service, because it was expensive. Moreover those on distant farms could not readily obtain such service. The Water Carriers were employed by most landowners for important ceremonies, such as weddings, when large quantities of water were needed. Service to the village included bringing water for all temple ceremonies and sweeping the village office. They were also supposed to assist visiting government officers by bringing them water and hay for their horses, and performing whatever other services were required. However, this was only theory; most government officials came from Mot and could return in a short time, hence did not need such assistance. The caste had traditional ritual duties in many important ceremonies. Both households owned a little land, but one had acquired it just prior to 1954. Both received *bālutā,* though one got rather little.

One of the two households of Barbers (Nhāvis) was a new resident by my criterion, but as he was employed in the *bālutā* system, he will be included in the discussion. The traditional services involved shaving the head, face, and armpits, as well as performing other services, such as paring nails and opening boils. Shaving the face was done about once a week, the head about once a month. Ceremonial duties included performing at the tonsure ritual—which was held for male children less than one year old. There were other ritual duties; for example, on Nāgapancami, the day on which cobras were worshipped, the Barbers made small mud images of snakes for all important households of the village, and one Barber made a large mud snake for the whole village.

One Barber worked in Mot and in Gaon. He was able to dispense traditional services as well as to cut hair in the "modern" fashion. He was a young man of about eighteen, whose grandfather had come to the village about twenty-five years before. He lived at some distance from the main settlement and received *bālutā* payments from a few neighbors. His main source of income was from Mot. Many people in the village did not even know of his existence. The other Barber, the new resident, was known to all and was considered the one to whom *bālutā* must be given. He did not object to the young man taking some *bālutā,* because he had all the clients he could handle, about fifty per cent of the old-resident landowners. He also owned land and leased it out for additional income.

Only one of the two households of Blacksmiths (Lohārs) in Gaon practiced their traditional occupation of iron working, and it also did carpentry. The other household practiced carpentry and did agriculture. There were no Sutārs (traditional carpenters) in Gaon; the Blacksmiths got *bālutā* for working in wood. The household that did iron work had left the village some years ago and had returned shortly before 1954. In the interval many landowners had turned to Blacksmiths in Mot. As a result, the village Blacksmith had established *bālutā* relationships with only a few farmers. This household did only minor repair work in iron and little manufacturing of new implements. Both households made new wooden parts for agricultural implements. The Blacksmith caste had no special ceremonial obligations.

The Blacksmiths, like the Goldsmiths, considered themselves to be in the Pāncāl group. However, the households in Gaon used only village Brahmans for ceremonies.

The Muslims of the village had been much influenced by their Hindu neighbors and followed many Hindu religious customs. It was said (possibly exaggerating) of one Muslim, deceased in 1954, that he was more meticulous in observing Hindu holidays and in reading Hindu scriptures than the village Brahmans. The Muslims in 1954 did not perform Hindu household ceremonies, although they participated in communal ceremonies. One Brahman informant insisted that because they were not Hindus they were not a proper caste; however, everyone treated them as such.

The three Muslim households that were involved in village life were traditional butchers. They were usually referred to by the term *"mulāni,"* which means "butcher." They received *bālutā* for their services, and all owned and worked some land. By the criterion here adopted, one household was not old resident. The household head had been invited to the village when his brother, the regular butcher, died, leaving two minor sons. The newcomer raised his brother's sons, and these set up separate households when they married. The three households comprised a minimal segment; they allocated *bālutā* work informally among themselves instead of by formal rules.

The butchers slaughtered and cut up goats and fowl and, more rarely, sheep. Their services were used for Hindu religious ceremonies, especially weddings. At one time *mulānis* made animal sacrifices fairly frequently at the Mariai temple and at the Bhavāni Devi temple, but this had become rather rare. The sacrifice was made at a specified distance from the deity, about fifteen feet, but apart from this, it was done in the same manner as secular butchering, by cutting the animal's throat.

The one Washerman (Parīt) household in Gaon was primarily dependent upon its traditional occupation, for, in addition to serving villagers, it operated a laundry in Mot. Income was augmented by farming, although on a small scale. The full services of the Washerman, including laundering of everyday clothing, required payment in addition to *bālutā*. *Bālutā* was given for washing clothing (really only dipping them in water) on ceremonial occasions and for ritual services. On a death, for example, all household clothing had to be washed. A Washerman was required for a number of other ritual services, such as weddings and sacred thread ceremonies (*munjas*).[2] It was largely the wealthiest villagers who used the Washerman's full services, although a number of Rajputs did so, even though they were not well off.

Of the two households of Watchmen (Rāmośis) in the village, one did full-time agriculture. The job of the other household might be described as assistant to the headman, but without authority or prestige. The household head was supposed to help the headman apprehend thieves, but there was very little to do in this connection. Along with a member of the Scavenger caste, he helped guard the tax money collected in the village, and he accompanied the Scavenger who carried the money to Mot. When conditions were unstable, he was expected to patrol the village at night, once at midnight and once at three in the morning. This had not been done for some time. Whenever a government worker came to the village, he acted as escort. For example, when government veterinarians came to inoculate village chickens, he took them to the appropriate households. At weddings he guarded the possessions of the incoming party. The Watchman was responsible for the "temple" of the god Vetāḷa, who protected

---

[2] The sacred thread ceremony, *"muñja"* in Marathi, is undergone by males, usually at about eleven years of age if the full ceremony is held, to initiate them into their caste. Through this ceremony the individual becomes one of the "twice born," ritually fit to recite the sacred texts of Hinduism. After the ceremony it is a man's right and obligation to wear the sacred thread about his body, a symbol of his purity. This is a cotton thread made according to a special ritual design. Of the castes represented in Gaon, only Brahmans, Temple Priests, and Goldsmiths were reported to hold the ceremony regularly. Other castes in the village that wore the thread, the Marathas and Sagar Rajputs, usually went through brief token rituals at weddings instead of undertaking the full ceremony.

the village from ghosts and evil spirits. The temple comprised a circle of white-painted stones at the rear of the village. The Watchman held and farmed *īnām* land and received *bālutā* for his traditional work.

The Basket Makers (Kaikādis) were immigrants from southern India. Their social organization differed from that of other villagers, and they did not usually speak Marathi to one another, but rather a language they called "Telu." In one ethnographic source their language is referred to as a mixture of Telegu and Kanarese.[3] The Basket Makers said that they had once been a wandering caste in southern India and that they settled in Gaon "seven generations" back.

They interacted much with other villagers, especially Scavengers, whose houses were close to theirs, but their status as full members of the village was equivocal. Some villagers referred to them in casual speech as a wandering caste. When questioned directly on the matter, informants varied. Some said they were no different from other villagers; some compared them to a group of Vadāris (earth workers), wanderers from southern India, who had stopped beside the village for a few months and then left. The Basket Makers' houses were situated just outside what was once the wall around the main settlement. Because close to the main settlement, they were, unlike the Bāgḍis, incorporated into village life.

Their traditional occupations involved raising pigs and donkeys and making basketry items. Only one of the households was entirely dependent upon these occupations. One lived solely by agriculture, and the other two owned and worked land in addition to practicing their caste occupations. Pigs, donkeys, and baskets were sold in Mot; baskets were

[3] R. E. Enthoven, *Tribes and Castes of Bombay,* Bombay, 1920, Vol. II, pp. 126–127.

either sold to farmers in Gaon or given on what seems to have been a semi-*balutā* arrangement.

The Leather Workers (Cāmbhārs), as well as Scavengers and Rope Makers, were Harijans (Untouchables). Only three of the thirteen village Leather Worker household heads dealt in leather in 1954, although it was said that in the early part of the century all had done so. One of the three, an elderly man, sold leather items but rarely worked the leather himself. The other two made and repaired footgear and made leather straps for bullocks, parts of children's toys, bags for drawing water from wells, and other goods used by farmers. These two received *balutā*. All Leather Workers were at least partly dependent on agriculture.

The Leather Workers were fairly well off, considering their caste rank, and had been upwardly mobile in the recent past. Their rank relative to others, however, remained unchanged.

The main obligation of the Scavenger (Mahār) caste was to dispose of dead animals, especially cattle. They would not touch dead dogs or pigs. They were messengers, especially in delivering news of death to kinsmen of the deceased in the region. They carried and stacked wood for cremations. They were considered village servants. If a high-caste villager wanted a job done, for example, to bring a heavy object from Mot, he told the headman, who had some Scavenger appointed for the work. Small tasks to be executed on the spur of the moment were expected of any available Scavenger, to bring a lamp, for example, or to buy something from one of the village shops. When a government official came, a Scavenger was placed at his service. A Scavenger helped collect taxes, assisted the village Watchman in guarding them while they were in the village, and carried them to Mot, accompanied by the Watchman. (It should be mentioned that before paper money was introduced, carrying coins was heavy work.) Scavengers also kept the Mariai temple clean and worshipped the deities in it.

All Scavengers were liable for minor services at all times, but the heavy work was rotated among them. Difficult tasks were the responsibility of on-duty Scavengers. There were twelve households or minimal segments on duty in a given year, and only these received *balutā*. Although other Scavengers, not on duty at the time, were not entitled to *balutā*, some of them went around with the on-duty workers, and they were sometimes given something. These were called *"ādane,"* the "others." Farmers gave to them "because all will be on duty one day," but the payment was not considered their right, rather something like *bakṣīṣ*, a gift. Scavengers held *īnām* land in addition to receiving *balutā* payments, but many had so little that they did not trouble to work the land. A number of Scavengers worked as field hands for landowners, but in most cases this was seasonal rather than steady employment.

In exchange for *balutā* payments, the Rope Makers (Māngs) supplied landowners with a variety of ropes for use in farming, as well as slings, muzzles, brooms, bindings for unrefined sugar, and other similar items. These were given at the appropriate time, for example, the bindings when the sugar cane was being crushed, the slings when the crops began to ripen and were threatened by birds. Ropes used on bullocks were given at the Bāil Poḷā ceremony, the ceremony in honor of bullocks, but also at any other time they were needed. They performed ritual duties for "their" landowners on Bāil Poḷā and on a few other ceremonial occasions. It was considered a good omen to meet a Rope Maker at the village outskirts, and the landowners gave small sums of money when met by the Rope Makers who served their households.

Like the Scavengers, the majority of Rope Makers were primarily dependent on their traditional occupation for subsistence. Very few owned land. Four households subsisted on agriculture alone, either on their own land or through steady employment for landholders. Most gained additional income by part-time work for farmers, though some did only traditional work. One man worked as a barber in Mot in addition to making rope. In the 1940's a few Rope Makers had started selling their wares in Mot several days a week; the number doing this had gradually increased since that time.

They were said to have been at one time traditionally "*tāskar*," murderers and looters, but they did nothing of this kind in 1954. Indeed, Gaon's Rope Makers were reputed to be a mild-mannered group. In the ethnographic literature one of their traditional occupations is reported as hangman, but this was not known to residents of the village.[4]

[4] R. E. Enthoven, *Tribes and Castes* . . . , p. 441; Arthur Steele, *The Law and Custom of the Hindoo Castes Within the Dekhun Provinces Subject to the Presidency of Bombay, Chiefly Affecting Civil Suits,* London, 1868, p. 121.

 7

The Distribution and
Organization of the Castes

ALL of the castes found in Gaon are referred to in the ethnographic literature as distributed fairly widely in the area formerly called Bombay State. Most of them were found throughout the deccan region of Maharashtra and some beyond this, for example, the Potters, Barbers, Iron Workers, Leather Workers, and of course, the Basket Makers.[1] Most of the castes are referred to in the literature as divided into subcastes, usually so defined by area of origin.[2] In some cases the subcastes referred to were recognized by villagers. For example, Śegar Dhangars are described in the ethnographic reports as a subcaste of Dhangars, whose traditional occupation is shepherd.[3] Śegar Dhangar was the subcaste designation formerly used for Sagar Rajputs. However Sagar Rajputs considered themselves to be a subcaste affiliated with northern Indian Rajputs. They said they differed from the North Indian Rajputs primarily in that the northerners were vegetarians. Goldsmiths, whose caste name was Sonār, are mentioned as having a subdivision called Pāncāl, which was the title claimed by Gaon's Goldsmith.[4] Members of one subdivision of Muslims [5] are mentioned in the Poona District

[1] R. E. Enthoven, *Tribes and Castes of Bombay,* Bombay, 1920, Vol. I, pp. 244, 268, 311; Vol. II, pp. 22, 275, 384, 401, 434; Vol. III, pp. 73, 174, 297, 339; James M. Campbell, *Gazetteer of the Bombay Presidency,* Vol. XVIII, Pt. I, *Poona,* Bombay, 1885, p. 407.

[2] R. E. Enthoven, *Tribes and Castes . . . ,* Vol. I, pp. 244, 263, 311; Vol. II, pp. 27, 130, 256, 384; Vol. III, p. 343; J. M. Campbell, *Gazetteer . . . ,* pp. 284, 349, 380, 440, 481.

[3] R. E. Enthoven, *Tribes and Castes . . . ,* Vol. I, p. 314.

[4] R. E. Enthoven, *Tribes and Castes . . . ,* Vol. III, p. 339.

[5] J. M. Campbell, *Gazetteer . . . ,* p. 484.

Gazetteer as "mutton butchers" and as tending to follow Hindu religious customs; this seems a fair description of Gaon's Muslims. In some cases subcaste distinctions noted in the literature were not known to the villagers. Scavengers, for example, are alleged to be much subdivided,[6] but Gaon's Scavengers denied the existence of any subcaste distinctions.

While the castes and subcastes referred to in the old ethnographic literature do not have the significance once given to them, they are not entirely to be ignored. It is true that the names employed often refer to groups of people that probably had different origins, often nothing more than shared occupations. Clearly, intermarriage was not usually practiced within groups so defined; but then preferential rules of marriage limited the *de facto* endogamous groups quite narrowly, as we have seen. The explicit interdiction of marriage between subcastes was rarely brought into play. Some informants recalled such matters having been brought up at caste meetings, where violations were punished. But such cases were very infrequent, and the informants always spoke of them as occurring in different areas and in the distant past.

When contact was made between people of different subcastes bearing the same caste name, they tended to identify with one another. The village Goldsmith interacted fairly frequently with Goldsmiths of other subcastes in Mot, for common occupation brought them together. He considered himself a member of the Pāncāl Sonārs, who allegedly had a common origin with four other Pāncāl castes of different occupations, including Blacksmiths (Lohārs), carpenters (Sutārs), and two others called Pāṭharvaṭ and Ṭāmbaṭ. Yet the Goldsmith had no more to do with "Pāncāl" castes than with anyone else in the vicinity, less to do with them than with other Goldsmiths, who were not called "Pāncāl." Brahmans

[6] J. M. Campbell, *Gazetteer* . . . , p. 440.

in Gaon were of the Deśastha Brahman subcaste. There were
a number of Koṅkanastha Brahmans in Mot, and while intermarriage was forbidden, interaction, including interdining,
was quite frequent. For example, small groups of Brahmans
met regularly in Mot to discuss religious matters under the
guidance of a learned man, and these included Brahmans of
both subcastes. A Koṅkanastha Brahman from Mot owned
land jointly with a Brahman from Gaon. Brahmans, of course,
did not comprise a tightly knit group, but some loyalty was
directed to Brahmans in general. This was more evident
among Brahmans than others, but it was found to some degree in all castes.

Even where interaction was not frequent, the broader
"ethnic" groupings subsumed by caste names still had some
significance. They were important when economic need, a
pilgrimage to a shrine, or some other purpose called an individual to places far from his home village. When a man was
alone in a distant place and needed assistance, he first tried
to find a relative, no matter how remote. If none was available and if he did not have a friend in the region, he then
turned to someone of his caste name. For ordinary villagers, it
was inconceivable that when in need in a distant place they
should turn to some formal organization or to a village headman. It was considered that hospitality must be given to
those of one's caste who appeared in the village. Food and
water were given and, if necessary, a place to sleep, although
one of the temples in the village was usually thought adequate
for sleeping purposes. The Rope Makers are a case in point.
When they visited Poona they did not know whom to contact
except other people called by their caste name. The Poona
Rope Makers gave them hospitality and advice. It is from
the Poona people that Gaon's Rope Makers learned of rope-

making machines, which they were, in 1954, trying to get for themselves.

There was no precise geographic definition of such a group in most cases. Even the distribution of a caste name did not limit it. Village Leather Workers said they were of the same caste as a group in Bombay city called Moci, who were of lower status than they, but who also traditionally did leather work. "It is the same caste but a different name." Identification extended to groups that were very unlikely to meet, such as Gaon's Washermen (Parīṭs) and northern Indian Dhobis, Gaon's Leather Workers (Cāmbhārs) and the northern Camārs. What comprised one's caste differed in different contexts. When speaking in terms of India in general, Brahmans, Rajputs, Dhobis, and so on were each conceived as one caste by people of the particular castes; smaller groups were then referred to as subcastes. But in more ordinary discourse the limits of caste were usually defined by the linguistic region. For most people in Gaon this meant the deccan Maharashtra. In ordinary parlance the group was not usually divided into subcastes. The village Washerman said his subcaste was "Gāngnā Dhobi"; but it was a term rarely used by him or by anyone else in the region. Similarly Deśastha Brahmans, despite the fact that they frequently contacted Brahmans who originated in the Konkan, usually referred to themselves and were thought of as Brahmans, without qualification. It was the same with Goldsmiths, despite their frequent contact with Goldsmiths of different subcastes. People in most castes, whether or not they thought of themselves as having an all-India distribution, did not concern themselves with subcaste designations. The only exception was the Sagar Rajputs, who, because they had become recently upwardly mobile, used their subcaste designation fairly frequently.

Clarity of definition in geographic extension and internal differentiation differed in different castes. Some were fairly clearly structured. Brahmans, for example, were identifiable as such and identified with one another throughout Maharashtra, probably throughout most of India, and the subcastes of Brahmans were clearly marked off from one another. Sagar Rajputs were even more clearly defined, for they had a limited geographic scope and no subdivisions. Other castes, however, were less structured. The Water Carriers (properly, Koḷis) are an example. They were a highly heterogeneous group when viewed from the broadest regional basis. The term "Koḷi" was applied to a large number of groups of different occupation, probably of different ethnic origin, who had little in common apart from a shared name and a status inferior to Marathas but above Untouchables.[7] It was an easy matter to assign this or that individual to the Koḷi caste in the area covered by this research, but it seems not always to have been so simple in other parts of the district.[8] Scavengers were quite similar to Koḷis in caste structure.[9]

The Marathas were an extreme case of this kind. When viewed from the perspective of Maharashtra as a whole, the caste was amorphous. It is hard to tell in some cases whether a group was Maratha or of another designation, Kunbi.[10] Within Gaon and other villages of the region this difficulty did not arise. After initial confusion of terminology was overcome, a Maratha could be well enough distinguished from other castes. But within the Maratha caste there was much uncrystallized differentiation. The term "subcaste" was not

[7] R. E. Enthoven, *Tribes and Castes* . . . , Vol. II, p. 243.

[8] J. M. Campbell, *Gazetteer* . . . , p. 389.

[9] Alexander Robertson, *The Mahar Folk, A Study of Untouchables in Maharaṣṭra,* Calcutta, 1938, pp. 49–51.

[10] R. E. Enthoven, *Tribes and Castes* . . . , Vol. III, p. 9; Irawati Karve, *Kinship Organization in India* (Deccan College Monograph Series: 11), Poona, 1953, pp. 155–156.

used to designate any particular Maratha subdivision. However, many households referred to others as "lower" or "less pure" Marathas and asserted that they did not intermarry with them. These, in turn, referred to others as yet lower. This kind of accusation was made in other castes—the Sagar Rajputs are an example—but it was much more frequent among Marathas.

What existed here were roughly ranked bilateral kindreds. A bilateral kindred, as has been noted, tended toward endogamy (without actual normative endogamy) and overlapped with other bilateral kindreds. The distinctive feature of Maratha bilateral kindreds was the extent to which honorific distinctions were made among them. Such distinctions were based in part on the proud traditions of particular *bhāukis,* allegedly royal lines with different amounts of royalty. However, the rank of many bilateral kindreds was uncertain because many *khari bhāukis* carrying the surname of royal *bhāukis* were allegedly false claimants, descended from improper marital unions. Indeed most honorific distinctions were made on the basis of an alleged taint in the marital history of a group, either a quasi-marital relationship between Marathas or, worse, between a Maratha and another caste. Many of the "tainted" groups were explained as due to the Maratha interdiction on widow remarriage and its frequent violation. Marathas sometimes went to elaborate lengths to investigate the "purity" of potential spouses in order to avoid such groups. For example, one man told of a case in which he claimed to have stopped an "improper" marriage between a woman and his brother's son. The parties had agreed to the marriage, but he was suspicious. He was not known to the woman's family. On a pretext, he stopped by their home and made casual inquiries. When they spoke of the marriage, he said he knew of the prospective groom (his brother's son), and advised against the union. The boy was, he said, a "mixed Maratha," part Water Carrier. The girl's father was unconcerned and said something to the effect that she was not quite pure either. As a result, the match was stopped. While I am not certain of the literal truth of the man's story, it is illustrative of the extent to which Marathas were concerned about the "purity" of potential spouses. Where a prior affinal link existed, which was often the case, then little investigation was necessary.

The internal structure of the caste was further complicated by the fact that wealthy households of "lower" Marathas sometimes married into "higher" ones that were less well off. Informants reported that in such marriages the recipient of the bride was almost always of the "superior" but relatively poor household. Thus we probably have a tendency toward hypergamy, although not normative hypergamy within the caste.

In areas where Kunbis were being assimilated to the Maratha status, the uncrystallized heterogeneity of the caste was likely to be heightened. It is thus evident that Marathas were a heterogeneous group with vague boundaries within Maharashtra, that there were numerous distinctions of rank within the group, but that the distinctions were not so sharply drawn as to allow for any particular subdivision to be named as a subcaste.

Despite the considerable geographic extension of most castes and the loosely structured organization of some, the members of a caste thought of their group in terms of kinship. There was a tendency to slip back and forth in speech between kin group proper and caste. In discussing the conflict between Marathas and Rajputs, for example, people sometimes referred to it as a conflict between Kokes and Marathas, although it was intended as a general reference, extending to all

Sagar Rajputs. Questions asked about intercaste relations were sometimes answered in terms of kinship relations and vice versa. One man of Potter caste was quite explicit in this identification: "When I meet someone of my caste in Poona or Pandharpur, we think there might be some relationship between us. We ask about different names and tell about different names. We do not usually find a relationship, but there usually is one, and we may not know of it. We may not be able to trace it."

The identification of kin and caste obtained not only with regard to whole castes, but also in many people's conceptions of the subdivisions of a caste. This may have existed among the Scavengers at a time prior to this study. An ethnographic report indicates that Scavengers considered themselves to be subdivided into groups that they called subcastes, but some of which were clearly *bhāukis*.[11] I found a similar confusion in people's conceptions of Maratha subdivisions. The ill-defined, partly hypergamous elements of the caste were conceived sometimes as exogamous and sometimes as hypergamous or endogamous groups. One version had it that Marathas were divided into ninety-six groups, of which five were high, the others low. The precise nature of the groups was unclear; some used the term "sect" for them, some *"gharāṇe"* (roughly equivalent to *bhāuki*), some *"kuḷi,"* and some "subcaste." In any event, it was believed that the first five could intermarry, but should not marry into the other ninety-one. They may have been tempted by money to do so in some cases, it was said, but this was conceived as a violation of custom.

One of the most complete "explanations" of the Maratha caste, offered by a rather speculative Maratha, had it that the caste originated in Vedic times from eighteen Ṛṣis (seers to

[11] A. Robertson, *The Mahar Folk* . . . , pp. 49–51.

whom the Vedic hymns were revealed). These, the informant asserted, gave rise to the "eighteen subcastes of pure Marathas." Enquiry revealed that the informant thought of these subdivisions as customarily allowing intermarriage; he then referred to the eighteen as *"gharāne."* The original eighteen, he explained, had had illicit relations with women of other castes, and the result was "fifty-two castes of mixed Marathas." Later the same informant referred to "ninety-six *gharāṇes* of Marathas," five of which were pure, the rest impure. When asked to explain, he said that the original eighteen had given rise to fifty-two mixed castes and these, in turn, to the ninety-six castes. All of the "Maratha" castes apart from the original eighteen were identifiable, according to the informant, as Barbers, Rajputs, Potters, and others, each with their own caste name. (This theory fits well with the tendency to speak loosely of a number of different castes as "Marathas." See second section, Chapter 8.)

The informant was especially given to theorizing, but his constant moving back and forth between kin group proper and subcaste was done by many villagers. It should be mentioned that his notions and other similar ones were "little-tradition conceptions,"—attempts at systematic formulations of a highly fluid social condition by ordinary folk. I infer that there exists in Maharashtra a regional great-tradition counterpart that removes many inconsistencies by defining the elements of the caste as groups of *bhaukis,* each group in a hypergamous relationship with others and, thus, similar to a subcaste.[12]

[12] I. Karve, *Kinship Organization* . . . , pp. 157–158. For a discussion of the Maratha caste, see my article, "Caste and the Concept 'Maratha' in Maharashtra," *Eastern Anthropologist,* Vol. xvi, No. 1, pp. 1–9.

SOCIAL CONTROL WITHIN THE CASTES

It was probable that the identification of kin and caste was fostered by the fact that the overwhelming majority of caste fellows with whom one had frequent relations were, in fact, kinsmen. Interaction was most intense, of course, at the village level, where it coincided with the *khari bhāuki,* usually with attached *soyare.* Beyond this it took in a bilateral kindred. In one caste, the Sagar Rajputs, this very nearly coincided with the boundaries of the caste itself. Kokes' *soyare* were found in over fifty villages, almost all of the villages in which the caste existed, excluding the Koke villages themselves, which were twenty-two in all. In other castes, however, the *de jure* endogamous group extended well beyond the bilateral kindred. For example, Potter *soyare* were found in under twenty villages and Brahmans' *soyare* in thirty-five villages and Poona city, yet these castes extended over most of Maharashtra.

However, bilateral kindreds were in fact the groups within which marriages usually took place; they were the groups wherein most extravillage caste interaction obtained and wherein social control was exercised. Also, bilateral kindreds overlapped extensively; the result was that communication over fairly large parts of a caste's total area occurred.

If a man was alleged to have committed some transgression against caste regulations, this matter would be discussed at large gatherings. If the caste did not hold regular meetings, the man was informally accused. If judged wrong, he would be likely to promise to mend his behavior, for this was the very group within which he was most likely to marry his children and the group with which he most frequently interdined. If he did not conform, he was, in effect, "outcasted." He would not be invited to weddings, and he would not be able to find a spouse for his children. He could attempt to form marital ties by going outside the usual channels, but this was in itself suspect. His *khari bhāuki* would isolate him; they would act as a barrier in any attempts he might make to effect a marriage, and they would not cooperate in death rituals.

In castes that did not hold formal meetings the occasion of communication was primarily the marriage ceremony, for this was the largest single gathering of people in the caste. If not at a wedding, communication occurred during visits to kinsmen, usually when fairs were held in their villages. In any event, news travelled quickly over a considerable portion of a caste by these means. These informal means of communication and social control were the sole forms among Marathas, Brahmans, and Temple Priests, although the ethnographic literature mentions formal means for the latter two,[13] and they may have had such in the distant past. Other castes had held formal meetings in the recent past, some at regular intervals and some whenever it was thought appropriate. Meetings of this type were not held in most castes in 1954; the description I give is based on informants' reports of conditions about ten to twenty years prior to this study.

The areas covered by formal meetings were not markedly different from those over which the bilateral kindred extended. Estimates in different castes varied from twenty to forty villages. Scavengers' meetings had a wider scope in that neighboring areas, not included in the meeting, sent representatives who in theory had the right to veto decisions. Some castes, the Leather Workers, for example, held meetings every year on a designated day; others held them whenever

[13] J. M. Campbell, *Gazetteer* . . . , pp. 160, 379; *but* cf. D. R. Gadgil, *Poona: A Socio-Economic Survey,* Pt. 2 (Gokhale Institute of Politics and Economics, Pub. 25), Poona, 1952, p. 179.

the occasion arose, though they usually favored religious holidays. Most castes held formal meetings but had no regular officers to call the meetings or to preside at them. When a difficulty arose, some messenger—any interested party, generally from a village involved in the matter—would be sent around to other villages of the area. He dispensed information on the nature of the dispute and the date and place at which the meeting was to be held. Formal caste officers existed among Potters, Barbers, Washermen, Leather Workers, Scavengers, and Rope Makers. The offices were inherited by *khari bhāukis,* as noted earlier. The following details on the Rope Makers are typical of the others.

The most honored officer among the Rope Makers was called the *"mhetre."* It was this officer who was supposed to have been the original head of the caste, and it was he who allegedly assigned the remaining officer to particular *khari bhāukis.* The other offices were called *"pāṭīl," "coguḷa,"* and *"gāund."* The main *bhāuki* of Rope Makers in Gaon were *pāṭīls. Mhetres* were all from Mot. The particular individual in the *khari bhāuki* who carried out the duties of the office was not fixed. Selection was allegedly based on ability. There was some suggestion, however, of a tendency toward inheritance of offices in particular households, in that one individual was often repeatedly selected to perform the duties of the office, and his son was frequently selected for the same duties when the office holder died.

Technically, the *mhetre* was supposed to judge disputes and decide on punishments, but in fact decisions were made by the assembled group. The *mhetre* presided over the meeting, quieted disputes when they became too heated, tried to reconcile divergent opinions, and then announced the decision of the group. The duties of the *pāṭīl* were to make the official announcement of a meeting—"to call the meeting." When a dispute came up, it was referred to him, and he decided whether or not a meeting should be held. If he decided on holding one, he informed the other officers. The *gāund* acted as messenger. He spread the news of a meeting among Rope Makers of surrounding villages. He carried a written account of the nature of the dispute and the time and place of the meeting. The *coguḷa* provided for the comforts of those who were to attend the meeting. He supplied lights, seats, and similar necessities, as well as seeing to it that food was available for the caste. He also kept written records of the proceedings of the meeting and the decisions reached. He recorded the name of the *mhetre* who conducted the meeting and collected the signatures—or "marks"—of all those present, in order to certify that the decision was valid.

The official activities of caste officers were limited to about forty villages. Rope Makers from outside this area could attend a meeting if they were interested, but they had no official voice in the proceedings. Meetings could be called on the occasion of any difficulty, but they were usually held during a fifteen-day period in the Hindu month of *Bhādrapad* (August-September). Each meeting usually lasted two or three days.

The duties of the officers differed slightly in the other castes, and all did not have the same officers. For example, Scavengers had no *pāṭīls* and their *coguḷa* acted as messenger. But the general characteristics of the offices and the meetings were similar in the six castes. However, the caste officers had little real power. Indeed, few, if any, individuals in a caste were likely to hold a preponderance of power. In an attempt to identify leaders, a number of household heads in Gaon were asked who they thought were caste leaders and who village leaders. Almost all gave some names for village leaders, but a large number said that there were no caste leaders.

Many answers took the form of "everyone is his own master" or "all are equal." Power was probably highly dispersed throughout the caste. The group as a whole had its say at formal or informal meetings.

The purposes for which meetings were held were much the same for all groups. Sometimes offenses in the ordinary sense were not the subject, but some action was taken to bring a member up to the standards of purity considered appropriate by the group. After a stay in prison, for instance, a man had to be "purified." The Goldsmiths required that ex-prisoners sit in a large pot which was then symbolically "heated," that is, a fire was built at some distance from it. (Metal cups were purified by being heated red-hot after use by persons considered unclean.) Most frequently, however, meetings were held in order to correct offenses against caste custom and to punish grave affronts by one member against another. They could be used to minimize competition in matters pertaining to traditional occupation. Most cases had to do with marriage, sex, and caste occupation.

One kind of case which often came up involved the violation of *bhāuki* exogamy. A Water Carrier case is illustrative. A man of this caste had gone to inspect a prospective wife, a widow. He decided to marry her, the bride price was fixed, the invitations to the wedding distributed. At this point, someone heard of the proposed match and advised the man not to marry the widow; apparently she had formerly been married to a man of his *bhāuki*. This had been overlooked by the groom-to-be, for the former husband of the woman had taken another name. Still, such a union would have broken the rule of *bhāuki* exogamy. The prospective groom became very angry at the father of the widow for having attempted to deceive him. He brought up the event on an occasion when a large group met (at another wedding), and it was decided to fine the father of the widow 100 rupees.

The breaking of occupational restrictions was not infrequently a cause for penalty. In one case a man of Watchman caste started performing some of the traditional duties of Scavengers. He took a job which involved carrying government funds, and Watchmen were supposed only to guard such funds, never to carry them. At a ceremonial occasion, when a large number of Watchmen from the area were collected, a meeting was held on this issue. He was told to give up his job. However, the offender insisted on keeping it. He left his home village and continued his activities. As a result, he was outcasted. He was invited neither to the ceremonies of his caste fellows nor to their homes. For two years he continued in this way. Finally he yielded and gave up his job. At this time, he was made to promise never again to do such work, and he had to pay a fine which was used for a feast for the caste. Then he was officially taken back into the caste.

In some cases alleged offenders were found innocent. For example, a Watchman had attended a wedding at which he had refused to take any food. This could be, and was, interpreted as a gross insult, for refusal to accept food often implied that the host was inferior, "unclean." For some time people avoided him. On the next ceremonial occasion, a meeting was held and the matter discussed. The man claimed that his child had died on the day before the event, and hence he was not able to eat feast foods. His accusers claimed that he should have explained his behavior on the day of the feast, and they demanded that he be punished. He retorted that he had explained to one person; and his accusers answered that he should have announced it publicly. The meeting finally decided that the hosts were the ones at fault for not requesting an explanation on the day of the wedding.

The penalties for offenses varied, but most often the

offender was fined, and the money was used for a feast for those who attended the meeting. Additional punishments might also be inflicted, such as requiring the offender to carry the footgear of all those present at the meeting. If an offender refused to correct his behavior and accept his penalty, he was outcasted. Outcasting did not extend to any offspring born prior to a caste's decision, though it did to those born after the decision. Fixed punishments were not strictly assigned to particular offenses, hence people who were generally well liked or of high status could be treated mildly for small infractions, while others might be dealt with more harshly. For example, a man of Water Carrier caste was discovered to have been living with a woman of lower caste. At a caste meeting, it was decided to "purify" him by the "heating" method described above. This very mild penalty was inflicted, according to the informant, "because everybody liked the man."

Whether intended to settle interpersonal disputes or to punish offenses against caste custom, the meetings assumed the form of "criminal" rather than "civil" proceedings. Thus, someone who insulted another person would be punished by having to pay a fine to the caste rather than to the one insulted. Sometimes the assembled caste members tried to settle interpersonal disputes by advising one or the other party to give in, but the penalty for refusal was either payment of a fine to the caste or some other form of "criminal" punishment.

In the Maratha caste, which was loosely structured and which did not hold formal meetings, outcasting could not be very effective. Improper behavior led to a stigma on the family name, and this could make marital arrangements difficult, but it did not totally cut off the offenders, even in cases of cross-caste marital unions.

 8

Caste Rank

CASTE rank was not a completely clear-cut matter. While some castes were always ranked in the same relative order—Leather Workers, Scavengers, and Rope Makers, for example—many were ranked only roughly. Connected with this rough ranking was the fact that when people were asked to rank the castes of the village, they showed little strong conviction or definite opinion; neither were their opinions normally overtly formulated or consistently stated. This was especially marked with respect to castes far in rank from those of the speakers. Some professed ignorance in this context, others varied in details from one interview to the next. Indeed, there was some vagueness and detachment in many cases whatever the distance between the speaker and the castes being ranked. People changed their opinion without hesitation when confronted with conflicting views. For example, a Brahman had ranked Goldsmiths above Marathas; I mentioned that many did not agree, and he responded, "Well, maybe Marathas are higher." A Leather Worker ranked Goldsmiths as low; his wife said she thought them a high caste, and he changed his view. Caste ranks were requested from a group of Scavengers, and they casually deferred to one another, usually to the eldest, when a difference arose. This personal aloofness was sometimes found even where castes were close in rank to the informant's, and where the positions of the two castes were in dispute. For example, a Maratha woman, when asked whether Marathas or Goldsmiths were higher, said that each thought themselves superior. A Maratha man made much the same kind of answer.

It is not that people were indifferent to caste claims concerning status. As will be discussed later, there was one severe case of hostility over this matter. Furthermore, when asked about caste rank, people were interested and, often after some thought, gave their opinions. But they were relatively uninvolved emotionally in the topic and did not normally discuss it in day-to-day living. I would explain this as a result of the absence of generally shared, usable definitions of position for all castes. There was uncertainty in ranking, and this can result in intense conflict over rank among people in close contact. When individuals were present who represented castes being rated, the raters were circumspect. For example, a Goldsmith ranked Sagar Rajputs fifth from the top when he was alone, but third from the top in the presence of a Rajput. Similarly, Rajputs ranked Goldsmiths much higher when the village Goldsmith was present. These shifts were undoubtedly consciously made. But the aloofness about caste rank was probably an unconscious reaction to the potentially severely disruptive situation. Without necessarily thinking the matter out, people seemed to have refrained from taking a strong stand on caste rank in order to avoid aligning themselves with one caste against others.

Although villagers were not deeply committed to a general scheme of caste rank, each individual practiced caste taboos or believed that he should practice them. For example, some people avoided interdining with some castes from whom they would accept water, while both of these practices were interdicted as respects other castes. Hence, despite the lack of precise, overtly stated agreement among villagers, it is possible to construct a general view of caste rank. This is given in Chart II. The chart is based both on general caste ratings by informants and on assertions made by large numbers of particular individuals as to the castes with which they would not interdine and which were in other respects polluting to them. The numbering within each group gives the order within that group. The letters used in II, number one, indicate that though the castes were about equal in rank, their ratings involved an emphasis on different criteria, the Temple Priest's on religious and the Maratha's on secular criteria. In group II, number three, the castes were ranked as about equal by

CHART II

Caste Rank in Gaon

I. BRAHMAN	III. LOW CASTES
	A. 1. Muslim
II. HIGH CASTES	2. Washerman
1. a. Maratha	3. Watchman
b. Temple Priest	B. 4. Basket Maker
2. Goldsmith	
3. Potter; Rajput;	IV. UNTOUCHABLES
Water Carrier	1. Leather Worker
4. Barber	2. Scavenger
5. Blacksmith	3. Rope Maker

the same criteria. In group III, I set off Basket Makers with the letter B because they are possibly to be included in group IV, and, more important, because they were conceived as separate and different from other castes. The sharp lines implied by the Roman numerals are misleading; the classification is merely for convenience. If we ignore the implied sharp boundaries and consider the ranking as a continuum, we have a good approximation to an all-village view of caste rank. These and other details pertaining to the construction of the table are discussed in Appendix B.

There is a reason to believe that this hierarchy is, in general outline, widespread and fairly old. A report published in 1868, covering the area around Poona city, ranked a large number of castes, and those represented in Gaon were given in an order similar to that in Chart II. The ranking was made by a group of *"śāstris"*—Brahmans learned in sacred law. It was based primarily upon their own general estimations, but was accompanied by another rank system "according to the books." Gaon's castes, by their general estimations, were ranked as follows: Brahman, Goldsmith, Maratha, Temple Priest, Barber, Potter, Blacksmith, Water Carrier, Washerman, Watchman, Leather Worker, Scavenger, Rope Maker. Dhangars were ranked between Potters and Blacksmiths, and though Sagar Rajputs denied the title, their rank in the village was close. Muslims were discussed as if they ranked between Water Carriers and Washermen (consistent with the view in Gaon), although the *śāstris* did not deign to assign an actual rank to them.[1] Basket Makers were not mentioned. The discrepancy between the rank of Temple Priests in this system and that of Gaon will be brought up later. The remaining discrepancies are that the position of the Goldsmith caste was lower by Gaon's standards, and that Barbers and Blacksmiths, in that order, were rated beneath Potters and Water Carriers. It should be pointed out that the two Brahman informants I employed from the village were closer to the system of the *śāstris* than was the general village system. Like most of the villagers, they ranked Temple Priests just beneath Brahmans, but both ranked Goldsmiths just above Marathas, and Blacksmiths just below Marathas. Unlike the *śāstris,* however, they ranked Barbers beneath Blacksmiths. One rated Barbers as equal to Potters and Water Carriers, the other above them.

THE CRITERIA FOR CASTE RANK

One important reason why individuals varied in their formulations of caste rank is that different criteria for caste rank

[1] Arthur Steele, *The Law and Custom of the Hindoo Castes Within the Dekhun Provinces Subject to the Presidency of Bombay, Chiefly Affecting Civil Suits, London,* 1868, pp. xi-xii, 79, 91, 100, 104, 105, 108, 112, 113, 116–117, 118, 119, 120, 122.

existed. Some of these were religious or "ritual," others primarily secular. The religious criteria were probably more important. People thought of caste rank largely in religious terms. Often when they wished to indicate that a man was conservative regarding caste strictures, they would say simply, "He is religious." When I enquired about some instances of close friendship between Harijans and others, it was explained that though the men could not eat with one another and that some even maintained untouchability, no offense was taken, "because it is a matter of religion, not friendship."

The aspect of religion involved in caste was the idea of pollution. The term used by villagers was *"vitāḷ."* The same term was used for all conditions of pollution. People subject to death pollution, *sutak,* were "in *vitāḷ.*" People also used the term for birth pollution, with the exception of Brahmans and some Temple Priests and Goldsmiths, who called this *"soher."* However, even these said that *soher* involved *vitāḷ.* The condition of menstruating women was called *"vitāḷṣi."* If one touched a dead organism, man or animal, one was "in *vitāḷ.*" The condition was "contageous"; contact with polluted persons induced pollution in oneself. Harijans were conceived as in a permanent severe state of *vitāḷ,* and contact with them defiled. Eating in the same row with a Washerman or some other low caste was considered polluting by those much concerned with purity, especially Brahmans. Low castes were in a much milder state of *vitāḷ* than Harijans.

The different forms of *vitāḷ* were terminated in much the same ways. The main variations were for those in *sutak, soher,* or *vitāḷṣi;* these persons had to wait a specified period of time before becoming pure. But at the end of the time they underwent the same purificatory process as others—bathing. The *vitāḷ* associated with caste status, of course, could not be removed. However, pollution by contact with any of these,

Harijans or people in *sutak, soher,* or *vitāḷṣi,* was removed by the same means. The most frequent method was bathing —really only pouring water on oneself or, preferably, plunging into a river. Sprinkling oneself with water or touching a cow were considered satisfactory purification for mild *vitāḷ.* Drinking cow urine was an efficacious way to "cleanse" oneself. Sprinkling cow urine about a room or on a thing purified it from contact with polluted persons. If less pollution obtained, sprinkling water was thought to be sufficient.

Pure things or persons were particularly sensitive to pollution. Temple Priests, Goldsmiths, and especially Brahmans were more careful than others in matters relating to *vitāḷ.* For example, if while eating they heard the voices of persons in *vitāḷ,* whether Harijans or others, they were supposed to stop eating, throw away the food, bathe, and begin again. This was also done by some people of other high castes who were "strict" regarding defilement. Deities were very sensitive to pollution; they could not be approached too closely by Harijans or by temporarily polluted persons. Harijans could not enter temples, except for the Mariai temple. In castes that wore the sacred thread—Brahmans, Temple Priests, Goldsmiths, Marathas, and Rajputs—children who had not yet put it on were less susceptible. If they contacted a menstruating woman, for example, they had only to be sprinkled with water. In other castes the same rule obtained, but was applied simply to very young children. Adults in similar circumstances had to undergo more thorough purification—bathing, for instance.

In part, caste rank is explicable by reference to the bodily processes of birth, death, and menstruation. In some instances villagers explicitly recognized this. Scavengers were said to be low because their traditional occupation involved handling dead cattle. They were generally associated with death. They delivered news of deaths, stacked firewood for cremations, and had the right to rummage in the ashes for gold left on the body. Possibly the degraded status of Rope Makers was due to their having been traditional hangmen, but villagers did not know of this. Both Scavengers and Rope Makers ate beef; the cow was a deity, and if the consumption of its flesh was traditionally condoned by one's caste, one was especially defiled. The occupation of Leather Workers was obviously consistent with their low rank. The low rank of Washermen was said by some villagers to be due to the fact that they handled clothing in an impure state, the clothing of the dead and of women who had just menstruated. At the opposite end of the hierarchy, the highest castes tended to be traditionally vegetarian, thus avoiding contact with death. This was the case with the Brahmans, Temple Priests, and Goldsmiths.

It should be noted that these relationships involved castes, not individuals. Some Harijans did not practice their traditional occupations and were vegetarians. They were given more respect for this—when others knew of it—but were still defiling on contact. It was an open secret that some young men of Brahman, Temple Priest, and Goldsmith caste in the region ate meat (not beef), but they were still considered of high rank.

However, many castes cannot be set off by any specially pure or polluting attributes. Most castes ate meat, but not beef, and did not have particularly defiling traditional occupations. Yet they were ranked and, in the case of the Marathas, were even rated higher than a "purer" caste, the Goldsmiths. It is evident, then, that some ranking criteria were employed that were in no sense derived from the concept of pollution. These are secular criteria, and some castes were conceived to be high in this special sense. Indeed, there existed a peculiar category by which reference was made to secularly high castes. This was the category "Maratha."

Most people used the name "Maratha" to refer to that caste proper and also to a number of other castes, each of which had a regular caste name. Frequently villagers of caste affiliation other than Maratha referred to their own caste as "Maratha." On doing a census of the village, much of my data were initially confused because a number of Sagar Rajputs and a Potter, when asked their caste name, answered "Maratha." Identification of one's own caste with "Marathas" was most frequent with upwardly mobile castes or castes whose status was felt as threatened. Thus, Rajputs were vehement in claiming "Maratha" status. According to one Rajput, there were but two "Maratha" castes, Sagar Rajputs and Marathas proper. It is possible that this was also true of the Watchman caste. In 1954 the village Watchman gave his caste name as "Beraḍ Rāmośi." In 1961 he said, "I am not Beraḍ Rāmośi; I am Maratha Rāmośi, and everyone in the village will take tea with me—though I will not take it from [all of] them." This may be an instance of upward mobility —I did not find out if others of his caste were also dropping the "Beraḍ" designation—or it may be that he felt his status threatened. A number of Watchman households lived in Vāḍi; Gaon's Watchman claimed that these were a lower sub-caste, and he protested that others confused his group with the Vāḍi group. In 1961 he referred to them as "Beraḍ." Substituting the "Maratha" designation in his own caste's name for "Beraḍ" may have been a way of defending his caste against identification with what he believed to be a lower group.

Although almost all villagers used the term "Maratha" in a broad as well as a narrow sense, everyone clearly distinguished the two meanings of the name when specifically asked about the matter. Some insisted that the broad usage was improper. Those who spoke of a number of castes as "Marathas," according to one elderly Rajput informant, "speak wrongly." Similarly, one Maratha insisted that castes like Rajput, Potter, and Barber were not "mixed Marathas" or in any way related to Marathas; they were not Marathas at all. Marathas proper varied much in this respect. Some insisted on an exclusive and precise designation; others followed the majority and allowed the general category alongside the precise one. It should be pointed out, however, that these were opinions elicited by specific questions on the subject. In actual usage practically everyone, including most of those who denied the propriety of the broad usage, employed the name in the two senses.

The castes included in the general classification "Maratha" varied, and variation was related to the caste of the speaker. When Harijans referred to "Marathas" they often meant all non-Harijans in the village, excepting only Basket Makers and sometimes Washermen. When they were explicitly questioned, they always excluded Brahmans, usually also Goldsmiths and Temple Priests. Much the same attitude was taken by the low castes, group III, except for Basket Makers. They claimed "Maratha" status for themselves and all other castes, excluding Harijans, Basket Makers, Brahmans, Goldsmiths, and Temple Priests. Brahmans and high castes, group II, generally reserved the term for high castes, excluding Brahmans, Temple Priests, and Goldsmiths. The broad classification "Maratha" seems to have corresponded to the speaker's conception of a high caste whose rank was more secularly based as against those whose rank was based more on ritual purity.

If the secular prestige of a group was great enough, it could affect its position despite traditionally polluting customs. The main Muslim *bhāuki* had the traditional occupation of butcher, thus its members were associated with death. Furthermore, Muslim tradition permitted the eating of beef. By "ritual" criteria Muslims ought to have been ranked among Harijans. Yet the political rulers in this region, as in much of India, had at one time been Muslims, and the local Muslims were identified with them; hence they were ranked as touchable, albeit a low caste.

Secular phenomena were probably most important in caste mobility. The Marathas, emulated by many castes in the region and always ranked very high, were probably once less elevated. Marathas of Gaon associated themselves with the Kṣatriya *varṇa* and wore the sacred thread. The caste was probably upwardly mobile as a result of Sīvājī's conquests, but as late as the nineteenth century they were described as "pure Soodras of the Books" by Brahman religious specialists.[2] However, villagers never thought of them as being in the Śūdra *varṇa;* no one questioned their high status or referred to them as having been lower in the past.

The Sagar Rajputs had been upwardly mobile within the memory of living informants. Other villagers asserted that they were formerly called Śegar Dhangars, and that they held a caste meeting at which they changed their name, claimed Kṣatriya status and the right to wear the sacred thread. In speaking to me some Rajputs gave their caste name as "Kṣatriya Sagar Rajput." One Rajput claimed to have gone to a *"paṇḍit"* in Poona, who uncovered the true genealogy of his caste. This allegedly traced them back to one of Sīvājī's chief officers and thus assimilated them to the "Maratha" category. Sagar Rajputs also spoke of themselves as a subcaste of the Rajputs of northern India.

The traditional occupation of Dhangars as represented in the ethnographic literature and as attested by villagers is that

[2] A. Steele, *The Law and Custom* . . . , p. 100.

of shepherd. But references in the literature indicate that for a considerable time Śegar Dhangars had been soldiers, village headmen, and landowners.[3] The Sagar Rajputs were traditional village headmen and the dominant caste in Gaon as well as in a number of other villages of this region. Only two houses of Rajputs kept any sheep, and few had more than one or two goats.

Some villagers were amused by Rajput "pretensions" and some, especially Marathas, were annoyed. But criticism or ridicule rarely occurred in the presence of Rajputs. When it did, there was likely to be violent conflict. Some villagers of different caste backed their claims, even when they were not present. But whatever the stand taken, their claim was respected to the extent that everyone referred to them by the Rajput title, whether they were present or not.

While secular phenomena were central in mobility, sacred ones may also have played a role. It is possible that the Temple Priests achieved high rank by "ritual" means alone. In a report dating back to the late nineteenth century, they were said to have acted as temple servants and to have been beggars and musicians.[4] Begging and music making are usually low-caste occupations. In 1954 the Temple Priests of this region did not beg and, apart from chanting *bhajan,* were not musicians. In the 1868 estimation made by the *śāstris,* as has been noted, this caste was ranked below Marathas. Moreover, according to the rating given in sacred books, as interpreted by the *śāstris,* they are ranked below Potters.[5] Nearly everyone in Gaon ranked the caste just beneath Brahmans, and the all-village rating reflects this. I conjecture that be-

[3] R. E. Enthoven, *Tribes and Castes of Bombay,* Bombay, 1920, Vol. I, p. 314.

[4] James M. Campbell, *Gazetteer of the Bombay Presidency,* Vol. XVIII, Pt. I, *Poona,* Bombay, 1885, p. 379.

[5] A. Steele, *The Law and Custom* . . . , p. 104.

cause of their association with temples and their vegetarianism they achieved higher caste rank.

Whether or not mobility took place in this case, it is clear that a high degree of pollution acted as a barrier to upward mobility. The chance for mobility among Harijans was slight, not only because they were often poor and powerless, but also because it was very difficult to discard the stigma of so much pollution. The Leather Workers achieved a fairly good economic standing for a caste of their rank. This was the case, in any event, in this particular village, as can be seen from Table 8. One member of the caste from Gaon, deceased in 1954, had established a successful shoe shop in Bombay, and he helped another to do the same. The latter returned to the village and purchased land, while his son remained in the city. Through the assistance of the deceased man's son, other Leather Workers in the village had also been able to buy a little land. Perhaps because of the existence of the two well-off Leather Worker households, many villagers considered all Leather Workers in Gaon to be well off. Some said of village Leather Workers that "they" were landowners, whereas, in truth, most owned little land. The caste was taking steps in the direction of greater purity. Only two of the thirteen households in Gaon did leather work in 1954. The caste is reported in an early ethnographic account [6] traditionally to have permitted the eating of beef, but in 1954 representatives of the caste in Gaon claimed not to do so. Other villagers accepted their claim. (Some members of other Harijan castes also publicly denied eating beef, but other villagers disbelieved them. In private they admitted the practice.) Many village Leather Workers were as strict in avoiding pollution from contact with "defiling" castes as people of castes in group III. Probably as a result of the fact that their wealth

[6] R. E. Enthoven, *Tribes and Castes* . . . , Vol. I, p. 327.

was estimated as greater than that of other Harijans, their standards of cleanliness and personal appearance were considered by other villagers to be better. They were considered more "respectable" than other Harijans. In the eyes of some they were seen as much higher than Scavengers or Rope Makers, and a few villagers ranked them above Basket Makers. Some disabilities were probably removed in the course of time. Brahmans provided a curtailed wedding service for other Harijans, in the course of which a symbolic distance was maintained between the priest and the celebrants. A full service was given at Leather Worker weddings, and the symbolic distance was not kept, although touching people was avoided. I conjecture that this was a fairly recent phenomenon. The Water Carrier's hereditary right to pour water at weddings was sometimes exercised at Leather Worker ceremonies, never at those of other Harijans.

Yet Brahmans and others still considered it entirely improper for them to enter temples. Of those who maintained touch pollution in 1954, the majority included Leather Workers as well as other Harijans in the prohibition. The rank of Leather Workers relative to other castes remained unchanged in the eyes of most villagers. Furthermore, many villagers considered them only slightly higher than other Harijans (see Appendix B).

It seems likely that, though the secular aspect of rank was primary in mobility and often of much significance in rank, the very basis of rank was *vitāḷ*. High status, even if achieved largely by secular means, was always asserted through exclusiveness in the matter of *vitāḷ*. This is evident in the area of greatest sensitivity to pollution, commensality. With few exceptions, high castes had more restrictions on interdining than low castes. Interdining was taken to be the ultimate measure of rank by the villagers. As was mentioned, villagers often had to give some thought to the matter when questioned about caste rank. In assessing the relative rank of two castes the question informants repeatedly asked of themselves was who took food from whom. (See Appendix B.) Thus, caste rank, however determined, was always translated into the "terminology" of pollution.

9

Interpersonal Relations Among the Castes

Most of the behavioral manifestations of caste rank were unobtrusive taboos. Avoidances of interdining and the like were not conspicuous. Other consequences of caste were equally unobtrusive. For example, a Brahman was supposed to take a ritual bath before eating when he had been shaved by the Barber. People sprinkled a little water over clothing after the Washerman delivered them. Conservative Brahmans when taking food with high-caste people placed themselves at a symbolic distance from them. For example, where people ate in one row separated from one another by about one foot, the Brahman would separate himself by about two feet. Most strictures among non-Harijan castes were of this unobtrusive kind. In fact, ritual avoidance was mild among Brahmans and high castes, even including low castes, with the possible exception of Basket Makers. In many matters, Brahmans treated high castes as equals. There was no prohibition on their taking water from Brahman wells, for example. One Brahman, a religious man, was known to have brought up a Maratha boy in his home.

Caste taboos were marked only regarding Harijans. At a time prior to anyone's personal recollection, every Scavenger had been made to carry a pot suspended from his neck for use as a spittoon, while from behind he trailed a branch to obliterate his footprints. The shadow of a Harijan was supposed to have been defiling. In the remembered past and to some extent in 1954 non-Harijans considered any contact with Harijans to be defiling. Transactions between Harijans and others were made at a distance. When it was necessary for things to change hands, for example, in paying Harijans for services, the object was placed on the ground and picked up by the other party. The personal prestige of particular individuals did not mitigate pollution. Education gave prestige, but educated Harijans were still untouchable. For example, on one occasion, an illiterate woman asked an educated Harijan to write the date for her on a piece of paper. He did so and, forgetting, stepped foward to hand it to her. She stepped back, shocked. He then put it on the floor, and she picked it up. In the recent past it was rare for a non-Harijan to enter an Untouchable's home, even more so to take food or water while sitting near him. It was unthinkable for most people to take food or water from the hands of an Untouchable. Not long prior to 1954 Harijan children sat apart in schools. When it was necessary to correct the work of Harijans, one Brahman schoolmaster, to show his contempt and maintain maximum distance, marked the students' slates with chalk held in his foot. In administering corporal punishment teachers threw objects at Harijans, but did not deign directly to beat them. Of course, no Untouchable could enter a temple, apart from the one dedicated to Mariai, which stood in the Harijan quarter. When a Brahman priest performed marriage services of Scavengers and Rope Makers, he kept an understood distance, usually about ten feet, between himself and the assembled party. This precaution was not observed at Leather Worker marriages, but the priest always took a ritual bath when he returned from a Leather Worker's wedding.

On the river, where one washed clothing, bathed, or took water for cooking and drinking, the places of the castes were roughly allocated. Rope Makers were the farthest downstream, although temporary village residents of very low rank were sometimes assigned a place beneath them. Just upstream from the Rope Makers were Scavengers, and after them the Leather Workers. Farthest upstream were Brahmans, Temple Priests, and Goldsmiths. Between these and the Harijans the order was not fixed.

The behavior of Harijans was restricted even where pollution did not enter. In the recent past they were forbidden to use a horse at marriage ceremonies. The groom rode on the shoulders of a man or bullock. Even if he attained sufficient funds, the Harijan could not build a large house within the confines of the village, for such would be considered pretentious. Abject deference was expected of Harijans. When someone of higher caste passed a Harijan on the road, the Harijan stepped aside. When a Harijan walked by the *cāvḍi,* the government office in the village where the leaders often sat, he stopped, removed his shoes, and saluted before going on.

The ritual distance between Untouchables and others was reflected in spatial separation. Houses of the same caste in the village tended to cluster, as can be seen in Map II. This was most marked in regard to Harijans. They were clearly set off from others, and, despite their numbers, they tended to maintain themselves in their own sections, only approaching one another in one place, where Rope Maker and Leather Worker homes adjoined. Among other castes, only Brahmans, Temple Priests, and Potters strictly banded together. Marathas formed one major cluster in the northwest, invaded by Rajputs and the Watchman, but had some members in different parts of the village. Although Rajputs tended to cluster in the center of the village, they were found scattered throughout, except, of course, in the Harijan quarters. The two Water Carrier households were not contiguous.

Among non-Harijans, rank counted little when patterns of clustering were broken. Thus, Rajputs were found, not only among Marathas, but also beside a Brahman. A Water Carrier's house was also contiguous with a Brahman's. The Watchman was among Marathas, the Washerman near the Goldsmith. A new resident of Ghadṣi caste, which was ranked below Watchmen, was located among Rajputs.

Basket Makers were situated outside what was formerly the village wall, perhaps reflecting their peripheral social position in the village.

There was a pragmatic element in intercaste relations. In some situations pollution was thought to be less "contageous." One of these was work. Harijans handled many things later used, even eaten, by others without qualms. Polluted persons, whether through caste or other means, could handle uncooked food. Harijans, therefore, could work on one's fields, thresh grain, carry grain to the door of one's house, and in most cases bring it into the house itself. They could work at the manufacture of raw sugar, which was, in fact, cooked, but was not defined as such. Furthermore, in the course of labor in the fields or at sugar crushers, casual contacts with people were not considered of great moment. Field laborers usually did not return home for their midday meal. If Harijans and others worked together, they simply separated by a slight distance while eating. Some men who worked with Harijans and some who did not took a perfunctory ritual bath when they returned home in the evening to cover any possible polluting contacts; but many did not take the trouble. When children returned from school, some parents sprinkled them with water as a caution against defilement; but, again, many did not do this.

Casual sexual relations did not seem to intrude very much

in the matter of pollution. Some men of high caste had relations with prostitutes or semi-prostitutes from the village or from Mot. Such women were often Harijans. Some of the men bathed on returning home, but some admitted that they did not. Women who were sexually promiscuous disregarded the caste of the men with whom they had sexual relations. There was one case in which a rather promiscuous Rajput woman had sexual relations with a Scavenger. Yet the same woman was much disturbed when she thought she would have to wash dishes used by Scavengers. A Temple Priest girl was said to have had relations with many men without regard for their caste affiliation. In one case, I think a rather rare type, a Brahman girl was alleged to have had sexual relations with numerous men of low caste. This was openly discussed by non-Brahmans and, in private, rather shamefacedly admitted by a Brahman.

The relationships were not always casual. A number of men of "Maratha" castes had concubines in the village whom they regularly visited. The caste of the women made no difference. A number of these women were of Scavenger and Rope Maker caste, probably because of the economically and politically low position of their groups.

Such relationships were open "secrets." They were considered scandalous by "respectable" villagers, but they were tolerated, however unwillingly, so long as they were purely sexual. When a man and woman of different caste took up residence in one house, the condition approached *de facto* marriage, and the castes usually acted against the persons concerned. However, even here it seems that offenders sometimes managed to circumvent punishment or correction, especially among Marathas.

Lack of restraint between castes, regardless of rank, was also present in emergencies. In sickness very few considered the caste of the physician. There was a Christian physician in Mot who was alleged to have been a Scavenger formerly. Conversion did not remove the taint of Harijan status; he was said to be a "Christian Scavenger." Yet some people of this and other villages used his services without thinking about his status. Village midwives served people of any caste. A Rajput midwife assisted Harijan women in childbirth. In emergencies a Scavenger midwife was sometimes called to help women of non-Harijan castes, although this was done only if others were not available.

Although there were these areas of "pragmatic" interaction, large differences in caste rank remained an important determinant of prestige and esteem. It is true that a fairly well-to-do man with a reputation for proper behavior usually had prestige even if of a low caste, sometimes even if a Harijan. A man of high moral standards and propriety was esteemed irrespective of caste. But in fact, where such men were of Harijan status, their qualities were often not known to others. This applied especially to Scavengers and Rope Makers. They were conceived of as so polluting that the idea of physical dirtiness and moral baseness was associated with them. "The Scavenger is dead, the dirt is gone," goes one Marathi proverb; another, "Hens and goats are not wealth, Scavengers and Rope Makers not castes." [1] The Scavenger quarter, it was said, was always on the east, "because the wind blows that way." If a man was thought to be of little dignity or worth, he was sometimes said to be "like an Untouchable." A Rope Maker boy sat at the door of a Rajput, who, after having asked what his caste was, ordered him to go. The gesture of dismissal the Rajput used was one

[1] These proverbs and others like them have also been recorded in Alexander Robertson, *The Mahar Folk, A Study of Untouchables in Maharaṣṭra,* Calcutta, 1938, p. 3.

used in "shooing" animals. Culture encouraged a conception of Harijans as in some way less human than others.

Under such conditions one might anticipate antagonism between Harijans and others. Some hostility did exist, especially between Scavengers and the upper portion of the caste hierarchy. Not only was the Scavengers' occupation highly polluting, but they were stereotyped as "idlers" and "beggars." Some Scavengers did very little work, running occasional errands and depending upon others for handouts. These, though not a majority, were conspicuous, and they helped reinforce others' conception of the group. Furthermore, they were stereotyped as willful and violent. It was said that more than any other group they were prone to vindictive acts against farmers, such as poisoning cattle, or stealing or burning crops. Their reputation as cattle poisoners was fairly widespread; members of the caste from other areas were reported in Marāṭhi newspapers to have poisoned cattle.[2] There were a few Scavengers in Gaon who were said to have done so, and it is probable that some did. One case of cattle poisoning occurred shortly before 1954, and the circumstances of the case leave little doubt that Scavengers were involved.

It was difficult, although not impossible, for an individual Scavenger to gain recognition as "a good man." Mature men of this caste who were, by village standards, of high moral character were, with few exceptions, not known as such by other villagers. One young man of Scavenger caste attempted and failed to gain acceptance from "respectable" young men of high caste. The Scavenger was educated and met the standards of behavior of the others, but the onus of pollution and the stereotype of the group were too much. Individual Scav-

[2] E.g., "The Poisoning of Cattle" (in Marāṭhi), *Sakāḷ,* July 10, 1954, p. 1.

engers who were "well behaved" were accepted as such, albeit
at a distance, by most villagers. In a few cases the barriers
were overcome, and friendships developed with high-caste
people, as will be mentioned; usually individual Scavengers
of good behavior were simply tolerated as acquaintances.

In fact, Scavengers had little in the way of respectability
to lose by being "idlers" and "beggars." They had something
to gain by violence. Scavengers had the traditional right to
dead animals and used them as food. Their reputation for
violence resulted in farmers being more generous, if not especially willing, when handouts were requested. The result was
that some Scavengers were feared and disliked by other villagers. As a group they were esteemed even less than the
Rope Makers, who were lower in rank. In turn, many, though
not all, Scavengers were hostile to high-caste villagers.

There was one instance of an open break between the
Scavengers and important village landowners, probably
mostly Rajputs. The quarrel took place some time in the past,
and so only its general outlines were remembered. The Scavengers had demanded that their duties on the *balutā* system
be lessened, and village landowners did not agree. The Scavengers then refused to work; they left the village and settled
on the outskirts. After some time had elapsed, landowners
went to a distant place and convinced some Scavengers to
immigrate to Gaon. At this, the old Scavenger group gave in;
they "begged forgiveness" and requested that their old rights
be restored. The landlords relented, and both Scavenger
bhāukis shared the duties and perquisites of the caste.

Rope Makers in 1954 were also hostile to high-caste villagers, indeed even more so than Scavengers. However, this
was in part at least a recent phenomenon. Rope Makers were
busy most of the time at their craft; people of higher caste
recognized this and thought them industrious. They did some

begging, but this was a traditional privilege; other villagers did not consider that they abused their privilege. High castes expressed no hostility toward Rope Makers. The caste was almost entirely landless and dependent upon *bālutā* payments from "their" landowners. As will be observed later, the payments were relatively large, especially in the recent past. In speaking to me of their grievances, Rope Makers asserted that several years ago they had had no cause for complaint, although an elderly man spoke with resentment of mistreatment by high castes in the distant past. One cannot say to what extent Rope Makers identified with the village formerly, but it is clear that the extent of their hostility was a new thing. It will be discussed when we consider the changes taking place in the village.

The caste system tended to bring about mutual rejection between people far apart in rank, especially between Harijans and others. It also tended to encourage antagonism between groups close in rank. Antagonism might be anticipated because relative rank was frequently not precisely fixed and because, in a rough way at least, the rank of any caste had to be defined by reference to groups higher and lower.

The emotional detachment over rank discussed earlier helped to minimize rivalry. The Goldsmith caste, in what was evidently an effort at mobility, prohibited interdining with any other caste, even Brahmans. Yet no Goldsmith in this region ranked his caste above or equal to Brahmans, and some ranked their caste below Marathas. The organized caste was attempting mobility, but individual members, although they followed caste regulations, remained aloof. The only evidence of antagonism was found in a few Marathas, who ranked Goldsmiths as a low caste. Even these were not antagonistic to the Goldsmiths with whom they actually came in contact. A similar phenomenon occurred with Scavengers, whose caste custom forbade interdining with Basket Makers, yet who always ranked themselves below Basket Makers. Basket Makers and Scavengers showed no signs of conflicting in actual interaction.

However, caste antagonism did occur between Marathas and the upwardly mobile Rajputs. Marathas were most prone to sneer at Rajput claims to high rank. Maratha women, who prided themselves on their reserve and more frequently remained indoors, were critical of the "shameless" behavior of Rajput women. As one Maratha woman put it, "They go running after processions." Some Marathas of the two original hamlets, when asked about their identification with the village, answered (in the words of one), "What do I care for this village? It is a Rajput village." Marathas were the only ones to give answers of this kind. Marathas were usually the first to tell outsiders, in private, that "Sagar Rajputs are really Dhangars." When Rajputs heard of a Maratha making such an accusation, they were furious. They often reciprocated by casting aspersions on Maratha morals and claimed that many Maratha marriages were not "real" marriages. Thus, an angry Rajput: "We do allow widows to marry. Why should a young woman of sixteen have no husband? They [Marathas] say they do not allow it. If a [Maratha] man dies, then his three brothers will share the woman and the children will take the dead man's name. Is that better?" As one villager put it, "Marathas and Rajputs are daggers drawn."

While dispute over caste rank was generally minimized by the aloofness with which people handled the matter, it was very difficult to remain aloof in this case. Rajputs and Marathas were socially too similar to one another. Both claimed the traditional occupations of landowner and soldier. Both claimed Kṣatriya status. Rajputs were dominant in this and a number of other villages; Marathas were dominant in most villages of Maharashtra. Furthermore, the Rajputs' claims were recent, hence stood out clearly and stimulated rivalry with Marathas.

Beyond these cases there is little evidence of caste antagonism. Cases of conflict cropped up now and then in respect to *bālutā*. Two such cases, for example, involved Barbers and individual landowners and pertained to the size of *bālutā* payment. The Barbers refused service to the landowners, and the latter agreed to give more *bālutā*. These were clearly not cases of caste conflict, but simply bargaining over a share of the produce.

There was occasional sensitivity along caste lines that did not leave a deep mark on daily life. For example, until 1930 or thereabouts it was customary on the day of the village fair to give a feast in which Brahmans, Temple Priests, and some Rajputs participated. The feast was considered a village affair despite the limited participation, and other castes in the village resented their exclusion. They protested, and the arrangements were changed. A feast was thereafter held in which all could participate. However, a separate feast was held for Brahmans and their guests, at which a Brahman cook was employed. The guests were, as before, Temple Priests and some Rajputs. Hence the resentment remained, but it only appeared at the time of the fair. It was not very severe, and merely resulted in the abstention of many from the feast.

There were many stereotypes of castes that had little effect on interpersonal relations. For example, Deśastha Brahmans were said to be haughty, Goldsmiths mercenary, Rope Makers and Watchmen, thieves. But no one made these assertions about the particular individuals living in Gaon.

Furthermore, even the conflicts between Rajputs and Marathas and between Scavengers and "respectable" villagers rarely involved castes posed against one another as unified groups. Although Scavengers were stereotyped as a group, most individual Scavengers were accepted as peaceable villagers. The Scavengers who were alleged to have committed illegal actions against landowners were few, and a number of other Scavengers resented them for the "bad name" they gave the caste. In fact, the high incidence of *"bhāu bandaki"* mentioned earlier acted against unified action by a caste on the village level, where the *khari bhāuki* tended to coincide with the caste. Though all Rajputs resented Maratha aspersions on their rank, the Bal and Anna factions never worked together against Marathas. Marathas, in turn, were completely fragmented. Kinship relations among them were too remote to make for regular interpersonal relations. Many had little to do with one another. Those on the two original hamlets, especially, stayed to themselves. The caste as a whole had no formal organization, which might have affected its representatives within the village.

A number of factors overrode caste, chopping up the groups and creating new alignments. The most important of these was neighborhood. People with neighboring farms often needed one another's assistance, and hence often cooperated. Some of those who owned contiguous land were involved in semipermanent cooperating groups. These were formed through common ownership of equipment and the exchange of bullocks. Often a man did not own enough bullocks to plow his land properly; he either rented animals or exchanged with one or more neighbors. The terms of the exchange were related to the amount of land owned. For example, if one neighbor owned ten acres and another five, the latter would make some cash payment after his land had been plowed. Small differences in land did not require payment. Most of these groups included farm residents, but contiguity of land was most important, and some included residents of the main settlement.

I found nineteen bullock-exchange groups, containing forty-three household heads. Most of them were composed of people of the same caste, because the kinship ties within a caste resulted in much contiguity of land. Groups containing people of the same caste were thirteen in number, involving twenty-nine household heads. Six were of mixed caste, as follows: 1) one Scavenger, one Rajput; 2) two Scavengers, one Leather Worker, one Potter; 3) one Temple Priest, one Rajput; 4) one Brahman, one Rope Maker; 5) one Brahman, one Rajput; 6) one Maratha, one Blacksmith. The Rajput in the first group had dispersed holdings and also often cooperated with the members of the second group.

There were six jointly-owned sugar-cane crushers, two of them by people of different castes. One group contained two Brahmans and a Rajput, the other a Rajput and a Maratha. One Brahman and the Rajput in the former group were also involved in bullock exchange and, along with three other Rajputs, in the joint ownership of an irrigation well.

Adjacency of land often led to cooperating groups of a more casual and vaguely defined nature. Many people feared injury to their crops or animals, and they sometimes cooperated with neighbors in guarding against this. When lands were contiguous, people often borrowed equipment from each other. The fact that they worked close by would lead to discussion of problems pertaining to farming and other matters. While I have no count of these casual neighborhood groups, there is little doubt that they were numerous and that their composition was similar to the semipermanent ones.

Contiguity of land or even participation in a semipermanent cooperating group did not necessarily lead to close friendship. There was one instance of conflict within a semipermanent group; the two Brahmans sharing a crusher and a well with Rajputs were on bad terms and tended to use a Rajput as a link in communicating. However, many of these groupings did, in fact, lead to friendship or, in any event, to relationships of mutual trust. For example, a Brahman living in the main settlement had three neighbors on farms adjacent to his, a Maratha, a Leather Worker, and a Scavenger: "I am friendly with them but not intimate. I just borrowed a bullock cart from one of them. . . . We may borrow grain even and return it when the crop is in. [We] help one another when there is need."

Other factors helped cut through caste barriers. Association in work or play often resulted in friendship across caste lines. For example, the village Watchman and a Scavenger on permanent village duty were close friends. A few young men of Scavenger and Basket Maker castes were semiprofessional wrestlers, and they were often seen together. Friendships were formed simply because of common age and interest; young men were often friendly, although of different caste. Men sometimes were friendly (on the surface at least) because they were village leaders, all of whom, as we shall see, were not of the same caste. There were other friendships formed for less explicable reasons. Most frequently they involved individuals in castes close together in the hierarchy— Maratha and Rajput or Scavenger and Rope Maker—but here and there one found even intimate friendships spanning considerable differences in caste rank, a Rajput and Leather Worker, for example, or a Scavenger and a Potter. There was even one friendship, a cordial rather than an intimate relationship, between an elderly religious Brahman and an educated Scavenger, although it should be mentioned that the latter was a government officer who had not lived in the village for many years and only visited on occasion.

Similar conditions obtained between men and women. Under ordinary circumstances men did not form open friendships with unrelated women of about their own age, for such relationships would have been conceived as sexual in nature. People of opposite sex who were acquainted did not even greet one another in public. There were some open friendships between men and women, but they were brought about by a special technique. In much of India people who have studied under the same religious teacher, *"guru,"* can assume a relationship of fictional kinship and may consider one another as *"guru-bhāu"* or *"guru-bahīṇ,"* that is, brother or sister by virtue of a common *guru*. In this area the pattern had been further fictionized. If a man and a woman wished to be openly friendly, they visited the priest (*gosāvi*) at the Datta temple, he gave them perfunctory religious "advice," and they were thenceforth *guru-bhāu* and *guru-bahīṇ*. Relations of this kind followed the same pattern found among males. Many of them were between members of the same caste, but they often crossed caste lines, usually castes of about the same rank. There were also a few relationships between individuals far apart in rank; for example, a Temple Priest man and a Scavenger woman, a Scavenger man and a Potter woman.

CASTE AND WEALTH

In Table 8 I give the distribution of capital wealth in the village by caste. The averages are given in terms of total numbers of individuals and of households. The latter figures are at least as significant as the former, possibly more so, for a household head who controlled much capital wealth was likely to get much prestige and power, even if he had to provide for a relatively large number of people. The table takes account of productive wealth only—land, bullocks, sugar-cane crushers, and so forth.[3] It does not subsume all factors determining prestige, power, and living standards. Thus the village Goldsmith, who appears in the poorest bracket, was not really in such bad shape. His son had a good job in Mot; this and his own work gave him an income considered to be fair by village standards. The Washerman household was also better off than appears from the tabulated data, for the household head owned a laundry service in Mot. Similarly the Leather Workers had a better economic standing than the table indicates. Some of the poorer Leather Worker households received economic assistance from their Bombay kinsman, and the wealthiest household head of this caste was even better off than is shown by the table, for he had economic ties with a Bombay shoe shop, where his son worked.

There was a relationship between caste rank and wealth, as the table shows, but it was rough. Brahmans along with high castes averaged 13,958 rupees per household, 2108 per person, while low caste along with Harijans averaged 2291 rupees per household, 457 per person. Exceptions to the relationship were numerous. The well-off Watchman household is one such. His total wealth was 24,500 rupees; that he is not in the second highest bracket in the table is an accident of my classification. The Leather Worker average is as good as or better than most other castes of the village. Despite their high rank the Water Carriers, the Barbers, and the Goldsmiths are clearly to be classed as poor. Similarly many individuals in the Rajput, Maratha, and Potter castes were poor.

The distribution of wealth in the village gave a potential basis for class. Eighteen households, less than ten per cent of the total, owned forty-eight per cent of the productive wealth of the village (Rs 1,800,575). However, these eighteen were of Brahman, Maratha, and Rajput castes, and caste differ-

[3] See Chapter 3, note 8, on the computation of capital wealth.

TABLE 8

Caste Wealth (in 1,000's of rupees)

Caste	Total Wealth	Average Wealth by Population	Average Wealth by Household	Distribution of Wealth by Household (irregular intervals)							
				0– .59	0.6– 2.9	3.0– 4.9	5– 8.9	9– 17.9	18.0– 24.9	25.0– 50.9	51– up
Brahman	133.62	4.95	26.72					1	1	3	
Temple Priest	17.93	0.82	4.48	3	2		2				
Maratha	485.14	1.56	10.11		15	10	3	9	1	6	1
Goldsmith	0.30	0.06	0.30	1							
Potter	44.30	0.66	4.92	3	3	2	2	2			
Rajput	956.85	3.29	20.80		4	3	9	10	3	9	5
Water Carrier	1.55	0.22	0.78		2						
Barber	0.53	0.13	0.53	1							
Blacksmith	6.85	0.69	3.43	1			1				
Muslim	1.85	0.31	0.93		2						
Washerman	0.80	0.13	0.80		1						
Watchman	24.50	2.45	12.25	1					1		
Basket Maker	5.48	0.46	1.83		3						
Leather Worker	50.47	0.69	3.88	4	7			1	1		
Scavenger	67.68	0.58	2.82	3	13	5	3				
Rope Maker	2.75	0.03	0.13	21	1						

ences obviously interfered with persistent common political action on their part. Poorer villagers, it is evident, were similarly divided. This point will be discussed again later.

In fact, power was not determined along strictly economic lines. Unified action of large groups was another important determinant, for power in Indian villages is often also related to the number of able-bodied men that can be mustered in the event of conflict. The groups most likely to display unity in this context are castes. The potentially most powerful castes will be those large and wealthy. This is reflected, albeit approximately, in column one, where total wealth of the castes is given. In this regard, Marathas and Rajputs stand out clearly, as might be expected. Marathas were dominant in the region. However, they lacked unity of action in the village (as well as over broader areas). Kinship ties, although they often produced conflict, were still the main means whereby common action was achieved, especially in a large group. Marathas in Gaon were lacking in close kin ties. The Rajputs had this basis for common action, and they had a large, wealthy population. As we will presently see, they were dominant in power in the village, although their dominance was qualified by divisions within the caste.

Village Politics

IN OUR consideration of caste, it was seen that power was so much dispersed within each group as to make politics difficult to distinguish from the social organization itself. It was otherwise in village organization. The village incorporated much inequality, and, predictably, power was asymmetrically distributed. Marked inequality in power can result in political rather than social domination in a group—coerced association, wherein there could be no solidarity throughout the whole. This is especially likely where one subdivision of the whole, having its own solidarity, possesses a monopoly or near monopoly on positions of power, and where there are other solidary groups whose status is very low relative to the dominator's. These conditions existed in Gaon, as we shall see. Yet political domination did not exist, because the power of the dominant group was qualified. This came about, as I will now show, largely through the nature of conflict in the village. First I will describe the formal political offices, then turn to informal leadership.

THE HEADMAN

There were two headmen (*pāṭīls*) in the village, the revenue headman and the police headman. Both positions were inherited in the Koke *khari bhāuki,* as described earlier. Most Kokes reported that they had received their rights in the distant past for services rendered to the government. The rights were allegedly given to Kokes for Gaon and one other village, whence they were said to have spread to the "fourteen" Koke-dominated villages.

As was mentioned previously, the Kokes of Gaon were divided into four *ilānās,* and the jobs of headmen were rotated among these every ten years. When the time came for one *ilānā* to relinquish the headmen's positions, a formal procedure was carried out before the *prānt* officer (see Chapter 2). Two men from each *ilānā* appeared at his office, and he enquired as to whether the ten-year period was really over. Then everyone present "voted" on whether the incoming headmen were qualified. The vote was only a token, for the incoming headmen were always endorsed.

As remuneration for his services, the revenue headman received a percentage of the taxes collected for irrigation. He and the police headman received a percentage of the land taxes, usually about 100 rupees each per year. The police headman also received four annas per rupee collected from the village cattle pound. (An animal's owner had to pay a fine if it strayed and was impounded.) In addition, all Kokes of the main *bhāuki* in Gaon had rights to *īnām* land regardless of whether they were likely to hold one of the headmen's positions.

The legal qualifications for headman were few. Aside from the appropriate hereditary position and age, he need only have been educated through the fourth grade.

The duties of the revenue headman were to supervise the village accountant in tax collection and in the maintenance of land and property records. The income from taxes was kept by the revenue headman until he had it delivered to the office of the Revenue Department in Mot. (The delivery was made by a member of the Scavenger caste accompanied by a Watchman.) In the execution of his duties, the revenue headman was supposedly superior to the village accountant, but the accountant was always more competent in these matters and usually had a free hand in his job. As one former revenue *pāṭīl* put it, "When I was headman [I did nothing]; I just gave the *mamlatdār* tea when he came and sent him home."

Because the two positions had recently come to be held by men in the same household and because the revenue headman's duties were light, it had been the tendency for one man to do the work of both headmen. This was the situation in 1954 and in 1961.

The responsibilities of the police headman were to try to prevent violence and crime in the village and to make written reports to the police in Mot if they did occur. He had charge of the cattle pound, and he investigated matters such as fire, theft, suicide, and physical conflict. The office involved an active role in village affairs, although it was much subject to influence from informal village leadership. He sometimes handled interpersonal disputes, particularly between people who were not kinsmen. As one headman put it: "A Scavenger has stolen [grain]. I ask the man to return it, [and that] the other party should not go to court. My job is to keep quarrels out of court." If the matter was one of some importance or difficulty, the headman usually consulted some informal village leaders before reaching a decision. Thus, a past village headman: "In my job, I act according to what others think. I must be on good terms with everyone. If [an] important man does something wrong, I may not report it if advised not to do so. But sometimes I am told to make a report. Then I do. When I make a report it is a good one, and something is done about it."

However, the headman was not devoid of independence. If he was sufficiently self-willed and if he could get a few informal leaders to back him, he even acted so as to antagonize the majority. For example, on one recent Hanumān Jayanti (the birthday of Hanumān, the "monkey god") there had been a fight between the Bals and the Annas, in the course of which someone had been seriously injured. The next year, after consulting two village leaders, the headman called the police in from Mot for the day of the ceremony. This was done despite the fact that the majority of villagers, including most of the leaders, strongly disapproved of bringing outside authorities into the village.

It was much the more usual thing for the headman to attempt to insulate the village, to keep outside authorities away. He often did not report crimes. Instead he tried to solve interpersonal problems, criminal or otherwise, in accordance with the principles of justice prevalent in the village, without recourse to the police. He usually turned to the police only as a last resort. The action of a former headman is illustrative. A man had been run down by a bullock cart, and it was believed that the driver had done this intentionally. The injured man wanted to take the matter to the courts. The headman tried to get the offender to make some payment to the injured man and thus to keep the affair within the village. But the bullock driver refused. In order to frighten him into settling, the headman gave the information orally to the police in Mot, telling them to hold off action for the time being. However, the offender bribed the police and refused to make restitution. "What I did was make a report, and I worded it so they would have to prosecute. I had witnesses. But the police had already taken the bribe, so we had to compromise. The man who was hurt got something—two hundred rupees—I got something, and the police got something [from the offender]." The *pāṭīl* was well aware that a bribe had been given and that court action would be unlikely. He used the report as a way to get satisfaction for the injured man.

Village justice was not symmetrical. Wealthy, "respectable" villagers were likely to get more protection than the poor and lowly. The headman acted so as to give some immunity to important villagers, as the incident described on pp. 187–188 shows. In contrast, "little" people were often ignored. For example, the village Washerman had taken a dangerous job that necessitated his staying away from home all night, leaving his mother, wife, and children. The work made him enemies, and these attempted to discourage him from continuing by frightening his family while he was away. Cries for help were often heard at night from the Washerman's mother, but no one came to her assistance. The headman, although he was in the vicinity at times when she called for help, did nothing. He said, "I make reports that are effective. I will not make a report on what the Washerman is complaining about. There is nothing in it." As he well knew, there was something to the woman's complaint. There is little doubt that something would have been done had it been an individual of greater importance in the village. The Washerman had low status, not only because of his caste position, but also because he was relatively poor, and "not respectable."

The position of headman carried with it some power, not primarily because of the formal right to the title, but mostly because it involved the right (and duty) to make reports to the *mamlatdār* or the police in Mot. Yet the headman had to get along with his fellow villagers; he knew that these wanted little to do with outside authorities (and, indeed, usually agreed with them) so he could not use this, his main weapon, very much. As a result, if a headman was to be effective, for example, in resolving disputes, he had to be responsive to the wishes of at least some of the wealthy, assertive men in the village, who would, then, back up his decisions, tacitly or actively. These were the informal village leaders. Even if, by chance, he were one himself, he could not proceed without others. The formal allocation of the headman status, then, did not fix who was actually to exercise domination.

THE ACCOUNTANT

Another position that yielded some power was the office of village accountant, *kulkarni*. This was inherited in the main *bhāuki* of Brahmans. The descendant of the eldest son of the original village *kulkarni* had the legal right to keep the post permanently if he wished, but it was customary to rotate the work among the households every five years. In return for his work, the accountant received a percentage of the land taxes, usually about 150 rupees a year, in addition to the sum of fifty-one rupees every year. The duties were to collect taxes and to keep records for the village. Many different types of records were kept, totalling eighteen, pertaining to such matters as cremation grounds, different types of tax-free land, animals owned, and land owned by each farmer. The crops were checked three times a year by the *kulkarni*, sometimes accompanied by the *pāṭīl*. The most important record was the Extract of Land Rights, which detailed the position and amount of land owned by each villager, whether it was mortgaged and to whom. Copies of the Extract were often needed by farmers for such matters as law suits, land transfers, and irrigation rights. Everyone had the right to call upon the accountant for copies of any records in his care in return for a nominal fee, less than one anna. It was customary, however, to give the accountant a small "tip" on these occasions.

The power of the accountant was considerable. He had a fairly free hand in his work, for, as I have mentioned, the headman did not usually supervise very closely. The accountant's power came from his knowledge of how to assure transmission of property to an heir, how to secure loans, to clear a mortgage, and so on. People frequently went to him for advice in disputes on economic affairs, for his knowledge of such matters usually surpassed others'. Moreover, he held the records that guaranteed to the villager that the land he worked was his. An unscrupulous accountant could withhold records when they were needed or even alter them and ruin those who did not have the knowledge or power to fight back. The gross misuse of his power was unlikely, for he was a villager himself, and hence was subject to informal sanctions. Still the *kuḷkarṇi* was respected by everyone and feared by many. This gave some personal benefits. A former *kuḷkarṇi* recalled his position thus: "On Guḍhi Pāḍvā [New Year's Day in Maharashtra] we Brahmans used to go around to our families for *dakṣiṇā* [gifts to Brahmans], and we would collect a little bit, one or two pice, from each. We would normally end up with a few rupees. But when I was *kuḷkarṇi,* it made a difference. People would welcome me, treat me as if they liked to give me *dakṣiṇā.* When I was *kuḷkarṇi,* I would end up with twenty-five rupees or even more."

The hereditary right to the accountant's office supplemented Brahmans' religious authority with secular authority. Villagers knew that out-of-office Brahmans would be *kuḷkarṇi* one day and hence treated traditional village Brahmans with respect and caution. This probably made it easier for traditional village Brahmans to assume positions of informal leadership.

The headmen and accountant were the only formal offices in the village that yielded power. There was no formal village *pancāyat* (local governing body elected to deal with community matters). Informal village leaders often sat in front of the *cāvḍi,* where quarrels were sometimes brought to them for public discussion. Quarrels also were sometimes brought up on important holidays, like Sāṅkrānt, when all villagers gathered together. Different villagers might then give their opinions, and the village leaders sum up and decide the issue.

It was more frequent, however, to submit quarrels to individual leaders to be decided in private.

INFORMAL LEADERSHIP:
THE DETERMINANTS OF POWER

In composing an initial list of leaders, I asked a number of household heads to name the men they thought to be village leaders. Most named but one man, a few two or more. In Table 9 I tabulate the householders' responses by the caste of named leaders. (Where a respondent named himself as leader, I have not included it.) I give the number of people naming each "leader," the age of the "leader," and his capital wealth expressed in thousands of rupees. All were household heads, and the wealth given is that for the entire household.

Most of those named as village leaders were, in actual fact, leaders. Some of them organized community affairs, and many led in the collection of funds for such affairs, for repair of village temples, and the like. Some were sought to settle disputes. The village headman usually sought the advice of some of them, at least, before making important decisions. They were, by and large, men of much influence in village life.

There were two exceptions. One was the Leather Worker. He was named as a leader by the faction leader, Bal, for reasons that will be mentioned later. Although he was accepted as a man of good character, he was not especially well known and, in any event, had neither power nor influence. The other exception was the third man in the Brahman column, named by one Harijan. His father had immigrated to Gaon, hence he was a new resident by my criterion. He had some effect on village affairs, but his status as a leader was marginal. A fairly good western type of education gave him some influence. One young man of Scavenger caste, not named as a

TABLE 9

Persons Named as Village Leaders, by Caste, Wealth (in 1,000's of rupees), and Age

	RAJPUT			BRAHMAN			MARATHA			LEATHER WORKER	
No. Naming	Wealth	Age	No. Naming	Wealth	Age	No. Naming	Wealth	Age	No. Naming	Wealth	Age
18	33.7	62	9	34.3	42	17	38.9	35	1	2.9	50
17	50.4	31	6	32.2	74	1	?	40?			
16	62.9	55	1	11.3	25						
10	15.2	28									
8	70.6	35									
6	75.4	42									
3	68.1	26									
2	25.9	34									
2	34.1	40									
2	47.7	44									

leader, was similar to the Brahman in that he also was educated and was marginally a leader, although only of Harijans. He and the Brahman will be discussed when we take up the subject of change.

The second Maratha, named by one man, was no longer a resident of the village in 1954. He had left a few years prior to this and lived in Mot, although some of his land was still in Gaon. Because of his place of residence he was not as much involved in village affairs as other leaders, but he was very powerful and did, at times, exercise his power within the village. I did not get enough information on him to estimate his total wealth, but all agreed that he was unusually affluent. His age, as given in the table, is my own estimate, based upon his appearance.

The faction leader, Bal, is fourth in the Rajput column. Nine of the ten who named him as leader were Harijans. The tenth was a member of his faction. For reasons that will be given later, I do not class him as a sanctioned leader.

All of the remaining leaders were wealthy. They fall in the upper two brackets as given in Table 8. Age and "personality" were also determinants of power. By and large, leaders ranged between thirty and fifty-five years of age. The one man who fell below this age limit, the seventh Rajput in the column, had considerable wealth and was a fairly assertive man. He was not among the most powerful of village leaders. There was really no upper limit on age for leaders, but most old men were not sufficiently active to maintain power. The elderly Rajput and Brahman were unusually vigorous men for their ages. The most important "personal" qualification for leadership was simply a willingness to assume the center of attention. As will be mentioned later, one need not have been very aggressive to be a leader, but one had to be willing to step forward so that others might follow. As a comparison of Table 8 with Table 9 will show, there were many wealthy people who were not leaders. These were, by and large, retiring men, who rarely showed themselves on public occasions.

Membership in the appropriate traditional *bhāuki* was an important determinant of leadership. The most significant *bhāuki* was, of course, that of the Kokes; all of the Rajputs listed were of this group. All Kokes in Gaon were thought of as the *"pāṭīls"* of the village, and they thought of themselves in this way. As a result, Kokes believed that they had a "natural" right to lead others. More than any others, therefore, they were prone to seek power, either by direct assertion of themselves or by subtly placing themselves in positions of influence. Others accepted their leadership more readily precisely because their *bhāuki* held "legitimate" rights to power.

Membership in the traditional Brahman *bhāuki* was also important. Although there were but two Brahman leaders, it should be recalled that there were only five Brahman households in the village. As was mentioned in the discussion of formal leadership, the post of *kulkarṇi* was probably partly responsible for their secular prominence. Some years before this study they lost their right to this post, but expectations in these matters tend to persist, and Brahmans who were well off were still looked upon as secular authorities.

Caste rank, as such, was probably a secondary determinant of power. Neither the village Goldsmith nor any Temple Priest was a leader; though of high caste, they were not wealthy. The Marathas were of high rank and had a number of wealthy members. They had forty-eight households in the village, yet only two village leaders. The second man in the Maratha column, the man from Mot, was named as a leader by another person of his caste. Of the seventeen who named the first Maratha as a leader, nine were Marathas.

Both of these men were very aggressive, especially the village resident, who by sheer assertiveness had made himself one of the most powerful men in the village. Part of the reason for the paucity of Maratha leaders was that a number of Marathas were indifferent to village affairs. Also the caste did not have the highly centralized kin ties found among Rajputs and Brahmans, hence a potential leader would have had difficulty in mustering as much support as the latter. The most important reason, related to their dispersed kinship ties and their apathy, is the fact that they did not have a *bhāuki* with a traditional place in the scheme of village authority. Hence, unlike Kokes, they did not conceive themselves as "naturally" village leaders.

Low-caste membership was probably an obstacle to the assumption of power. The wealthiest Leather Worker (noted in Table 8) had many qualifications for leadership. Because of his Bombay connection, he was wealthier than the table indicates. He was of the proper age, and he was a self-confident, assertive man. Yet he remained aloof from village affairs, and no one considered him a leader.

There were other determinants of village leadership, for example, education, but these were secondary. Among the more important secondary determinants were caste rank and age. The primary determinants, it is clear, were wealth and membership in the proper traditional *bhāuki*.

THE NATURE OF VILLAGE LEADERSHIP

Leadership may be conceived on a power continuum, extending from those men who used nearly no coercion to those whose leadership was based nearly completely on force. Leadership that employed very little coercion I call "passive." Men of this kind were leaders largely because their behavior was emulated. I use the term "active" for leaders who employed coercion or the threat of coercion, but whose leadership was based upon adherence to community norms. Leadership that had little or no basis in traditional values and that was, therefore, nearly naked power is properly termed "unsanctioned" and will be discussed later.

The types will be described in a purer form than actually existed. Only a few leaders were completely to be identified with either the active or passive type; most approximated the types; a few were intermediate. Nevertheless, I will refer to leaders as of one or the other type, making qualifications where necessary.

PASSIVE LEADERSHIP

An important characteristic of passive leaders was that their behavior very nearly coincided with the ideal moral code of the community. It was considered necessary to give much respect to the family of one's daughter's husband, and, ideally, this respect should have been reciprocated; but in fact reciprocity was not expected, and indeed some people took liberties with their sons' wives' families. Passive leaders insisted that it was necessary to give formal respect to one's son's wife's family, and they followed these precepts in their own behavior. More than any others, men of this kind tended to merge kinsmen to immediate consanguineous relatives (see Chapters 3 and 5), and their actions approximated the ideals. They scrupulously respected elders. Taking intoxicating beverages was morally disapproved, but in fact most people considered it a forgivable fault; passive leaders were teetotalers. Their adherence to ideals was elaborately formal at times. For example, after the Barber cut his toenails, one passive leader always "saluted" him—that is, a respectful apology was tendered. "It is," he said, "as if I had touched him with my foot." Generosity was a highly valued ideal, and leaders of this kind were unusually generous. One man was known to "lend" seed to poorer people at planting time and then quietly to refuse payment when harvesting was completed. Passive leaders were more than ordinarily religious. They performed all, or almost all, the proper ceremonies. They were not, however, other-worldly in their religiosity. One of them mentioned, on observing the destruction of a hornet's nest, that "killing is a *pāp* [sin], but to kill what is injurious to man is not a sin; it is a *puṇya* [blessing]." Their religiosity usually resulted in careful avoidance of pollution from caste interaction.

Interpersonal conflict was, ideally, undesirable; but it was, in fact, expected to exist, especially among the powerful. Passive leaders, however, carefully avoided conflict. They refrained from using "bad words" about others in public, no matter how blameworthy they felt them to be. They refused to take sides in intracaste or intercaste conflicts. One Rajput leader of this type had numerous Marathas turn to him for advice. Even if their own caste was defamed in their presence, such leaders did not strike back; they either left the area or pretended not to have heard. Many villagers privately ridiculed the Rajputs' recent upward mobility. Passive leaders did not do this; one Brahman leader privately and publicly supported their claims.

Passive leaders did not participate overtly in competition for power. One of them denied his own position of leadership. Most active leaders named themselves as leaders in my survey, but in answer to my question as to whom he thought was a village leader, this passive leader chose to name no one. He said, "I never take the initiative myself, so that relations in the village will not be strained. I always follow the majority." To the extent that such leaders directly interfered in village affairs, they did so privately, or, if publicly, unassertively. One passive leader objected to the fact that during Āmbīl

Ghugriya (ceremony to honor the goddess of smallpox) a man who was regularly "possessed" by a goddess always trampled the sacred fire (*hom*) in the Devi temple. The only action he took was to leave the temple as soon as the objectionable performance started. In this way he indicated his disapproval without a verbal protest. Direct interference in village affairs was likely to be done quietly. One instance of this involved a Brahman leader who altered the Holi ceremony, which required the worship of a village bonfire, in a direction that he thought closer to the spirit of the *śāstras* (sacred laws of Hinduism). Food offered to the village fire had customarily been given to members of the Scavenger caste, and the Brahman thought this sacrilegious. He suggested to active village leaders that the food should be thrown into the fire, and that, to prevent dissatisfaction, the Scavengers be given an equivalent amount of food made especially for them. His suggestion was taken. This same man objected to the customary sacrifice of an animal to the god Khaṇḍobā because the sacrifice coincided with the "birthday" of Hanumān. Hanumān, he said, was a *brahmacārin,*[1] hence animal sacrifice was inappropriate on the day set aside in his honor. The leader's wish was not followed.

In these matters passive leaders often acted through active leaders. They were important, also, as style-setters in behavior, for they, more than others, embodied the moral ideals. Although they did not assert that they were leaders, and one even denied it, they knew that they were followed. One passive leader spoke of a visiting "holy man," protesting that he was spurious, really interested in profit rather than religion. "The man tried to get me to give him a silk *dhoti,*

---

[1] *Brahmacārin* refers to a celibate student of the Vedas, a member of the first *āśrama* (one of the traditional life stages of Hinduism). A *brahmacārin* is in a more sacred state than a householder and would be ritually polluted by an animal sacrifice.

because he knew that if I gave him something, everyone else would do so too. I would not give him anything." Because they were conscious of their positions, their public behavior and statements were especially guarded. One man, for example, spoke very strictly on the practice of untouchability—passive leaders were reputed to be strict in this context—yet I discovered that he was more lax with Untouchables in private.

Important activities of passive leaders were private advising and resolution of quarrels. The cases they decided were varied, but most were related to land disputes and the like, for instance, the equitable distribution of family wealth at the breakup of a joint family. I give one quarrel as an illustration. A man had been unable to repay a government loan, and as a result his land was offered at public auction. Under such circumstances, it was customary for close relatives to buy the land and resell it to the former owner at the original purchase price when the latter was able to repay. In this case the purchase was made by the defaulter's sister's son, who not only bought the land, but also took the former owner into his home, fed him, and helped him in other ways. Meanwhile, the nephew invested in the improvement of the land; a diesel pump, for example, was installed. The value of the land had soon gone up out of all proportion to the original purchase price, partially as a result of the improvements and partially due to market conditions. At this point, the original owner expressed his desire to buy back the land at the original purchase price. A quarrel ensued, and no decision could be reached. The two men took the quarrel to a passive leader, who decided that a portion of the land should be returned without any payment. Though antagonism continued between the disputants, the decision was accepted without further delay.

Because passive leaders remained aloof from conflicts,

resolution of quarrels could continue without respect for village factionalism or intercaste rivalry. Disputants felt that they could turn to such leaders without fear that factional or caste partiality would be shown.

Strict adherence to ideal norms was not the only basis for leadership of this kind. As for all sanctioned leaders, it was necessary for passive leaders to be wealthy. One man of Maratha caste was known for his strict morality, his eloquence, and his religiosity—he was a *kīrtankār,* a type of preacher—but he was a tailor, a poor man, and hence not a leader. Furthermore, leaders had to be the kind of people who wanted, or in any event were willing to accept, positions of prestige in the village. Other villagers—Kokes, Brahmans, and Marathas—were wealthy and highly moral but were too retiring to be much noticed or too hesitant in their judgments to be called upon to decide disputes.

ACTIVE LEADERSHIP

Active leaders were distinguished by wealth, assertiveness and pride. Wealth alone was not enough to give leadership. If a man was willing to have himself seen in demeaning positions, he could not be a leader. One example of this was an elderly, aggressive, rather boisterous and well-to-do Koke. He was known as a man too pleased to accept a handout of tobacco or tea, and hence he was held in contempt, much more so, indeed, than if he had been poor. One young man went so far as to shout at him in public that he was "like a Harijan," a shocking thing to say to anyone of high caste, especially to an elder.

To be an active leader one had to conform to village norms and, further, one had to use one's wealth to exceed expectations in some respects. The wedding ceremony was an especially important occasion for this. It was supposed to be an elaborate affair, involving a sizable dowry, the exchange of much new clothing, and so on. The behavior of ordinary people approximated this norm to the extent that their wealth permitted, but the weddings of active leaders exceeded it. At their weddings, two bands might be present to play music; a team of professional dancers might be called upon; the bride was more heavily laden with gold than others. Some active leaders plunged themselves into debt, all strained their resources to make the proper impression. Their weddings were more elaborate than those of men as wealthy, and in some cases, even wealthier than they were.

Generosity was not merely an ideal; it was a concrete expectation. Leaders of this type were more than usually generous. They gave liberally to beggars. Their *balutā* payments and tips to *balutedārs* were often larger than was considered necessary. They always gave to the Scavenger *ādane* ("others"—off-duty Scavengers), and all used the village Washerman's full services, although the service was considered to be poor and the fee high. Their contributions to village ceremonies, collections for temple repair, and the like were always very large. Their generosity was usually a public matter. It was an advertisement of it. It encouraged the idea that others were indebted to them, that indeed the village as a whole was beholden to them. Thus by defining them as "creditors," it enhanced their position as leaders.

These leaders vied with one another for positions of honor at ceremonies. For example, they were the ones on Bāil Poḷā (the day on which bullocks were ceremonially honored) who attempted to outwait one another for the honor of being last in the procession (see second section of Chapter 11). They were the men in the village most deeply involved in status competition.

While their behavior was consistent with village norms, it

was less so with moral ideals. Joking with one's *mehuṇi* was rougher with these men, and one's son's wife's parents were often treated with more haughtiness than the ideal required. A new daughter-in-law was less likely to be treated "as a daughter" than in the households of passive leaders. Locally distilled rum found an outlet in many of their households. Many were present in the audience at a *tamāśā,* a traditional show involving bawdy singing and joking. A few of these leaders kept women, sometimes women of lower caste, and many had casual extramarital sexual relations.

Active leaders directly ran the village. They were not usually employed to decide disputes in private, but along with passive leaders they sometimes considered such matters in public. Such leaders would, on occasion, directly order other villagers about, for example, to disperse an unruly group on the village streets or to chastise someone whom they thought behaved improperly.

In caste matters, most active leaders were concerned about pollution but less solicitous for the niceties of it than passive leaders. They were more attentive to secular status. They insisted that lower castes, especially Harijans, keep in their place, speak "softly" to important persons, and obey orders. Many active leaders were curt and domineering in their relations with Untouchables.

As was mentioned, headmen usually consulted active leaders before making important decisions. Important ceremonies were, in theory, planned entirely by the headmen. In fact, the headmen planned these in conjunction with informal committees of village leaders. The active leaders planned the village fair, saw to it that money was collected, and that proper supplies and hired performers were present. They decided whether or not to hold Āmbīl Ghugriya and how much to spend on the ceremony. When I was about to leave the village in 1955, it was decided to hold a farewell celebration; these men carried through the decision and passed on the nature of the celebration and on the gift to be given. The Rope Makers had wanted to give me a separate celebration, but village leaders quickly stopped them, fearing, I suspect, that it would reflect on the unity of the village.

If one wished to have one's way in a dispute, the most economical, rapid, and effective way was not to go to court, but to gain the favor of active leaders. For example, one Rajput had mortgaged land to another; he wanted to repay the money and regain his land, but the mortgagee raised technical difficulties and refused to relinquish it. Both were men of good standing in the community, but the mortgagee was wealthier and more powerful. If the mortgagor turned to the courts it would be, he realized, a long, expensive, and possibly futile procedure. Instead he invited four of the most important active village leaders to dinner and served them liberally with rum. "I knew they would be pleased with this. When they were drunk and happy I told them about the land. I said [the mortgagee] should return the land. They said they would back me. . . . The land was returned."

The power of active leaders was used not only to run the village, but also to ensure privileges for themselves. For example, when a well was constructed, allegedly for the whole village, it was placed at the edge of the village, inconveniently for most people, beside the home of one of the most powerful leaders. The power of village leaders gave them greater leeway vis-à-vis the law. On a ceremonial occasion a village leader got drunk and misbehaved badly in public. A policeman from Mot was present and wanted to arrest him for disorderly conduct. However, a number of people, including the village headman, interceded on his behalf. They protested to the policeman that he was an important man, that it would be a disgrace to the village if he were arrested. Under much pressure, the policeman agreed to forget the affair.

UNSANCTIONED LEADERSHIP: THE BALANCE OF POWER

Although caste was not the sole determinant of leadership, all leaders were of high caste. Were this the end of it, we might find lower castes to be very nearly powerless and unprotected, their rights neglected. Abuses could easily occur, especially of Untouchables, most particularly Scavengers and Rope Makers, whom many active leaders held in contempt. At least verbally, Rope Makers were dismissed as of no consequence by many leaders, and some referred to Scavengers repeatedly as "first class brutes" . . . "drunkards" . . . "whores." Yet the rights of Untouchables were not bypassed. This was partly due to the fact that power in the village was divided; village leadership did not act as a unit, and, more important, the Koke feud created a political force on the side of the Untouchables, especially the Scavengers and Rope Makers, who most needed it.

As has been mentioned, there were seventeen households involved in the feud, nine Annas and eight Bals. The Anna faction had six high-caste, well-to-do households allied with it. This group included some of the wealthiest men in the community. A number of them were village leaders. The Bals had but one allied household of Rajputs. He was a *soyare,* the only wealthy man associated with the Bal faction. He was not deeply involved in village affairs. (He had left the village just prior to 1954; by 1961 he had returned.) Hence the Annas would have had a considerable advantage in the conflict if the Bals had not employed additional weapons. Their way of handling opposition was often to resort to threats of physical violence. If anyone acted against the interests of Bal or his group, he was likely to be warned (to quote the terms actually used on one occasion): "Do not continue the dispute or Bal will take care of you in his fashion." Their power did not come only from the readiness with which they, themselves, threatened force; they also gained strength by supporting Harijans, especially Rope Makers and Scavengers, in their differences with villagers of high caste. Villagers said that this relationship with Harijans went back into Bal's family history as far as anyone could recall.

Bal and others in his group kept the sympathies of Harijans by associating with them in a friendly fashion and by protecting them from abuse by others. An incident illustrates this. A young man from an important Koke family, the son of a village leader, met a Rope Maker woman alone in the fields and made sexual advances to her. The offended woman rushed home and told her family. Her sister later met the Koke on the road and started to upbraid him. In the ensuing quarrel she lost her temper and slapped his face. The enraged Koke went home and collected a number of his kinsmen, who entered the Rope Maker's quarter and beat the offending woman's husband. The Rope Makers wanted to go to court over this, but village leaders threatened them. Then Bal came to their aid. He and some of his followers beat the young Koke who had offended the Rope Maker woman. He then called together three village leaders, one of whom approximated the passive type. A public hearing was held at the village *cāvḍi*. The Kokes who had attacked the Rope Maker confessed their offense, paid fifty rupees to the injured man, and asked his pardon. The Rope Makers were thus satisfied.

Another example of Bal's actions toward Harijans took place on Independence Day not very long after the assassination of Gandhi. The young men of the village, of all castes including Harijans, had been dancing in the ceremony in honor of the day. A pause was called because of the heat, and it was suggested that the dancers go to their homes for water. At this point a Brahman, whose house was near by, invited Bal into his courtyard for water. Bal then invited all the dancers, Harijans included, to follow him. Rope Makers and Leather Workers drew water from the well. The Brahman, although he found the matter very distasteful, was helpless. Some anti-Brahmanism existed, and Brahmans were sensitive to it. Furthermore this was an occasion on which everyone was supposed to be treated as equal, when overt discrimination against Harijans would have been unseemly. Bal thus used circumstances; he knew that anti-Brahmanism and the ceremony, which emphasized unity and equality, would prevent the Brahman from protesting. He used them to declare openly his sentiments regarding Harijans, and in this way to establish more securely the idea that he was a "friend" of Harijans.

Harijans recognized the assistance given to them by members of the Bal group, and many sympathized with them. Most Harijans, however, preferred to avoid giving open aid to Bal, for this would be tantamount to out-and-out defiance of sanctioned leaders. One group of young Harijans, a Leather Worker, two Rope Makers, and a number of Scavengers, openly joined the Bals. These were considered by other villagers to be the least reputable element in the village, "loafers," "beggars," and petty thieves. They were feared by "respectable" villagers, for they were said to be liable to steal or burn crops or to poison cattle. The allegiance of these men to Bal gave him considerable strength, for there was apprehension among "respectable" villagers, especially Annas, that Bal would call upon them for aid in the event of an open fight. The reputation of the group as destroyers of crops and cattle lent further strength to Bal, for farmers were very vulnerable in this regard. It was said that Bal had, at one or another time, instigated the destruction of crops and cattle of some Annas, but there was no proof.

"Respectable" villagers tried to dispose of the group but never caught them in a criminal act, and all efforts were unsuccessful. According to some informants (five Harijans, three of whom were of the "disreputable" element) one farmer gave some of them *jāgāri* (raw sugar) as *bālutā* and then later claimed they had stolen it. However, he was unable to prove that he had not given it, and so the men remained at large. A concerted effort was going on in 1954 to have four of the least reputable Harijans "externed" (required by court order to stay out of the district). A number of village leaders, and others they had persuaded to help, testified that the four men were idlers who harassed the farmers. If this charge had been allowed to stand without some reputable villager coming forth as a character witness for the defendants, the men would have been externed. The Harijans turned to Bal. He and three of his kinsmen travelled to Poona to testify to their good character before a magistrate. As a result the young men were not molested. In this way Bal held the allegiance of the group and helped keep his power intact.

As has been noted, the Bal group did not protect only its Harijan allies but village Harijans in general. Bal's support of Harijans came up in connection with his having named a Harijan as a village leader on my survey. The man he named was obviously not a leader. This was clearly more an expression of Bal's attitude, in any event his publicly expressed attitude, in favor of Untouchables than an opinion as to who was, in fact, a village leader. Probably his support of Harijans was a way of solidifying his hold on the small group that actually supported him. It is possible that the Annas feared

Bal would get further support from Harijans and tried to prevent this from happening. Informants from the "disreputable" group of Harijans asserted that Annas gave money to young Harijans on occasion and told them not to back Bal. On one occasion, which occurred after 1955, the Annas employed two young Leather Workers in a manner which might substantiate the claim of these informants (see last section of Chapter 13), but I have no further evidence on this point.

It is possible that, in his general support of Harijans, Bal was trying to give some moral sanction to his power. Yet he cannot properly be called a sanctioned leader. The defence of Harijans had little relation to village customary values. His frequent threats of force could not be justified by village ideals or norms. His relative youth and lack of wealth helped to disqualify him as a "respectable" leader. Bal, himself, seemed to see his power as improper. When asked to identify village leaders, many active leaders mentioned themselves first, then perhaps another; Bal did not. His attitude when not actually involved in a dispute was mild and retiring. He was neither boastful nor ostentatious. He avoided central positions in village ceremonies. When a photograph was taken of all important villagers, he stayed to one side; only after being coaxed, finally pulled over, did he consent to be included. Many village leaders made speeches on important ceremonial occasions; he never did. He was sometimes involved in the status struggle on Bāil Poḷā, but this was only against members of the Anna group; he refused to make way for them when they met on a village street. This was a matter of asserting himself against his rivals rather than claiming status, for it was only the Annas whom he contested on the occasion. Generally he did not strive for the symbols of power and prestige that active leaders wanted.

Five members of Bal's group were questioned about village leaders, and only one named him as a leader. The others named men equivalent to or approximating the passive type of leader. Thus even his own group did not consider him a proper village leader. Although nine Harijans named Bal as a leader, many Harijans named others. In one interview with a large group of Harijans, some of whom had earlier named Bal as a leader, and in further casual encounters, specific enquiries were made regarding Bal's position. The sense of their responses was that he was not a "real" leader.

We may but conjecture as to the motives that led Bal to seek power. Prestige was uninvolved. It was probably not for economic gain. It was said that Bal sometimes extracted money from the Annas. It was also reported that when his Harijan allies wanted to intimidate farmers who refused them handouts, they would sometimes steal large quantities of the farmers' standing grain. They could not have kept this themselves, for it would be too easily discovered; and so, it was said, they gave the stolen crops to Bal. However, these accusations were made by informants who disapproved of Bal. No one was able to give an example of a large quantity of crops being stolen, and the extraction of money from the Annas was also unsubstantiated. In any case, if any of this did happen, it could not have involved very much economic value. I think it likely that Bal's wish for power derived from his conflict with the Annas. A number of the Annas were active leaders, and it was only by marshalling power that Bal could oppose them. As he could not gain power by sanctioned means, he turned to open threats of violence and alliance with Harijans.

While Bal's leadership was sustained by the belief that he might use violence against the person or property of anyone who went against him, he did not, in fact, use violence very often. It should not be thought that "respectable" villagers stood in constant fear of him. Like other village leaders, he was not continuously active as a political force. His primary concerns were those of the other villagers, his land and his household; in the course of day-to-day living he did not often employ political pressure. He could be called upon by Harijans for help if a major crisis arose, and the knowledge of his support acted as a restraining influence on high castes in their dealing with Harijans; but minor matters, insults, for example, did not usually come to his attention.

Most villagers disapproved of Bal, but, apart from the Annas, they did not consider him a mere *"gunda"* (a kind of bandit), and they did not feel toward him such extreme indignation as might have led to united action against him. Bal knew of others' disapproval, and he did not wish to exacerbate matters. His political activities, while contrary to traditional village proprieties, were limited by those proprieties. As was mentioned, he did not attempt to force himself to the forefront at village ceremonies; indeed, he deliberately chose to remain in the background. He gave respect to village leaders, excepting Annas, and even helped to maintain the authority of village leadership. As we shall see, he was not averse to reprimanding Harijans who overstepped their "places" vis-à-vis village leaders. In the Rope Maker incident he had other village leaders decide the issue; he did not attempt directly to participate in the decision-making process. Individual Annas were not attacked or in any way abused when they came to the main settlement. Violence against Annas only occurred when they (the Annas) took drastic steps, as in the Rope Maker incident, or during ceremonies, when emotions were intense and the two groups met face-to-face.

Because Bal accepted the system of relations and authority in the village, his power, though resented by others and not sanctioned by village tradition, was accepted as a part of the scheme of things. He was tacitly allowed his sphere of influence, and other villagers, including leaders, worked within this sphere. If unable to handle Harijans, some villagers, even active leaders, turned to Bal for aid. I give an illustration. Late one night an active leader, intoxicated on locally distilled rum, wandered into the Scavenger quarter of the village. He found a group of Harijans performing *bhajan* (religious singing) and stopped to listen. He ordered a Scavenger to bring him cigarettes. (Scavengers' traditional duties included running errands for "respectable" villagers.) The Scavenger complained that the shops in the village had closed and that cigarettes would only be available in Mot, rather a long distance to walk at that hour for a few cigarettes. An argument started, and the Scavenger threatened the leader with violence. An Untouchable rarely openly threatened important villagers; the leader, befuddled by drink and alone among the Harijans, was angry and frightened. The man who threatened him had to be put down, but he was in no position to do it. So the leader hurried off to Bal's house, woke him and complained. Bal returned with the leader and scolded the Harijan, warning him to choose his words carefully when speaking to important men. Bal was then told of the circumstances of the threat. He forced the drunken leader to return to his home, occasionally threatening him when he misbehaved.

As had been brought up in connection with village factions, the fact that the Bals lived in or near the main settlement constrained most of the other residents to keep up an outward show of good relations with them. This held for leaders as well as for others. More than any of the other leaders, the active leaders in the main settlement maintained a façade of good relations with the Bals, despite their sympathy for the Annas. For most of them this involved concessions to Bal's well-known attitude toward Untouchables. They were almost all more careful and less overbearing than other active leaders in their relations with Harijans and were sometimes even helpful to them. The two active leaders who, along with the passive leader, "tried" the offending Kokes in the Rope Maker incident were from the main settlement group.

One man, whom I will call Śankar, will serve as an illustration of most other active leaders from the main settlement. He was a typical active leader, very wealthy, aggressive, and much given to ostentation to validate his status. His sympathies were with the other active leaders of the village, and when in Mot he often associated with leaders from the Anna group. Yet in the village he got on well with the Bal group and usually showed reserve and care in his dealings with Harijans. At times he even assisted the Untouchables. He did so, for example, in connection with the Mariai temple. This structure was in the Harijan section of the village. It was not only a place of worship—compared with other temples it was rarely used for worship by any but Harijans—it was also the only sheltered place in the village in which numbers of Untouchables could gather. The temple had fallen into a state of extreme disrepair, and a new one was felt to be needed. A member of the Bal group started a movement to collect money for a new building. However, he would have had difficulty getting enough if he had worked alone. The Annas, for example, would have been unapproachable. He needed a man of prestige to back the drive, and for this he turned to Śankar. Śankar cooperated with much overt enthusiasm. He became head of the collection committee, and a sufficient sum was soon raised for a new structure. As the villagers, including Harijans, saw it, this procedure had gone on for the benefit of the village Harijans.

I give another example of the way Śankar behaved. A

friend and frequent associate of Śankar, who was also an active leader of considerable importance, was unusually antipathetic to Scavengers. His dislike was well known, but he generally did not show his feelings in the presence of Scavengers. On one occasion this leader while with Śankar accosted a group of Scavengers and without provocation started cursing them. He called them thieves, looters, and the like, and cried out that they should, one and all, be punished. He apparently expected Śankar's support. Instead Śankar discreetly signalled to the Scavengers that he was neutral and turned his back on his companion. Encouraged, the Scavengers shouted at their defamer, who was abashed and backed down.

Śankar behaved as he did in order to disassociate himself from his companion's extreme position. He avoided antagonizing the Harijans and thus was in a better position to remain on good terms with the Bal group. It should be noticed that Śankar did not actively support the Harijans against his associate—this is what Bal would have done—but instead subtly gave permission to the Scavengers to strike back without allowing himself to become personally involved.

The Annas resented main settlement leaders for their toleration of Bal. One Anna recited a Marāṭhi proverb intended to absolve the village at large, while condemning Bal and those, like Śankar, who did not oppose him; it went something like this: "One rotten mango in a basket spoils a few around it, but it does not spoil the whole basket." The "rotten" and "spoiled mangoes" comprised a political force that worked apart from or even against the remainder of village leadership, dividing and balancing power, and thus giving greater protection to the politically weakest elements of the village. In this way identification with the larger community was facilitated.

11

Village Cohesion

ALTHOUGH conflict, by dividing power, allows for solidarity, it is plain that solidarity cannot be brought about by these means alone. One rather obvious element that helps produce identification is sheer contiguity. This was seen in our data on neighborhood groups, in the divorce of Vādi from Gaon, and in the partial separation of the original Maratha hamlets from community life. When people live close together for some time, complementary needs are often met and mutual aid is provided. With prolonged contiguity, common activities, values, and problems are recognized; this fosters identification. Yet contiguity alone is clearly not enough to produce solidarity in the context of such centrifugal forces as we have discussed. Other phenomena must help to produce cohesion if it is to persist.

It is well known that religion is often a factor in group cohesion. The close connection between religion and social groups has been briefly noted with regard to the family, the *khari bhāuki,* and the bilateral kindred. Caste was seen to be intimately involved with religious ideas. In the case of the village, as I will now show, there were many indications of the relationship of religion to the social group. These were primarily, but not solely, in the yearly cycle of all-village ceremonies. There were a number of such ceremonies; a full description of all would be beyond the scope of this book. I will illustrate with the most significant and emphasize the more relevant parts.

RELIGION AND COHESION

One important village ceremony was Āmbīl Ghugriya, held
in the Hindu month of Āṣāḍh (June-July). It was primarily in
honor of Mariai, the smallpox goddess, but it also honored
every deity in the village. There was first a procession of all
villagers, led by the headman and a Water Carrier, around
and through the village, the purpose being to make offerings
to all village deities. For Datta, whose temple was some distance from the main settlement, a village Barber was sent
with an offering. The procession ended at the Mariai temple.
The villagers formed a large semicircle about the front of the
temple, and special offerings were made to the goddess. In
the distant past a male buffalo had been sacrificed by the
headman with the assistance of a village Muslim, but this
was not done in 1954. Then, as in 1954, a number of people
were "possessed" by deities during the ceremony, and at the
Mariai temple these people, standing or dancing in the center
of the semicircle, were questioned by the assembled villagers. The questions, especially the initial ones, were stylized.
The first, "How do you like our ceremony?" was answered,
"Blessed by Mariai!" The next was, "When will there be rain?"
This was followed by a number of questions relating to village
crops and welfare. Later, individual questions were asked and
requests made, generally pertaining to health, childbirth, and
the like.

This ceremony was one of the most important all-village
religious affairs. Because the deity worshipped was in the
Harijan quarter and under the special care of Harijans, all
members of the village could participate fully in the ceremony. It was the one occasion on which all villagers paid
their respects to all village deities. Its primary purpose was
the worship of the smallpox goddess, hence it involved the

safety of the entire village. Furthermore, the traditional questions asked about village crops related to the economic well-being of all villagers. Everyone who was financially able made some contribution to provide offerings for the village deities. The ceremony might best be characterized as a symbolic effort of the village as a whole to stave off disease, crop failure, and other disasters.

It was rare to have people from outside the village attend Āmbīl Ghugriya. This is unlike the celebration of Hanumān Jayanti, the birthday of Hanumān, the "monkey god." The holiday, held on the fifteenth of the Hindu month of Caitra (March-April), was the occasion of Gaon's fair, hence many people attended it from the region. The ceremony started at sunrise, the time of the birth of Hanumān, with the villagers and a few outsiders gathered about the Hanumān temple. The moment the rays of the sun were seen, everyone threw colored rice and shouted, "May Rām be successful!" (In Hindu sacred literature Hanumān is a disciple of Rām.) After this, religious "cradle" songs were sung to the new-born god, and large offerings were made to him—primarily coconut, raw sugar, and ginger. All traditional *bhāukis,* as groups, made these offerings, which, after being presented to the deity, were distributed to everyone present as *prasād* (food offered to God and eaten as a blessing). In the afternoon there were feasts, one for the Brahmans and Temple Priests, who required a special cook, and one for the rest of the village. The Goldsmith, who accepted cooked food only from members of his own caste, was given uncooked food. In 1954 the general village feast was not well attended.

In the evening there was a procession, the high point of the ceremony and the main attraction for visitors from other villages. It was composed of male villagers of all castes, some dancing, some doing a stylized sword-play, many in masquerade costumes, dressed as women, animals, historical figures, and the like. There was a band, hired from Mot, toward the front of the procession and, farther back, extra drummers for the dancers. Fireworks were lighted as the procession moved along. Accompanied by religious singers (doing *bhajan*), an image of Hanumān was carried on a palanquin at the rear of the procession, which stopped at each household so the women could touch the deity.

On the next day there were wrestling competitions in which wrestlers from the entire region, some from rather distant places, competed for cash prizes. The celebration ended with another procession in the evening.

Hanumān Jayanti represented a general effort of the village which mirrored and reinforced community solidarity. The expenses were high, as much as 1000 rupees in some years. Everyone who was able contributed some money for the affair. Most Harijans were too poor, it is true, but the few who were well enough off gave something. Along with all other castes, they made offerings to Hanumān.

Most important, this ceremony was the occasion on which the village displayed itself to the region, hence one on which consciousness of village identity was heightened. One event illustrates this. The villagers were in procession when a Maratha woman, excited by a personal antagonism, referred to a Koke as a Dhangar. Her remark was overheard. A Maratha man, in an effort to prevent conflict, called out that the woman's remark was improper. He then attacked his own caste, saying sarcastically, "We know how pure Marathas are!" However, the Kokes were still excited, especially the younger men. They wanted to attack the Marathas. Some older Kokes, however, quieted them by reminding them that there were outsiders present; in the words of one, "If you fight, it will hurt the village." The Marathas were warned not to repeat such remarks, and the episode was passed over without further conflict.

There were other ceremonial events which helped to produce community integration. There was Holi, when people worshipped a village bonfire, to which practically all had contributed wood or dung, and from which each non-Koke household took a brand for its family Holi. (Kokes did not have separate Holis.) There was Dasarā, when the men went to the outskirts of the village on a mock raiding party. Everyone exchanged "gold" in the form of leaves, thus sharing the "loot" of their "raid." Harijans made their presentations to others by placing a leaf on the ground. The "gold" was then taken home and offered to the family deities. Another ceremony was Gudhi Pādvā, Maharashtrian New Year's Day, when the villagers gathered in and around the temple of Bhavāni Devi, and the prospects for the village crops were forecasted for the coming year. On Makar Sāṅkrānt (celebration of the winter solstice), in the same temple, a village Brahman read a horoscope for the general prospects of the village. On these celebrations Harijans sat just outside the entrance to the temple. These were not all the village ceremonies that helped to integrate the community, but they suffice to show that integration was strengthened by religion. Everyone who wished to do so participated in them, and the turnout was good at many of them.

Religious activities of the kind described are symbolic of cohesion and reflections of it. When group identity is symbolized, it is strengthened. But religion can also reflect and heighten conflict, for symbolic occasions are times when conflicting parties are most likely to assert their claims. Hence, as would be expected, the antagonisms in the village were often most intense at religious events. Hanumān Jayanti, for example, was a very important symbolic occasion; emotion was intensified during it, hence conflict frequently came to the surface. On one Hanumān Jayanti held a few years before this study, there occurred a fight between the Bal and Anna factions which resulted in a serious injury. The next year the headman called in the police from Mot to act as guards. This was a radical and shocking action, much censured by many villagers, for the intrusion of outside authority into community affairs was highly offensive. That he took so extreme a course in the face of popular disapproval was indicative of the explosive potentialities of the occasion. (It was probably also in part a result of a change in attitude toward government which will be discussed later.) On Hoḷi one of the Kokes, the most honored, was supposed to have been the first to make an offering to the village fire. Conflict for the honor was so acute that it was decided to have the Temple Priest currently on *bālutā* duty make the first offering. On Bāil Poḷā, the ceremony in honor of bullocks, there was a procession of bullocks to the Hanumān temple, in which the order in the procession was supposed to be determined by the prestige of the animals' owners. The struggle for position was so sharp that in the recent past the ceremony had often lasted several days, although it should have lasted but one. As a result it was decided that the position of honor should go to the last in the procession. Those who preferred not to compete could go through with it, while the others tried to outwait one another. The struggle continued, however. During the procession, if one of the Anna group met a member of the Bal faction on the village streets, neither would make way for the other. Hence the Annas decided in 1952 to stage their own Bāil Poḷā in their hamlet. Ceremonies of the kind described can be important in heightening solidarity, but to do so they must take place within an already solidary group, for they are likely to intensify extant social conditions, whether cohesion or conflict.

BĀLUTĀ AND COHESION

One of the most important factors which helped to bring about village unity was the traditional economy, the *bālutā* system. The system consisted of the provision of stipulated goods and services by villagers for other villagers. The defined goods and services were given in whatever amounts were needed and were paid for at a constant rate, a rough percentage of the crop when it was harvested, irrespective of year-to-year variations in the amount of goods and services received. At harvest time or just after sugar crushing, landowners sent word to *balutedārs,* those who served in the system, to come for their *bālutā,* that is, their regular payment. If crops were bad one year, then *bālutā* was necessarily less, but it was not smaller simply because fewer services were required and not larger if more was needed.

It should be observed, first of all, that *bālutā* was conceived as a system, isolated as such by the villagers. It was referred to as a *"cāl,"* roughly translatable as "system." It was synonymous neither with caste interaction nor that of class (using the term in the Marxian sense).

It was said that there were twelve groups operating in the *bālutā* system—*"bār bālutedār."* In fact, this was a customary number used in connection with *balutedārs;* in this village there were more than twelve, in some others, less. The social entities to which the term *balutedār* was applied were *khari bhāukis,* status positions, and sects. Castes employed in traditional occupations were incorporated in preference to others practicing the same occupations, but if there was no caste representing an important calling, then some other caste filled the position of *balutedār*. A carpenter was usually included in the list of *balutedārs,* yet there had been no representative of this caste (Sutār) in Gaon within the personal recollection of any villager. (One informant, a man of about forty-five, said there had been one before his birth.) There was one Sutār in Vādi who worked for a few people living on farms close to Vādi. Within the lifetime of other villagers, the *balutā* functions of carpenters had been filled by the two households of Blacksmith caste. One of these did only carpentry and was referred to as "the *sutār*."

A caste of long standing in the village, the Basket Maker, was only partly accepted as *balutedār*. Two of the three old-resident households of this caste claimed *balutedār* status, and these gave baskets to some farmers in exchange for grain on a yearly basis. A few villagers said they were *balutedārs,* but most denied it. The latter pointed out (correctly) that Basket Makers were often paid in cash, and when paid annually in kind, the amount given depended upon the number of baskets supplied, not on crop size, as in *balutā*. The hesitation with which Basket Makers were assimilated to *balutedār* status parallels their merely partial acceptance as really "of" the village. This was probably due to the linguistic and cultural characteristics that marked them off from other villagers, for other castes, native to the deccan Maharashtra, were taken in with less difficulty. It was reported that some years back a woman of Māli caste (gardeners), now deceased, settled in Gaon and was accepted as a *balutedār*. She provided flowers for religious rituals in exchange for *balutā*. In any event, although the Basket Makers were only partly accepted as fellow villagers and *balutedārs,* they were a caste interacting in the usual way with other castes. Their caste rank was no more imprecise than that of most other castes in the village.

Moreover, a status position was included in the system, the temple *gosāvi*. (Villagers did not use the adjective "temple." I use it to refer to the *bālutedār gosāvi* as distinguished from other *gosāvis*.) *Gosāvi* was the title given to Kokes in the general area of Gaon whose lives were dedicated to the god Datta. Within the area of "the fourteen villages of the god Datta," the "fourteen" Koke villages, there were a number of *gosāvis,* all chosen from among Kokes.[1] Generally a man became a *gosāvi* through a vow made by his parents. For example, if a child was sick, the parents might vow to Datta that if the deity preserved the life of this child, the next-born male would become a *gosāvi. Gosāvis* were celibates. They wandered about the area, begged for their livelihood, and devoted their lives to the worship of Datta. One of these was selected by the Kokes of Gaon to care for the Datta temple. This individual was a *bālutedār,* and he kept the position for life. Other *gosāvis* were not in the *bālutā* system.

Two religious sects, the Gondhaḷi and Vāghya, were sometimes included in discussions of the *bālutā* system. They were singers, dancers, and musicians, devotees of two particular deities, the Gondhaḷi of Bhavāni Devi and the Vāghya of Khaṇḍobā. Representatives of both groups were usually called for the same occasion. Their services were used by many villagers, especially at weddings, but most members of the sects lived in Mot, none in Gaon. They were clearly

[1] There was a difference of opinion in this regard. Some said that any Sagar Rajput could become a *gosāvi,* but most insisted that only Kokes were eligible. No case was known in which a temple *gosāvi* had been a non-Koke. In general usage the term *"gosāvi"* was not applied exclusively to Kokes, not even to Rajputs. Some people in the area were called *gosāvis,* although they were not celibates. They were referred to as "Soṅsāri Gosāvis" and were distinguished by a saffron turban. They could beg if they found no work, but apart from this right, possibly to be interpreted as a religious right, they were little different from a caste, for they were endogamous. There were four or five households of these in Vādi, none in Gaon.

bālutedārs in some villages of the area, where they lived within the village limits, but in Gaon few gave them *bālutā* for their services. Most paid cash, about fifteen rupees per performance for both groups. They had little to do with other villagers apart from their occupation. One informant employed the term *"ālutedār"* for the sects. *Ālutedārs,* he said, did not have the right to insist upon *bālutā* payment, as did *bālutedārs,* but they could be included if the farmer chose.[2]

Most of the *bālutā* positions were, in fact, occupied by village castes, or rather by the main *bhāukis* representing the castes, for others were not usually included. This took in all long-standing castes, apart from Basket Makers, as noted, and also excepting Rajputs and Marathas, whose traditional occupations were agriculture. However, the goods and/or services supplied were limited in many cases. For example, the Leather Worker repaired leather items, and supplied new straps for a type of plow and small toy drums for children, always with the landowner's leather. This was in the *bālutā* system. If, for example, new footgear was wanted, it was negotiated for separately. It was considered proper to purchase such items from one's regular Leather Worker, but it was not mandatory, and some turned to the market in Mot. Similar rules existed for other *bālutedārs.* The Potter gave a full complement of items to a man when he married, and he replaced small- or medium-sized pots later if breakage occurred; but large water pots or elaborate stoves required separate negotiation. The Goldsmith did minor repair work and polishing and made simple items such as anklets in return for *bālutā.* The metal was supplied by the client. Major

2 I first heard of this usage toward the close of my field work in 1961 and had no time for further questioning on the subject. I do not know whether it was in general use. It was clearly not prevalent, for other informants had made no mention of it despite prolonged discussion of the subject.

repairs and elaborate jewelry were not involved in *balutā*. Many of the better-off farmers had "house-Scavengers" associated with their families. The house-Scavenger cleaned the courtyard daily, smeared mud on the walls of the house on occasion, and performed other minor chores. House-Scavengers often had semihereditary attachments to particular landowners, but the relationship could be severed at any time by either party. The status of house-Scavenger was not considered to be part of the *balutā* system, and separate payment was made for the work, usually annually and in kind. Similar limitations obtained in regard to the *balutā* services supplied by Blacksmiths, Water Carriers, Washermen, Rope Makers, and Brahmans.

While caste was intimately related to *balutā,* the interaction involved in the two systems was clearly not identical. Obviously the inequalities in the two systems differed. The *balutā* system was focused on the traditional landowners of the village, especially the Rajputs; these were superior in the system, as will later be shown. But service castes included Brahmans, who were always ranked above Rajputs. They included Temple Priests and Goldsmiths, who were usually ranked above Rajputs; and also Potters and Water Carriers, usually ranked as equal to them.

The inequality within the *balutā* system centered on secular dominance; but it was not coincident with economic class. Many landowners—some with fairly large holdings—were *balutedārs*. It is true that when agriculture assumed importance, *balutā* duties were sometimes given up. A number of Potter and Leather Worker households had stopped serving in the *balutā* system. But these were complex matters. Leather Workers had been upwardly mobile, as I have pointed out. Their caste occupation was polluting, hence they were likely to stop it when they could. The Potter's traditional occupation was very time-consuming, and to practice agriculture on a fairly large scale practically precluded it. Brahmans, who were large landowners, had recently stopped going around to farmers when they announced that *bālutā* was being distributed. However, the Brahmans continued to serve in the *bālutā* system. A few farmers sent *bālutā* to them. It might be mentioned that the Brahmans' *bālutā* payments were small, while the "tips" they received after rendering each service were larger than those given to any other group, probably greater in total value than their *bālutā*. The Watchman, who was fairly well off, also remained in the *bālutā* system, as did a number of smaller landowners.

Class was reflected in certain aspects of the system. The traditional landowning castes, especially the Rajputs, were set off from the service castes. *Bālutedārs* asserted that they comprised a kind of brotherhood. They said that *bālutedārs,* irrespective of differences in caste, were *"bālutā-bhāu,"* *bālutā*-brothers, and that the term for brother could be used in addressing one another. This notion was not applied to landowning castes; Rajputs were said simply to be *"pāṭīls."* However, this was an ideal, not an actual expectation. The kinship term was in fact never used. The obligations of brotherliness were not really expected of *bālutedārs*. Brothers, it was said, should not accept payment from one another, hence *bālutedārs* should provide one another with services without expecting payment. This ideal was applied not only to the annual *bālutā* payments, but also to the "tips," to be mentioned shortly, that accompanied each transaction. The Leather Worker, for example, was supposed to give wedding shoes (*lagna joḍā*) to other *bālutedārs* free of charge, while from traditional landowners he was supposed to get one and one-quarter rupees for them. This aspect of the "brother" ideal influenced behavior to some extent, but it was not a compelling norm. *Balutedars* who were well off were, in fact, expected to give *baluta* to those who were not. Thus, one butcher who was fairly well off—he owned four and one-half acres of good land—said that he took *baluta* from all land-owners who were better off than he, whether these were *balutedars* or not. He said that he served anyone, rich or poor, but did not take annual payments from those poorer than he. He received the services of other *balutedars* but did not pay prosperous *balutedars,* while he did pay poor ones. Leather Workers who owned land gave *baluta* to Scavengers because they owned little, and Scavengers who owned and worked land gave *baluta* to Rope Makers, who generally owned none. A Scavenger who owned five irrigated acres gave *baluta* even to other Scavengers. The same man took *baluta* when he was on duty.

The effect of the ideal was that *balutedars* had a favored position in regard to payments. If someone who was not a *balutedar* lost his land, he was not entitled to *baluta* service, while *balutedars* who had no land continued to get service. Thus one Brahman lost his land due to a tax default but continued to receive service from a number of *balutedars,* including, for example, Temple Priests, the Barber, and Scavengers. When a *balutedar* paid another, the amount varied more than if a Koke was involved. Thus the Watchman put it: "As a *balutedar* I pay the Brahman what I feel is right. He would not ask for more [*daksina*]. But if I were not a *balutedar,* then I must give the Brahman what he asks for. It is the same for all. When I go to the Brahman, then he gives me what he feels is right, and I do not argue." When the Watchman said the Brahman must be given "what he asks for," he meant that payment had to remain within the prescribed limit for a given ceremony. These limits were more loosely held when one *balutedar* had transactions with another.

This ideal clearly posed *balutedārs,* as a group, against
"pāṭīls." But it was an ideal that had only slight effect on
mutual expectations. It was not totally inefficacious; some
landowners thought of *balutedārs* as a group and felt that
violation of *balutā* rules in regard to one group might set "the
village" against them. However, *balutedārs* were not unified
vis-à-vis landowners. Thus one Scavenger, in answer to my
questions about *balutedār* unity, said: "Scavengers stick together, yes. If Rope Makers had trouble with Kokes we
would not support them. We would not interfere. Rope
Makers are not Scavengers. [Ethnographer: Then why say
'balutā-bhāu?'] We say *'balutā-bhāu.'* It comes down from
the past, so we say it. But we do not act like brothers." In
crucial matters *balutedārs* did not act as a single group; each
balutedār group acted for itself. "Workers" were, in fact,
divided by caste differences as well as intracaste antagonisms,
just as Marathas and Rajputs conflicted, and Rajputs conflicted among themselves.

Caste and class were significant factors in village life. The
balutā system was superimposed upon them; it incorporated
them and, as will now be shown, helped to make of the community a unified whole.

The tendency was for practically all *balutedārs'* services to
be performed by and for residents of the village, especially
for long-standing residents. There were some exceptions.
When a village was lacking in important *balutedārs,* it often
employed those of neighboring villages. Thus, Gaon used the
Gondhaḷis and Vāghyas of Mot, although many paid cash
instead of giving *balutā.* Vādi, formerly a part of Gaon but
eventually socially separated, employed Barbers, Rope
Makers, Scavengers, and Brahmans from Gaon some years
prior to 1954. They gradually gave this up, however, and
by 1954 only Scavengers and Rope Makers took *balutā* from

Vādi. The two original Maratha hamlets, partly separated socially from Gaon, used Gaon's *bālutedārs.* This village was a bit more self-sufficient than most others of the *tālukā* in regard to *bālutā.* But all in this area attempted to maintain a fairly complete complement of *bālutedārs,* and they all tended to use the *bālutedārs* of their community exclusively.

There were other exceptions in Gaon. Eleven households used Leather Worker *bālutedārs* from a nearby village. In the case of eight of these, their Gaon Leather Worker had died, leaving a widow who recommended a *soyare* of hers in a neighboring community. This was improper; work was not supposed to leave the *khari bhāuki.* However, as has been observed, the Leather Workers of the village were giving up their occupation, and those who maintained it had all the work they could use. In explaining why he used an outside *bālutedār,* one landowner said of Gaon's Leather Workers, "They do not care for *bālutā.*" Another said, "They do agriculture now, not leather work."

A similar situation obtained in the case of the Potters. Three households gave *bālutā* to a Potter in Mot. The Mot Potter formerly lived in Gaon, and when he moved he took the trade of these clients with him. No objections could be forthcoming from the village Potters, because the same *khari bāuki* was involved. Furthermore, a number of Potters had given up *bālutā* service, and the remainder had all the trade they wanted. Apart from these exceptions and those previously noted, the system was entirely intravillage.

The rules of the system required that services be dispensed by *bālutedārs* to all landowners and to all other *bālutedārs* to the extent that it was practicable. There were, obviously, phenomena that prevented certain goods and services from being given to some people. For example, if a *bālutedār* owned no land, he was still entitled to the services of others, but he had little use for the services of such groups as the Rope Makers or Blacksmiths. More important modifications in *balutā* service were brought about by caste regulations. Brahmans did not serve Muslims, except where they served the village as a whole; the latter's household rituals did not require Brahmans. Similarly, the Muslims rarely served Brahmans and never Temple Priests or Goldsmiths. Some Brahmans called Muslims to slaughter animals when they feasted people of other castes. This could occur at an *īrjik* (described in the following section, "Cohesion") or on some other occasions. For example, feasts were held when a new well was dug and by those who owned sugar-cane crushers just before crushing started. *Bālutedārs* and those who worked on these occasions were feasted, and mutton was often served. When such conditions obtained, Brahmans gave *balutā* to Muslims. But only two Brahmans owned crushers, and the others rarely gave feasts. The Goldsmith and the Temple Priests had the right to call the Muslim but were not in a position to feast others on a large scale. Water Carriers' services were little used by Brahmans, Temple Priests, or Goldsmiths, for they could not accept water for drinking purposes from his hands. He did, however, perform ritual services for them at ceremonies. Most castes' services to Harijans, particularly Scavengers and Rope Makers, were either denied or abbreviated. For example, Brahman service to Scavengers and Rope Makers was slight. It was limited to weddings, where horoscopy was done and a much curtailed ceremony performed. The Washerman refused his services to Harijans and Basket Makers, both secular and ritual services. The Goldsmith did occasional minor repair work for Scavengers and Rope Makers (primarily in silver, for they had very little gold), but, for example, he would not put jewelry on the bride at a Harijan wedding, while this was usually done at weddings of other castes. The Barber did not serve Harijans and provided only a few ritual services to castes classified in the low group, except for Muslims. Muslims were allowed full service. Scavengers gave no service to Rope Makers or Basket Makers.

These are examples of the way in which *balutā* was modified by caste interdictions. It should be pointed out that these interdictions did not operate solely to the detriment of the lower groups. The ritually superior position of the Brahmans, Temple Priests, and Goldsmiths prevented them from taking some *balutā* service, for example. However the castes receiving the least service were clearly Harijans, especially Scavengers and Rope Makers. The *balutā* system had to be accommodated to caste if it was to persist.

The *balutā* relationship was fundamentally a generalized village-servant relationship; the tie was from the *balutedār bhāuki* to the village as a whole. This can best be seen in the methods *balutedārs* used to apportion *balutā* tasks among their members.

Some main *bhāukis* were composed of but one working household and did not need to allocate service; they always served the whole village. These were of the Goldsmith, Washerman, and Watchman castes. The three Muslim households comprised a minimal segment and allocated the tasks of butchering by convenience. The total *balutā* received was divided equally among them. Barber *balutedārs* were represented by two households; but, as was mentioned, one had very few clients and was only peripherally a *balutedār*. Of the two Blacksmiths, one did only carpentry. The other did both carpentry and iron work, but because he had left the village and only recently returned, he had few patrons. There were two Water Carrier households, father's brother's sons. These had been engaged in conflict, in the course of which one had very nearly retired from the *balutā* system, leaving most of the work for the other. The remaining *balutedārs* divided their work in customary ways. One method was to allocate a period of time to the *bhāuki* subdivisions. During its time on duty a subdivision served all clients in the village and received all *balutā* payments. This method was used by Brahmans, Temple Priests, and Scavengers. The Brahmans rotated yearly among three groups, two of which were composed of one household each, and one of two households. If duties were too numerous, as sometimes occurred, the on-duty group requested the assistance of the others. They kept the rights to all remunerations, though they often relinquished their *dakṣiṇā* rights to their helpers. (Helpers sometimes took advantage of this. After receiving *dakṣiṇā* that they had permission to keep, they asked for "something for me.") The Temple Priests were divided into four units of one household each, and, like the Brahmans, each took one year. For their tasks at sugar crushers, however, they allocated the crushers among the households. The bond was to the crusher, not to its owners, for if it changed hands, the tie stayed with the crusher.

The Scavengers were supposed to get *balutā* for twelve households during the year, each of the two *bhāukis* alternating every month. However, the rule was broken in that one elderly man served full time along with the others, which resulted in two on-duty Scavengers instead of one. The permanent worker was from the original *bhāuki,* the smaller of the two. This *bhāuki* was divided in half, and each half contributed an additional worker for three months. The immigrant *bhāuki* was divided into three *ilānās,* each of which took two months' work. The method by which they allocated duties has been described.

The Rope Makers, Leather Workers, and Potters allocated *balutā* tasks by dividing the land of the village into approxi-

mately equal parts and "giving" each part to a subdivision of
the *bhāuki*. The Rope Makers had three major *bhāuki* subdivisions, *ilānās,* and they divided the village lands into three
parts. One *ilānā* served Vādi, one served the two original
Maratha hamlets and the surrounding area, and one served
the rest of Gaon. The Leather Workers had but two working
households, and, omitting the eleven landowners who had
bālutā relations in other villages, they divided the land of the
village among them. The Potters had four households taking
bālutā, and these, similarly, divided the village land among
them. The right to serve landowners on a given part of the
village was allocated, not the right to serve particular landowners. Some landlords owned land in different parts of the
village, hence they gave *bālutā* and took service from two or
more *bālutedārs*. If a man lost his land, he lost the services
of the *bālutedār* who worked on that land; and if he bought
land in another part of the village, he paid *bālutā* to the man
who served that part. Landlords often owned the same plots
for many generations, so family-to-family ties were sometimes
formed. This is what happened in the case of the Leather
Worker mentioned earlier, where *bālutā* ties were formed
outside the village. However, it was within the rights of the
main Leather Worker *bhāuki* to protest, and probably to prevent it if they wished. The family-to-family bond was not an
attribute of the system. It was a situational phenomenon, like
the friendship groups formed on the basis of neighborhood.
The norm was to allocate *bālutā* rights in terms of the village.

Intracaste arrangements of this kind minimized competition for work, and this gave *bālutedārs* more unity. Furthermore, it was the *bālutedārs* who allocated work in the
system, not the landowners. As contrasted with a market
economy, *bālutā* gave the monopoly of a task to a particular
group in the village. Some of the poorer landowners did not

use all *bālutedārs,* and some used none; this went unpro-
tested. But landowners could not capriciously change workers
assigned to them. If a change was wanted, which was rare,
this could usually be effected, but it was with the consent of
the *bālutedārs* concerned. One man, for example, disliked
the services of his Potter *bālutedār* and told him he wanted
to change. The matter was discussed among the Potters, and
an exchange of landowners was made. Informants asserted
that if agreement could not be reached in this way, appeal to
the village headman was made, but no instance of an appeal
was known.

Another source of strength for *bālutedārs* was the organization (and the solidarity) in their castes. It would not have
been possible, for example, for an individual landowner to
turn to Mot Rope Makers against the wishes of those from
Gaon, for Mot was included in the area of social control of
the caste. However, this area was limited in geographic scope.
Hence it was possible, in the case mentioned, for village
leaders to import Scavengers from a far-off place. This was a
troublesome procedure, as is shown by the fact that only one
instance of it was known, and that was from the distant past.
It should be mentioned that the extent of caste organization
was not a phenomenon of *bālutā,* as such; in other parts of
India *bālutedār* castes are not invariably well organized, and
strong caste organization sometimes exists in the absence of
the system.

Bālutedārs' monopolies were conceived by them and by
landowners as legitimate rights (*hakk*). *Bālutedārs* could,
themselves, "mortgage" their prerogatives or even sell them
to someone of their own *khari bhāuki.* But if a landholder
violated a *bālutedār's* rights, it was felt that illegal acts might,
in turn, be committed against him. Again, this was not, as
such, a part of the system, but it was related. There was

something like the notion that "one bad turn deserves another." In connection with *bālutā,* a number of farmers expressed concern that their crops might be burned or their animals poisoned. I give one example. There was some anti-Brahmanism in Maharashtra, especially among Marathas. Marathas in some other areas, Satara, for example, took to using their own priests in place of Brahmans. A Maratha from Gaon contracted a marriage for his daughter with a family from Satara and agreed not to use a Brahman at the ceremony. At the last moment, however, he backed down and called Gaon's *jośi.* The groom's party (distinctly superior in the relationship, it should be recalled) was angry and protested to him. He explained: "I must live in Gaon, so I could not bring . . . another. For all the village would be against me if I started acting like that. They could burn my fields. Would you pay for this?" His fears were probably not justified. No cases of crop burning were reported from this village and very few from others. It is unlikely that the village Brahmans would have resorted to such action or that others would have done something of this sort for them. But, justified or not, the Maratha felt these anxieties and did not want to take any chances in the matter. Neither did most other landowners.

Such factors involve coercion and a balance of power. In actuality, these were of secondary importance. The overwhelming majority lived in accordance with the norms of the system without much thought about it. Interdependence in the system went beyond economics. *Bālutedārs* were considered necessary for household and village ritual. All important *bālutedārs,* except Blacksmiths, had specifically designated tasks in a number of ceremonies. We may take the village Holi ceremony as one example. The Water Carrier sprinkled the ground in front of the village *cāvḍi,* thus purifying a place for the sacred fire. On the purified spot all *bālutedārs,* in this instance including the Blacksmith, arranged in a great heap a quantity of wood and dung collected by the villagers. A Scavenger carried some of the wood and dung to the Devi temple; he gave these to a Temple Priest, who purified a small space in front of the temple and arranged them there. The village Brahman worshipped the wood and dung and then lit the small heap with fire from the Temple Priest's hearth. A Temple Priest made an offering to the fire, and then a Scavenger carried the fire back to the village heap, where it was used to light the main fire. Although a Koke was supposed to make the first offering to the fire, this procedure, as noted, had been changed and the first offering was made by a Temple Priest. After this, other villagers made offerings, usually pieces of sugar-filled wheatcake, which customarily had been destined for the Scavengers until the custom was changed by a village leader (see Chapter 10).

The marriage ceremony was a more striking case. Few self-respecting landowners would have considered a wedding proper without a nearly full complement of *bālutedārs;* they entered almost every phase of the ritual. Before the marriage was decided upon, a horoscope was usually made by the village Brahman. A few days before the ceremony, the village Barber shaved the groom (if the groom was from the village), and it was the Barber who delivered invitations to all in Gaon who were to attend the ceremony. Also before the ceremony the images of the household deities were cleaned by the Goldsmith; a procession was held to and from his house for the purpose. The incoming party was met by the Water Carrier, who poured water at their feet in order to counteract the evil effects of having crossed bodies of water on their journey. To ensure good luck, the party was stopped by a village Rope Maker. On the night before the wedding the

Hāḷḍi ceremony was held, and the first to "cleanse" the bride and groom with turmeric was the wife of the Washerman.

On the next day the village Goldsmith put jewelry on the couple. The groom and his mother left their residence. Their feet were not allowed to touch the ground, so a Washerman spread a cloth before them on their way to the marriage canopy. Just prior to the main ritual the groom, on horseback, the reins held by the village Barber, proceeded to the Hanumān temple to change his clothing. He was required to put on an entirely new set of clothing, including a special pair of shoes provided by the Leather Worker and intended for use only on this day. Meanwhile the Washerman or his wife prepared a *covk* to be used in one of the rituals. (A *covk* is a design made on the ground, consisting of grain and other foods, as well as small coins.) The main ceremony was performed by the village Brahman, except in some instances when the wedding was held by Temple Priests or Goldsmiths. In the course of the ceremony the Water Carrier brought water for the ritual washing of the groom's feet, and he ceremonially applied water to the groom's eyelids.

After the couple were married, they sat on a platform before a mud-brick wall on which a number of especially prepared clay pots had been placed. These pots, in addition to a full complement of kitchen equipment, were supplied by a Potter. Often a Potter also helped in the preparation of the feast foods, and a Water Carrier brought the water for cooking and drinking.

So long as the visiting party was in the village, the safety of its animals and other property was the responsibility of the Watchman and Scavenger. In many cases before the newly married couple departed, they went to the Datta temple to receive the blessings of the *gosāvi*. Toward the end of the festivities, the services of the Gondhaḷi and Vāghya were often employed in the worship of Khaṇḍobā and Devi. A Temple Priest prepared the *covk* they used, and a Muslim sacrificed an animal to Khaṇḍobā when it was desired.

This description refers to weddings held within the village. When some other village was host, landowners still tried to bring as many *bālutedārs* as possible. The well-off always brought a Brahman, a Scavenger, and a Watchman, often also a Washerman.

These two ceremonies are illustrative. There were many other ritual events on which *bālutedārs* were considered necessary. When a Satyanārāyaṇa Pujā ("good luck" ceremony) was held, a Rope Maker had to announce it. The Washerman purified all clothing in a house after a death. The Barber performed the tonsure ceremony. Leather Workers carried torches beside the deity in the procession of Hanumān Jayanti. Other examples of *bālutedārs'* participation in ceremonies were given earlier in the discussions of individual castes and village ceremonies.

On ritual occasions *bālutedārs* were considered particularly necessary. While there were individual exceptions regarding secular services, it was felt that one had to use *bālutedārs* for ceremonies, or had at least to request their services. For example, the Barber who worked in Gaon prior to the present ones had been considered an irritable and rather highhanded man. He had as many patrons as he wanted, discouraged some from using his services (especially if on bad terms with them), and ignored others who chose not to patronize him. These went to Mot for barbering. Yet even these villagers felt they had to request his services for important ceremonies, such as weddings or tonsures. He complied in some cases. In others he refused, with the excuse that he was too busy. But he was always asked. One villager of Maratha caste had the status of an honorary government official and as a result was able to call upon the police for their assistance. Despite this, when weddings were held in his family, he always used the village Watchman and Scavengers as guards. Temple Priests and Goldsmiths sometimes used their own priests at household ceremonies, but if the ceremony was held in the village, the *josi* was invited, not merely as a spectator but as a nominal priest. Thus one Brahman, amused at the independence of the two castes, commented: "Even when they have their own priest, they call us to weddings, but we just sit and take *pān* and *dakṣiṇā*." (*Pān* is a mild stimulant, the leaf of the "betel" or areca palm, chewed with a little lime and ground betel nut. *Dakṣiṇā* can be roughly rendered as "gift to a Brahman." It is much the same as the "tips" given to *bālutedārs,* to be described below.)

The nature of the *bālutā* payment gives reason to view the system as contributing to village cohesion. The payment was, by and large, given in two forms, small amounts when particular transactions took place and larger yearly or bi-yearly payments of grain or other produce. I will first describe the former and then turn to the annual payments.

Bālutedārs were often given something whenever they delivered goods or performed services. This was rare when general service to the village was rendered. For example, when the Brahman read the village horoscope on Guḍhi Pāḍvā (New Year's Day), he received no payment. The Water Carrier led the Āmbīl Ghugriya procession, sprinkling buttermilk and water to purify the ground; he was given nothing for this. Such service did yield returns in a few instances, however. The Temple Priest and *gosāvi,* for example, were entitled to all money and cloth and usually all foods offered to deities in the temples in which they worked. But in individual transactions some payment was always given. The village Brahman received, in addition to annual payment, remuneration in the form of cash, grain, and sometimes cloth. These payments to Brahmans were given the special term *"dakṣiṇā."* There was no term for payments to other *bālutedārs.* I shall call them "tips." Not unlike the tips in western society, these, as well as *dakṣiṇā,* were mandatory, and the minimum size was roughly fixed.

On ordinary occasions the tips were usually quite small. For example, the Temple Priest received half a millet cake when he delivered leaf cups and plates. The Barber was given a small meal, usually a millet cake and some chutney, when he shaved a client. Scavengers were entitled to a small quantity of cooked food from every household when they were on duty. When they performed service for a landowner, they were given food or a small coin. The Rope Maker got a millet cake and sometimes a cup of tea when he delivered ropes. (In addition to his tips and regular *bālutā,* he was entitled to all the molasses residue produced in the manufacture of unrefined sugar and all of the grain left on the ground after threshing *javari.*)

On ceremonial occasions the tips were larger. For his services at the tonsure ceremony the Barber was given cloth, one and one-quarter rupees, and sometimes miniature silver scissors. The Potter was given a full meal, "a feast," when he delivered the small pots used for ceremonies. For his services at weddings, he was given clothing—at least a turban and enough cloth to make a blouse for a woman. The Washerman was given ten annas, some fruit, and other edibles at a wedding. The Leather Worker received one and one-quarter rupees at weddings.

There was a permissible range within which a tip might vary, depending on the wealth of the landowner. For example, when a Brahman performed a marriage ceremony, the proper payment was two rupees and eight annas, enough

grain to feed five people, and some clothing. If the landowner was wealthy, he might give much clothing of good
quality. Otherwise, a single piece of inexpensive cloth suf-
ficed. A poor landowner could give as little as ten annas and
a small quantity of grain. The examples of tips we have
given represent but a small part of a much larger number.
Despite the variable nature of the tips, they constituted an
important part of most *balutedārs'* incomes. In the case of the
Brahman, the tips were a larger source of income than his
annual payments. Often much of the clothing the *balutedār*
wore and sometimes a considerable amount of the food he
ate was from this source.

Concerning annual *balutā* payments, the villagers did not
share consciously held and precisely formulated standards.
Villagers made generalizations about appropriate payments,
but these were often vague, varied from person to person, and were only approximated in fact. Landowners differed in the proportion of the crop given to each *balutedār.*
However, everyone said that the "twelve *balutedārs"* were
divided into three groups, ranging from highest to lowest paid.
There was some variation among informants as to the constitution of each group, but a large majority agreed. Most
put Harijans along with Blacksmiths in the highest-paid
group, the "big *balutedārs.*" Brahmans, Temple Priests, Goldsmiths, and usually also Muslims and Water Carriers were
classed as "little *balutedārs.*" Watchmen, Barbers, and
Washermen were considered "medium *balutedārs.*" Potters
were sometimes put in the "medium" group, sometimes in
the "little" group. Payments conformed to this scale in that,
by and large, farmers gave a larger proportion of their crops
to the different groups in proper order.

In an attempt to find out the relative size of the *balutā* payment, detailed figures were taken from thirty-seven land-

owners for a number of their *bālutedārs* in eight villages of the *tālukā*. The numerical data have been given elsewhere.[3] In general terms, it was found that when the market value of the goods given in the *bālutā* system was compared with actual *bālutā* payments (excluding tips and other extras), the *bālutedārs* usually came out ahead. That is, they received more in *bālutā* than they would have gotten in produce for the same goods or services on the market. The only exceptions to this were Barbers, who often suffered a "loss"— although it should be pointed out that the *bālutedār* Barber had a larger and more secure clientele than he could have had in Mot.

Paralleling this objective economic "advantage" of the *bālutedār* was the belief held by villagers that *bālutedārs* were paid equal to or more than the economic worth of their services. All landowners asserted that they overpaid *bālutedārs*. Some Rope Makers complained that their payment was unjust, but they said that this had not been the case in the recent past. Then, they claimed, they had received more than the value of the rope items given. The village Barber said that some of "his" landowners had paid him too little at one time; but he added that this was unusual, that his *bālutā* was usually "about right." A Brahman explained that his father, who had poor land, could barely have lived by simply selling his services. *Bālutā,* he said, made the essential difference. In an interview with the village Watchman on *bālutā* payments, we had first discussed the Rope Maker's payment, which, he said, was very large, much greater than his. He then added that his own payment was satisfactory, though it had been slightly decreased recently. We calculated its market value at about 200 rupees a year. I enquired whether he

[3] "Exploitation or Function in the Interpretation of Jajmani," *Southwestern Journal of Anthropology,* Vol. 18, No. 4, pp. 302–316.

could earn that much for similar services on a wage basis in Mot or elsewhere. He replied that his work in the village was very important, but part time; wage labor would require full-time work, and he would not be able to work his lands. Full-time labor would yield more than *balutā,* he said, but he would lose much in the long run. He then added that he also held *īnām* land for his work and went on, in some detail, to elaborate on the significance of his position in the village.

When specifically questioned on the subject, most *balutedārs* answered (to me, at any rate) to the effect that their *balutā* was about equal in value to their services. However, many *balutedārs* said that other *balutedār* groups, not their own, received very large payments, larger than the market value of the goods or services provided.

More revealing were parenthetical remarks made by villagers, not in response to specific questions on the subject. One Rope Maker had just finished saying that all of his patrons continued to use his services. Then he corrected himself, saying that it was not quite all—"the very poor buy in Mot." A similar statement was made by the main village Barber. Some Rope Makers had lost many patrons by 1954; these complained that they could barely live by selling in Mot. A Maratha woman who owned very little land was asked to name her *balutedārs;* she answered that she had never given any *balutā,* for it was too expensive. A number of other landowners who were by village standards not well off made similar statements, to the effect that they could afford no *balutedārs* or only a few.[4] It seems that it was implicitly understood among villagers that participation in the *balutā* system was an expensive matter, a luxury, for landowners.

[4] These statements were made in the course of a survey of household heads. Among other questions, each landowner was asked to name the *balutedārs* who served him. Similarly, some *balutedārs* were asked whom they served.

The ideas held about the *bālutā* payment and the nature of the payment provide some insight into the social asymmetry contained by the village and help us to understand how *bālutā* facilitated village identification.[5] The *bālutedārs'* services were not paid for when rendered—the tips, especially in secular transactions, were not usually considered sufficient payment—hence the landowner was under an obligation to the *bālutedār,* and the latter had to trust that his patrons would ultimately pay him. The annual payments were believed to be equal to or in excess of the value of the goods and services provided; when they were made, the *bālutedār* became the "debtor," and the farmer, in turn, had to trust him to continue to serve for the next year. The time gap between payment and service thus fostered mutual obligation and trust.

The superiority of the landowning groups, especially the Rajputs, was incorporated into the system. The quantity of food the landowner gave was not assessed with precision, certainly not by a careful comparison with market prices. This afforded the landowners the opportunity to believe and assert that they gave more than the economic worth of even the Barber's services, though this was objectively usually false. Thus landowners proclaimed their position as "creditors." The admission by a number of *bālutedārs* that they received more than the economic value of their services was tantamount to an acceptance of "debtor" status. They were dependents. Even where *bālutedārs* claimed that the exchange was "about equal," a degree of dependency was recognized. The landlord gave food, the essentials without which the others knew they could not live. He may have depended upon

[5] This analysis is partly based on A. W. Gouldner's "The Norm of Reciprocity," *American Sociological Review,* Vol. 25, No. 2, pp. 161–178.

them, but they well knew they depended more upon him. The *bālutā* system existed for landowners, especially Rajputs. Gaon, it was said, was a Rajput village; the Kokes, it was said, were the "owners" (*mālak*) of the village. Class, in the Marxian sense, was an important feature of village life; *bālutā* incorporated this inequality, limited its extent, and translated it from a potentially purely political and economic relationship into a social relationship.

There were yet other aspects of *bālutā* that contributed to village solidarity. The system involved nearly all castes of the village and gave them security of status and livelihood. For the landlords, it provided a means of manifesting their dominant position by enabling them to act as donors of benefits to others. More important, for service castes it gave economic security (to the extent that such is possible for villages like Gaon). But their economic security was largely circumscribed by the village and bound up with that of the landlord, for there existed the belief, approximated in fact, that the size of the *bālutā* payment was proportional to the yearly crop. How this contributed to solidarity can best be seen if we conceive it in contrast to market conditions. Where a market system predominates, the income of a worker is determined by variations in production and consumption over a wide region, where he knows neither the land nor the people who work the land that decide his fate. Under such conditions social identification is not likely to be enhanced by the processes of economic exchange. Where the *bālutā* system remains strong, the *bālutedār's* condition is, in his own eyes, similar to the landowner's in that it is inextricably bound to the agriculture of the village in which he lives. He is given an obvious economic motive for identifying with the system of relations within his village.

COHESION

A community divided by caste and faction and partly geographically dispersed cannot be expected to contain an equal
amount of group identification in all of its parts. It is obvious
that long-term geographic separation will often lead to loss of
cohesion. Vādi, the one-time hamlet of Gaon, was an entirely
separate community in 1954; its identity with Gaon was little
more than a remote memory for most villagers. Not only had
it been divided from Gaon by some distance for a long time,
but it had built up a fairly complete complement of castes,
giving the same potentiality for independence that existed in
Gaon. Maratha hamlets I and II were tenuously attached to
Gaon. They, too, had been spatially separated for a long time;
they had originated at a considerable distance from the main
settlement. The Maratha-Rajput hostility probably also fostered separation. Intense rivalry between similar and solidary
groups can diminish general cohesion, as can great differences
in rank among solidary groups. Hence the subdivisions of the
village identified with it to different degrees; Sagar Rajputs
identified the most, while other castes, especially Scavengers
and Rope Makers, somewhat less, Marathas the least. But
village identification was found in all groups to some extent.

Cohesion is an elusive phenomenon, but some evidence can
be given for its existence. Village identification was not entirely unconscious; at times, concern for the village and for
harmonious relations within it was verbalized. One instance
of this was given in connection with the Maratha-Rajput
conflict on Hanumān Jayanti, when a Maratha ma-
ligned his own caste in order to prevent an open fight, and
Rajputs spoke of the need not to "hurt the village." People
who professed "radical" sentiments sometimes said that they
could not act on all of their beliefs, because, they explained,

they must live with and get along with their neighbors as
smoothly as possible. This kind of statement was not frequent, but it was heard more often in connection with the
village than with caste. This does not mean that the village
was more solidary than caste. On the contrary, the fact that
the need for cooperation was verbalized might indicate a
more fragile solidarity. In any event it probably is indicative
of a different kind of solidarity, "organic" rather than "mechanical," to use Durkheim's terms.[6]

As I have mentioned, *bālutedārs* divided the work among
themselves by allocating time or the land of the village, not
households of landowners; and most relationships were restricted to the village. This gives reason to believe that the
bālutedār saw his tie as one between his group and the village
as a whole, rather than as a person-to-person or a caste-to-
caste relationship.

Of the people who lived outside of the main settlement,
many lived closer to Mot or to some other community; yet
almost all came to Gaon for important village religious ceremonies. Most of those in the two original Maratha hamlets
came in for Āmbīl Ghugriya, the ceremony in honor of the
smallpox goddess, and usually also for Hanumān Jayanti.
However, in regard to other communal ceremonies, they held
their own celebrations in the hamlets. The majority of the
others who lived on the farms came in for all important ceremonies. Sixty-eight of the household heads on farms other
than the two Maratha hamlets were asked whether they came
to Gaon for Bāil Poḷā and Dasarā (described in this chapter,

---

[6] Auguste Comte implies that the tie involved in the division of labor
outside the family is more "intellectual" in nature than it is "moral."
See Harriet Martineau, *The Positive Philosophy of Auguste Comte,*
New York, 1855, pp. 508–511. It is possible that the kind of bond involved in kinship groups, including castes as well as other groups like
them, tends generally to be less conscious than is "organic solidarity."

second section, "Religion and Cohesion"). This amounted to a rough sample of the farm residents, something approaching but not equal to the entire old-resident population of households outside the main settlement, excluding the two hamlets (eighty-one).[7] Fifty-seven (eighty-four per cent) of these came to the village ceremonies; eight (twelve per cent) attended the ceremonies of the Maratha hamlets or held their own ceremonies; three (four per cent), two Marathas and a Rajput, did not attend the ceremonies at all. The Annas and some of their allies, a total of thirteen households, held their own Bāil Polā for the first time in 1952; but as this was a very recent change, and as they continued attending all other ceremonies, I have included them in the fifty-seven attending village ceremonies. A considerable number of those attending village ceremonies were closer, by my estimation, to other villages or to Mot. Forty-two per cent of those attending main settlement ceremonies said they had more reason to visit Mot, but this was primarily for economic transactions. None attended the ceremonies of Mot or of any other community, no matter how close to them.

Another indication of the social significance of the village was the custom of *īrjik*. This was a form of cooperative economic activity wherein large numbers of villagers contributed one day's work without wages to another villager. It was most frequently used for agriculture, especially the harvesting of *javari* (where the stalks were pulled up rather than cut), but also for plowing. Occasionally it was used for putting up the mud roofs used on most houses. All landowners did not have *īrjiks,* generally only the most wealthy and "village-minded," and these not every season. There were usually about two or

---

[7] Residents of Maratha hamlet III also held their own ceremonies. But the hamlet contained few old residents and was relatively recently formed, so the respondents from the hamlet are included in the total.

three a year. If a man wanted to hold one, he simply spread the word among villagers that he was "having *īrjik*" on a certain date. No formal channels of communication were used; the information simply spread from man to man, and anyone could come who wished. While doing the work, the participants sang special *īrjik* songs, and afterwards they were feasted. Meat was expected at the feast, but there was no other form of payment. While outsiders could come to an *īrjik,* the call was intended for fellow villagers; others were rarely called and rarely came. If an outsider lived on his farm and it adjoined the *īrjik*-giver's, he sometimes attended; but other outsiders usually never heard of it, even when situated closer to the *īrjik*-giver than people in Gaon who attended.

The most popular spectator sport in this area was wrestling. The athletes were semiprofessionals. They travelled about the villages of the region and held matches, in which the villagers put up prize money for winners. A few young men of Gaon were wrestlers; these were members of the Basket Maker and Scavenger castes. When matches were held in Gaon, villagers irrespective of caste cheered these men. Rajputs, for example, cheered for Gaon's wrestlers even when the opponents were Rajputs.

Money was contributed by members of all castes for ceremonies such as Āmbīl Ghugriya and to put on a worthy performance for the village fair. Some members of the Brahman, Rajput, and Maratha castes spent much time organizing and preparing for these events. Others in these and different castes put in much work prior to and during the events. Villagers contributed money, time, and effort to build and repair temples. As was mentioned, the Mariai temple in the Harijan quarter had fallen down in the recent past, so a new structure was built at considerable expense with contributions of money and/or labor from villagers of every caste.

One event can help to make the point. Just after the assassination of Gandhi there was a wave of anti-Brahman feeling throughout the region. Brahmans were sometimes attacked and their property destroyed. Demonstrations of this kind were taking place in Mot. One of the Brahmans living in Gaon had been a member of the R.S.S.,[8] the militant Hindu organization to which the assassin belonged, so he was a special target for demonstrators. (He had quit the organization some time before 1948, but they did not consider this.) A mob came into Gaon with the intention of burning his home and possibly attacking him. When they gathered about his house, however, some Rajputs of Gaon stood up, braving the anger of the bad-tempered mob, and defended the Brahman. Some of the Rajputs were friendly with the man, but some were not. One Rajput in particular was on distant terms with him; the Brahman thought him "a man of bad character," and the Rajput knew this and resented him for it. Yet this Rajput was one of the Brahman's main defenders. He did this because he was known in the region as a staunch Congress Party man, and he believed the mob would listen to him. It did. In the words of the Brahman (in English): "He said not to burn the house. They did not burn." The Brahman's defense was taken up not because he was a friend, but because he was a member of Gaon. This I take to be social solidarity.

[8] Rashtriya Swayamsevak Sangh.

Part III · Change

12

The Changing Village, 1954–1955 [1]

IN THE course of the past century or so the whole of India has been subject to a number of innovations, largely of western origin, that have had considerable effect on social organization. More efficient systems of communication and transportation are examples. These and other innovations were deeply felt in the region of Gaon during the forty or fifty years prior to this study.

In this area irrigation had been, perhaps, the most important single innovation, for it brought with it a number of other changes, economic, social, and cultural. An irrigation canal had been completed in 1894. Its effects, however, were not felt at once. Although some made immediate use of it, a large number of farmers refused the water, probably because of a suspicion of all major innovations in matters related to subsistence. At the start, the government had to plead with farmers to take canal water; as late as the 1930's farmers were able to irrigate as much land as they wanted. But by 1954 the demand for canal water was so great that the amount of land irrigated by it was strictly limited. Joint families that in fact owned land in common sometimes registered it as separately owned, thus permitting a larger percentage to be irrigated.

One of the immediate effects of the adoption of extensive irrigation was an increase in the role of cash in the economy. This can be illustrated from the expenses and income involved in unirrigated as against irrigated land. The figures in

[1] Propositions made in this chapter, statistical and otherwise, refer to all residents, new and old, excluding Bāgḍis, unless otherwise qualified.

Table 10 are per acre of *javari* and *bājari* ("spiked millet"), the latter always grown along with a legume (*tūr*), as of 1954. They are approximate averages, for different types of soil give different yields, and expenses vary also.

TABLE 10

Expense and Income per Acre, *Javari* and *Bājari,*
Irrigated and Unirrigated

| | IRRIGATED | | UNIRRIGATED | |
	Javari	*Bājari* *(and Tūr)*	*Javari*	*Bājari* *(and Tūr)*
Expenses per Acre	150	100	50	20
Income per Acre	275	200	75	40
Net Income	125	100	25	20

These were staple crops, the most important foods involved in day-to-day living, and prior to canal irrigation only small quantities were sold. Canal irrigation allowed for the introduction of new crops and a greater emphasis on old ones. The new ones were predominantly cash crops. The most important of these was sugar cane, which was grown in the past only on well-irrigated land and in small quantities. Among other crops of this kind were cotton and rice, which were said not to have been planted before the canal was created. Approximate income and expenditure per acre in 1954 for these crops are given in Table 11.

TABLE 11

Expense and Income per Acre,
Sugar Cane, Rice, and Cotton

	Expense per Acre	*Income per Acre*	*Net Income*
Sugar Cane	1800	3000	1200
Rice	100	350	250
Cotton	150	700	550

Market conditions, of course, result in much variability in such figures, but, however approximate, they illustrate the larger role played by money in the economy in 1954. This must not be exaggerated, for by far the larger part of village land was still devoted to the old crops, but the significance of cash crops was great in people's eyes, and this helped to alter economic attitudes.

The canal had other effects that increased the importance of cash. When the value of irrigation was fully realized, many farmers who could not get canal water turned to well irrigation, and the construction of these wells required considerable money outlays. After 1940, diesel engines became available, and pumps were installed in many cases in place of the old bullock-operated lifts. Furthermore, the sugar cane was converted into raw sugar in the village; the pre-canal crushers had been bullock operated, but recently diesel crushers came into use. In 1954 there were eight diesel crushers and four bullock crushers. The diesel engines, pumps, and crushers involved much expense. A diesel-operated crusher, for example, cost about 10,000 rupees.

More frequently than in the past people were employed for cash wages instead of letting out land on a sharecrop basis. The process of converting cane into raw sugar was usually done by contract labor, wherein the amount of raw sugar produced determined the wage, which was paid in cash. As regards other work, permanent laborers were paid about forty rupees a month, daily laborers about two rupees a day. Women, often employed for weeding, were paid about ten annas a day. These forms of labor, although they rarely involved high wages, meant that even non-landowners had more cash in 1954 than formerly.

In addition to bringing about a greater emphasis on money, irrigation helped to produce a new attitude toward time and the organization of work. The government limited the number of cash crops grown and rationed the amount of land to be irrigated by the canal for each farmer. As a result, the farmer had to decide well in advance what crops and how much of each were to be grown, and where each crop would be planted. He then made application to the Irrigation Department and was assigned specific dates and particular times of the day on which he would be given water. He had to be much more time-conscious than in the past. This applied, as well, to many artisans. When a farmer required new ropes or when he needed tools repaired, he could not delay the process for a few days. He had to have what he needed by a particular day, often by a particular hour. The precise assessment of time involved in work tended to spread to other matters, where it was not necessary; a man wanted his footgear repaired and his shave "on time."

Irrigation was probably a factor in increasing the number of immigrants in the village. As was mentioned, many villagers did not take to canal irrigation at once. As a result, it was said, outsiders who had learned of its value came in and offered what seemed to be high prices for the land (these prices were actually somewhat less than the value of irrigated land). Furthermore there was a greater need now for laborers, some of them of a type not available in the village, for example, sugar workers. The increase in population was considerable. In 1881 there were about sixty-eight registered landowners in Gaon.[2] In 1954 there were 242, although thirty-six of the names had been added in order to get more land under canal irrigation and did not represent independent households. Thus the population of landowning households

[2] This is based on land records. Residents of Gaon as against those of Vādi were distinguished by using an elderly informant. He was unable to identify sixteen names, which may have been those of absentee landowners or residents of either Gaon or Vādi.

alone had tripled in the seventy-three-year interval. I doubt that this reflects only population increase, for the population of Bombay State increased about seventy per cent from 1901 to 1951.[3] A considerable part of the immigration to Gaon had probably been recent. By the classification employed here, there were sixty-nine new-resident households in the village. That is, twenty-seven per cent of the household heads' fathers were not born in Gaon. Moreover, as was mentioned in Chapter 2, these households included members of seven castes that had not existed in the village before or, in any event, had probably been but poorly and temporarily represented. Thirty-seven of the new residents owned one or more acres of irrigated land, and twenty-nine owned two or more. The larger new-resident landowners were primarily Marathas. Of those who owned at least eight acres, with a minimum of four irrigated, there were eight Marathas, three Mālis, and one Rajput. Thirty new residents owned no land at all. They were found in nearly all castes that had new residents. Most of them, as well as some of the smaller landowners, worked for other landowners of the village.

Another probable effect of irrigation was that more villagers left the main settlement and settled permanently beside their farms.[4] Dry land requires only occasional labor. In growing *javari,* far the most important of the old crops, the farmer worked in the course of the year periods varying from a few days, for example, in sowing, to about thirty days, in harvesting. Of course, the amount of time spent was related to the amount of land owned, but for the most part it can

[3] Census Commission of India, *Census of India, 1951,* New Delhi, 1953, Vol. I, Pt. 1-A, p. 26.

[4] The evidence for this is presumptive rather than conclusive. See my article, "Irrigation, Settlement Pattern, and Social Organization," in A. F. Wallace, ed., *Selected Papers of the Fifth International Congress of Anthropological and Ethnological Sciences,* Philadelphia, September 1–9, 1956, Philadelphia, 1960.

be said that, however difficult the work was, there remained much idle time. Irrigation changed this drastically. Even in growing *javari,* more time was needed. For example, one had now to prepare channels for water (usually two or three times a year), to keep the channels clear, and to see to the distribution of water. The largest amount of time was taken up with money crops, especially sugar cane. Land had to be plowed several times, at least three. The crop had to be watered every ten days, at least thirty-two times; one type of cane had to be watered every ten days until it was cut. Sugar cane had to be weeded more often than the staple crops, and it required frequent use of fertilizers, while the other crops were rarely fertilized. Some other cash crops also required much time. Where labor was hired for the work, it had to be constantly supervised. Farmers who grew money crops—and these included all well-off men and some not so well off— found it trying to walk repeatedly from the main settlement to their farms, especially when the farms were distant. Apart from a very few men wealthy enough to maintain two houses, many farmers chose to live the year round beside their fields.

Thus, irrigation was probably an important factor leading to dispersion. This is shown by the data given in Table 12 on the dates at which farm homes were established. I was able to date most of the farm households by asking the oldest inhabitant in each for an estimate. Estimates were taken in terms of remembered events, such as epidemics, which could be dated fairly accurately. The estimates were then checked with an elderly informant who had been village accountant many years ago and who had lived in the village for most of his life. Where several households were derived from a single ancestor who made the move or originally settled on the farm, they are counted as one. The total number of households so defined was eighty-two, but I was unable to get reliable estimates for five. Dates for the remaining seventy-seven households are given in the table.

TABLE 12

Dates of Establishment of Farm Households

Pre-Canal	12
1894–1905	17
1906–1925	14
1926–1945	28
1946–1955	6

There are clearly some factors apart from irrigation that caused dispersion. Sixteen per cent of the households lived on farms prior to irrigation. These comprised primarily the two original Maratha hamlets, which were first settled by outsiders. The figures do not include Vādi, which was formed prior to anyone's knowledge. Vādi was, within the remembered past, an almost completely separate village with a fairly full complement of castes. Its formation was probably due to sheer distance from the main settlement of Gaon; it is probably attributable to a long-standing process of "budding," whereby new villages are formed.

The remaining data lend plausibility to the hypothesis that irrigation was one important cause of dispersion. Twenty-two per cent of the farm households were formed in the twelve years immediately following irrigation. The beginnings of the Anna hamlet were laid down at this time. In the following twenty-year period there were relatively few farm households established, probably because of the doubts with which some farmers viewed canal irrigation. In this period an immigrant first settled Maratha hamlet III, and two households moved to what became Maratha hamlet IV. In the next twenty years about thirty-eight per cent of the farm households were established.

Irrigation was also one of the phenomena that brought the cultivator under closer surveillance of and contact with government. Contacts with Irrigation Department officials were frequent—for example, with measurers, who checked the amount of land to be irrigated, and inspectors, who saw to it that water was taken at the proper time.

Government was becoming more important to the average villager; and this was coming about also as a result of factors unrelated, or not directly related, to irrigation. The Bombay Department of Agriculture had an office in Mot, the main function of which was to encourage innovations in farming technique. The office was first introduced in 1906 but did not start any important work until 1932–1935, when a propaganda campaign was undertaken to improve agricultural methods. However, the department had a small staff and served four *tālukās,* so its efficacy was limited. Overlapping with this organization, and probably of somewhat more importance, was the Mot Tālukā Development Board, established in 1936. It was in part a government agency—a cooperative society using some government funds and subject to government supervision. This society met once every four months. Its members were farmers from different parts of the *tālukā,* about 800 in all. (Four of Gaon's farmers belonged.) Each member paid twenty-five rupees for permanent membership or one rupee a year. Officers were elected. The Board's election struggles followed regional party lines rather than local alignments—Congress Party, Praja Socialists, and Communist elements competed (Congress had always been dominant). Funds were used to buy tools, seed, insecticide, and the like, which were rented or sold to members at low rates. The organization's main purpose was general planning for the development of *tālukā* agricultural activities; this involved making suggestions to government on land improvement, the reclamation of salted or otherwise inadequate land, the construction of dams, and so on. It was instrumental in originating a plan for the construction of sugar factories not yet built in 1955. It was said to be a fairly smoothly operating organization, far more so than the localized cooperative societies to be noted later.

The introduction of cash crops was followed by difficulties between farmers and merchants. As a result, around 1947 the government established the Marketing Committee, which served residents of the *tālukā*. Its tasks were to see that a fair price was given to farmers, that brokerage fees were not too high, and that farmers did not sell adulterated sugar or grain to merchants. It consisted of five farmers and four merchants, elected by their respective groups, as well as one representative elected by all *pancāyats* in the *tālukā*.

A movement to consolidate land holdings was under way in the *tālukā* in 1954–1955, but its progress was slow. According to one of the officers in charge, villagers resisted the idea at first because of traditional attachments to particular plots of land. Although the movement had begun in this *tālukā* in the late 1940's, it did not reach Gaon until 1961.

A further encroachment of government was represented by its efforts to "revive" the Indian village community, a movement which influenced the Indian constitution. Thus one writer on the constitution said: [5] "Having regard to the importance of the village panchayats in ancient Indian polity, it is provided that the State shall take steps to organize village panchayats and endow them with such powers and authority

[5] G. N. Joshi, *The Constitution of India*, London, 1954, pp. 109–110. See also B. Mukerji, *Community Development in India*, Calcutta, 1961, pp. 42–43. The movement is an interesting example of a "revivalistic-rational" nativistic movement presently going on in India, not so much in the society at large as in the most westernized elements, which are dominant in government.

as may be necessary to enable them to function as units of self-government."

Even before the constitution, as early as 1933, Bombay State had attempted to bring about the formation of village *pancāyats*. However, a *pancāyat* was not formed in Gaon until later—villagers said 1941, but the *pancāyat* records date back no further than 1947. In 1949 the original Bombay State act was amended, and as it then stood it required that a democratically selected *pancāyat* be formed in every rural area with a population of 2000 or more. In order to ensure proper representation consistent with the new egalitarian view, it was legally necessary to include on the *pancāyat* a woman and a stipulated minimum number of "Scheduled Castes and Tribes," the former including Harijans, if there existed a sufficient number of them in an area. The powers of the *pancāyat* were numerous, including limited civil and criminal jurisdiction, as well as the right to impose stipulated types of taxes, and to introduce innovations in village social and economic life.[6] Thus a conception held by government representatives of "ancient Indian polity," by no means an unquestionably accurate one, resulted in an effort to build democracy and equality into a village organization by nature undemocratic and inequalitarian. As we shall see, this attempt was proving ineffectual.

Another government-sponsored organization having much the same purpose as the *pancāyat* was the Cooperative Credit Society,[7] which was introduced in Gaon in the 1940's. It consisted of all registered landowners who wished to join, and was controlled by their elected representatives. It was a multipurpose organization, which could act as middleman in sell-

[6] *Gazetteer of Bombay State* (rev. ed.), Vol. xx, *Poona District*, Bombay, 1954, pp. 463–467.

[7] See B. Mukerji, *Community Development* . . . , pp. 42–43, 236–237.

ing government grain, purchase and rent equipment, and perform other economic activities. Its main function was the granting of loans. In this regard it was responsible to a central bank in Bombay, which could investigate any loans recommended by the society.

Other factors, largely ideological, impinged on the village from without and helped to alter social life. In the course of India's struggle for independence the Congress Party attempted to encourage unity at the expense of the old social divisions. This movement reached a high point in August of 1942 in the "Quit India" campaign. Gandhi had been arrested, and Congress had been declared illegal. The result was outrage; there were arson and rioting in some places, non-violent demonstrations elsewhere.[8] Party officials circulated throughout the area, calling upon people to forget their old quarrels and act as one. They were aggressively egalitarian. Speeches were made attacking "castism" and, under Gandhi's influence, especially denouncing untouchability. Ceremonies were held, intending to emphasize the unity and equality of all Indians. At some of these, Harijans prepared tea, which was drunk by people of all castes. In other demonstrations, numbers of men, including Harijans and others, grouped themselves about leaf plates (patrāvalās) laden with food, and each man took a mouthful. These symbols of equality made a deep impression on villagers, and they remembered them well in 1954.

The program was still being carried out in that year, although with somewhat less enthusiasm. Poona District had four Congress Party organizers, one of whom was stationed, along with his assistants, in Mot. According to the Mot party organizer, a Muslim, the program "is the main work of the

8 *Times of India,* August 10, 1942, pp. 1, 5, 7; August 11, 1942, pp. 1, 3, 5.

Congress Party. We cannot have progress without unity. We must break this castism." The organizer, or more frequently his Hindu assistants, travelled about the villages of the area in the company of Untouchables and publicly took food with them. Speeches were made in which Hindu scriptures were quoted against the practice of caste. Caste, they said, was a customary practice, not a religious one.

The ideals were introduced into the programs at school. Children were told stories of Indian heroes; some stories told of Gandhi, of course, and mentioned his programs regarding social reform and his antipathy for untouchability. In a book intended to teach children to read, one story was devoted to the activities of Mahatma Phule, a nineteenth-century reformer of Māli caste, who had admitted Harijans to his well.

Either in Mot or in the village itself people were frequently exposed to speeches exhorting them to take to new ways. For example, a man from the Prohibition Department appeared in the village at irregular intervals. His talks were largely about the use of alcohol, but he was an ardent Congress Party man and often took up other subjects. Government officials from the Mot area—Revenue Department officials or others—not infrequently presided at meetings of villagers, usually on ceremonial occasions, and discussed such matters as modern agriculture, education, hygiene, and birth control.

The fervor of the old movement was institutionalized in secular ceremonies. One new ceremony, intended especially to encourage education, was Children's Day, held on January 15. There was a procession, followed by flag-raising, and then by skits in which the school children were the actors. The children gave speeches, largely composed by the teachers, on subjects such as education, health, and agriculture; these talks were represented as "advice to parents." Adults then gave similar speeches. Other important new ceremonies were Independence Day, on August 15, and Harijan Day, on January 26. These were similar in general outline to Children's Day, the former stressing the idea of independence and unity, the latter emphasizing the need for raising the status of Harijans. On Harijan Day the meeting was chaired by a member of one of the Untouchable castes, and tea prepared by Harijans was drunk by other villagers. People of high caste then entered the Harijan quarters and symbolically swept the paths. A ceremony similar to this, not sponsored by the government, was Dr. Ambedkar's Birthday, held on April 14. Based on the egalitarian teachings of Ambedkar, it was primarily of interest to, and instigated by, Harijans, especially Scavengers.

The Congress Party attack on the old order of society was, in part, written into the constitution of India and the laws of Bombay State. As was mentioned, Bombay law required that seats be reserved for Harijans if there were a sufficient number of Untouchables in an area. The governing of Poona District, excluding Poona city, was in part in the hands of an elective District Local Board; here, too, a number of seats were reserved for Harijans.[9] In 1954 three members of the Board were from Mot Tālukā, and one of these was a Harijan. The Indian constitution forbids legal discrimination on the grounds of religion, race, caste, or sex. It also prohibits such discrimination in public facilities, such as restaurants and bathing places.[10] Many villagers interpreted these legal phenomena more broadly; they thought that all caste proscriptions were "against the law," even in private interaction. For instance, some believed the law required that they not object to sitting beside Harijans, even in their own courtyards.

Before turning to a consideration of the effects of these

[9] *Gazetteer* . . . , p. 459.
[10] G. N. Joshi, *The Constitution* . . . , pp. 70–71.

phenomena on village life, it should be mentioned that World War II probably acted as a catalyst to change. The war brought about a marked increase in the price of food grains without a proportionate increase in the cost of personal services or locally manufactured items. The village economy, having been partially moved into a market context, was much affected. The cash value of the subsistence crop now far exceeded its exchange value within the village; it, too, became a cash crop, at least temporarily. It should be pointed out, however, that this was not decisive in weakening the *bālutā* system; in 1954 and even in 1961 villages that were unirrigated, and especially those distant from Mot, still maintained the system without many signs of deterioration.

The war had another effect. It created a general food shortage, and the government's efforts to alleviate conditions influenced caste activity. Caste meetings such as we described earlier had been occasions not only for "legal" action, but also for feasting and merrymaking. On such events there had been, of course, much wastage of food. Probably to prevent this, and probably also as a political measure against the independence movement, the government put into effect a law forbidding unofficial meetings of more than twenty people.[11] As a result, most caste meetings were completely suspended for a few years. As we will note later, many castes never completely recovered from the blow. Again, this does not seem to me to be decisive, but it was probably one factor that helped in their decline.

CHANGING CASTE

One effect of government propaganda and legal action was confusion of values regarding caste customs. In the ideology

[11] This matter, as well as the inflation, was reported by people in this region. I did not further investigate these events.

of traditional India, caste—or its scriptural counterpart, *varna*—was contemplated as a part of the natural order of things. This ideology was rarely openly attacked until western conquest. Western egalitarianism had an effect, as is well known; but it remained an ideology associated largely with foreigners. In the independence movement many of the Indian leaders, known to and accepted by the masses of people, overtly espoused egalitarianism. In 1954 this was the ideology of the party in power. Some villagers were hostile toward the government; but in spite of the hostility felt toward it, the government was still accepted by villagers as the sovereign power—a native sovereign power, conceived as Hindu. This power was attacking caste with a vigor and persistence that had never before occurred in India's history. Again and again, people referred to the 1942 "Quit India" movement, when they had seen the leaders of their own village take food with Harijans. Thus, a respectable alternative to the old values existed.

As might be expected, the values of caste were too well established simply to be thrown aside. They were overtly upheld by some. Thus one Maratha said: "The Almighty has planned that life should be created from four sources—egg, womb, earth, and sweet. To try to create [life] in any other way would be going against the wishes of God. Creating a crossbreed between an ass and a horse would be against the wishes of God. . . . If you want to abolish caste, why not abolish everything? Why not have two brothers exchange wives?"

A Rope Maker complained, "Since the new government, we are confused with Scavengers." A Water Carrier blamed bad economic conditions on the alleged decline of caste. "People are not religious today. They want to destroy caste, so now we do not get rain on time. Grain must be measured [when it is given as *bālutā*], and then we do not get it right, while formerly a pile was just made on the ground."

Most men held both systems of values simultaneously. All important active village leaders overtly identified with the Congress Party. Yet they boasted of the proud traditions of their caste in public and in private. They made many, and often long, speeches on Harijan Day and on Independence Day, but the subjects were restricted to independence, education, Gandhi, and the like. "Castism" was sometimes denounced in general terms, but the position of Harijans was not mentioned. On the first occasion of Harijan Day village leaders symbolically swept the Harijan quarters; after that the task was relegated to schoolboys. An Untouchable chaired the meeting on this day, and the ceremony required that Harijan-made tea be drunk; but the sweets distributed after the meeting were never given by Harijans.

It still brought prestige to be "strict" regarding untouchability. For example, it was known that one man, normally quite truthful, permitted Harijans to enter his house to carry in grain or make repairs, yet he publicly denied that he would permit this. The same man in different contexts spoke in favor of the removal of untouchability. Some people denied that they would accept water from the hands of Harijans, although, as I found out, they did do so. Some of these same people claimed to identify with Congress ideals; for holding Congress Party ideals also gave prestige. Others boasted that they would take water from anyone, including Harijans, though they would not in fact take water from Harijans.

The tendency was toward a wider acceptance of the new ideals. Almost all young men overtly accepted it. In casual conversation some people spoke as if caste were no longer extant. When Scavengers were asked about the castes from whom they would accept food and water, some replied that "Marathas" took food from them, so now they took from anyone. In conversation with a group of men regarding caste meetings, one man said that caste distinctions were gone except for intermarriage. The others agreed. Then someone mentioned that Ambedkar, the Scavenger leader, had married a Brahman woman; so the group concluded that even this barrier was no longer significant. This was, of course, a gross exaggeration. But it was indicative of an attitude: those in power, rulers whom they themselves had favored, were against caste and were acting against caste, hence in their eyes caste was of little or no significance—although, as we shall see, people had not stopped living in terms of it. The notion that caste was "bad" had gained a foothold. Villagers knew that there was a proper and prestigious alternative to the traditional values of caste, and this was probably responsible, in large part, for the fact that some aspects of caste were being attenuated.

Holding the new ideals did not cause a reversal in daily behavior. Some people privately admitted that they took food and water with Harijans only at public ceremonies. "Normally," as one man put it, "we are orthodox." One young Brahman who accepted Congress ideals and publicly argued for them, said that he had taken water from Harijans, but that he could not bring himself to take food with them. On Harijan Day, Untouchables made and served tea; he sipped it and said, "It tastes like kerosene." But the notion of intercaste defilement had been considerably weakened. Many young men of Brahman, Temple Priest, and Goldsmith caste had taken food from people of other castes, excluding Harijans. Interdining was practiced by most men, many of them mature men, among all high castes, including also Muslims and

Watchmen, and in some instances Washermen. Some of this "laxity" was probably fairly old in the village,[12] but it was probably less extensive before the 1940's. After this time, especially after the "Quit India" campaign, caste taboos were weakened even with respect to Harijans. Women were conservative in this respect, but even they were less "strict" than in the past. On Nāgapancami, a celebration in honor of the cobra deity, the women of the village danced around an image of a cobra. About fifteen years prior to this study Harijan women went at a different time and danced separately. In 1954 all went at the same time, although restraint was still observed between Harijans and others.

Most men, especially young men, did not consider Harijans literally untouchable. In the 1930's Harijans held their own wrestling matches; afterwards they participated along with others. In 1954 most men did not object to entering a Harijan's home, a rare thing in the past. Many, but by no means all, permitted Harijans to enter their houses. Some did not even object to Untouchables in their kitchens. About twelve per cent of the households in Gaon contained at least one member who had taken water from an Untouchable's hands. No attention was paid to Harijan status in the village school.[13] The rank order on the river was followed by most women but not by most men. In religious processions men mixed freely regardless of caste. In recent times the village Barber began serving Leather Workers, partly due to their upward mobility, no doubt, but probably also because of the alteration in attitude toward pollution.

[12] N. G. Chapekar, "Social Change in Rural Maharashtra," in K. M. Kapadia, ed., *Ghurye Felicitation Volume*, Bombay, n.d., p. 175.

[13] The incidence of people accepting water from Harijans was ascertained by asking most men whether they would do so, and then checking each, name by name, with a number of Harijan informants. The information on treatment of Harijans in schools was taken from school children, Harijans and others, as well as teachers.

In Mot the change was even more marked. Restaurants were legally and in fact open to all. (Harijans jokingly remarked that the law was enacted in order to impoverish them.) The temples of Mot were entered by many Harijans. Some people who held to caste taboos within the village ignored them in the town.

Intercaste defilement persisted, of course, to some extent. Women and most elderly men still held fairly strictly to the rules. Harijans did not enter temples in the village, apart from the Mariai temple. On Āmbīl Ghugriya I observed a Leather Worker in a state of possession enter the Devi temple in front of the assembled villagers. Nothing was said about it, but I was told that it had never before been done. Very few men took food with Harijans except in the new Congress Party ceremonies. Some changed their ways but slightly. One man gave his house-Scavenger tea every morning; in the past the Scavenger had brought his own cup, but later, during the 1940's, the man set aside a special cup for his use and for other Harijans. Some Harijans, especially elderly men, were themselves hesitant to break the rules. When "liberal" villagers asked them into their homes, they refused. "I am all right here." When asked to sit down, they sat apart from others. On traditional ceremonial occasions untouchability was usually maintained. For example, a young Brahman of about twenty-five performed a marriage ceremony for Rope Makers; before and after the ceremony he mixed freely with the participants, but during it he maintained the traditional distance. On Dasarā when men exchanged "loot," Harijans continued to place the leaves on the ground rather than hand them directly to men of higher caste.

The weakening of ritual taboos was accompanied by changes in secular symbols. The abject respect shown earlier by Harijans before higher castes was no longer displayed.

Untouchables no longer stepped aside when passing others on the road. They did not remove their footgear when walking by groups of village leaders. At their weddings the groom could use a horse, a practice that had been prohibited before. Harijans were bolder and more literate than they had been.

The formal caste meeting had declined in the recent past. Only four castes were still holding them in 1954—Goldsmiths, Water Carriers, Watchmen, and Washermen. This was probably due in part to the government interdiction on large meetings during World War II; but the decline of the idea of pollution was probably more significant, for the traditional meeting was intended primarily as a means of maintaining caste purity.

However extraordinarily rapid these changes may have been, there is no reason to believe that caste, as such, was declining. As might be expected from the fact that parents arranged marriages, intercaste marriages were very rare. One case occurred just prior to 1954 between a Maratha man from Gaon and a Goldsmith woman, both young. The couple had met in Poona city, and they took up residence there. The marriage had caused severe conflict within the man's household, and during 1954 the division of family property was under negotiation, although the father was still alive. A similar case involving two people of high caste was said to have occurred in Vādi in the recent past. These were the only concrete examples of intercaste unions known. There were said to have been intercaste marital unions in the Koke *bhāuki* and in some Maratha *bhāukis,* but these allegedly took place in the distant past. In any event, there is no reason to believe that the two cases represented a recent trend.

There was talk in the area that subcastes were intermarrying. Barbers, for example, said that they once would have been outcasted for marrying fellow caste members from

Khandesh or Karnatak, but that this was now permitted. The Brahman subcastes were said to permit intermarriage. According to one villager, "This is because non-Brahmans are intermarrying and so consolidating, [therefore, we] must do the same." No cases of subcaste intermarriage were known. Marriages were contracted in the traditional way, preferably with *soyare* or with someone connected by marriage with one's *soyare*. If such cases did occur, they would involve, as the villager recognized, no more than a reformation of caste lines.

It is known that, in India at large, caste is not declining. Western-inspired innovations, such as a modern system of communications and democratic elections, have resulted in a clearer definition of caste allegiance. Formal caste organizations have appeared.[14] The associations are of two types. In one the explicit purpose is to effect changes in society on the state and national level, often through political means. This kind of organization does not restrict membership to any particular caste, but it usually attracts members from one caste or a limited group of castes. The other type of organization allows membership only to those in one caste and claims to represent the entire caste. Its relations to state and national action programs, either social or political, are tenuous. Instead of having explicit programs aimed at altering general conditions, this kind of organization emphasizes the "uplift" of caste members through education and other similar means.

Of the first type of association, the main example familiar to the people of Gaon was the Scheduled Caste Federation. The organization, started by the Scavenger leader, Ambedkar, was intended for all Harijans, but it was reported that its

14 See G. S. Ghurye, *Caste and Class in India*, New York, 1952, chaps. VII-VIII; and M. N. Srinivas, "Caste in Modern India," *Journal of Asian Studies*, Vol. XVI, No. 4, pp. 529–548.

members were mostly Scavengers. The intent of the organization was to improve the conditions of Harijans, and the methods employed stressed political pressure on the state and national level. Only a few Scavengers in Gaon were actively interested in the organization. However, most felt some affinity for it, while members of other castes were indifferent. Among Scavengers there was a related movement, also started by Ambedkar, to encourage conversion to Buddhism. The intention was to convert as many as possible, irrespective of caste; but the only ones in this area who showed interest were Scavengers, and in the village less than a handful, all young men, were really concerned.

Another example of this type of organization was a group called the Satyaśodhak Samāj, which was strong in this region in the recent past, especially in the district of Kolhapur. Its aims were explicitly anti-caste, but in fact it was anti-Brahman.[15] According to people in Gaon and Mot, most of its support came from "Marathas," that is, secularly high castes. By 1954 there were no signs of the organization in the *tālukā*. In its place there was a political party, the Peasant's and Worker's Party. Although there was much antagonism to the Congress Party in the village, no one identified with the P.W.P. In the *tālukā* as a whole it was of little importance.

The other type of organization, exclusive to particular castes, was also of minor importance in 1954. There were few signs of it either in Mot or Gaon. The Goldsmiths had an organization of this kind with central headquarters in Poona city, but I found no Goldsmiths in the area who knew

[15] G. S. Ghurye, *Caste and Class* . . . , pp. 178–183; M. N. Srinivas, "Caste in Modern India," pp. 532–537. The R.S.S., the militant Hindu organization, had also been active in this region in the recent past. I believe that most of its membership was drawn from Brahmans and castes close in rank to them, but I have little information on the subject. I found no traces of the organization in the *tālukā* in 1954 and only a few in Poona city.

of it. The Dhangars had a well-organized association, with a written constitution and other publications. The local representative of the Dhangar association lived in Mot. He was a candidate for the Bombay State legislature and sent post-cards to all Dhangars of the area requesting their votes. Not knowing that Gaon's Rajputs had changed their caste identification, he included them in his campaign. This was the only contact the Rajputs had with the organization. They claimed not to know of its existence.

Among Rope Makers and Basket Makers there were faint stirrings of organization. In Mot and in Gaon members of the Rope Maker caste wanted to purchase rope-making machines and hoped for government aid in the scheme. In order to effect this there were some pamphlets printed, there were some meetings, and there was much informal discussion; but a permanent, formally structured organization was never achieved. Among Basket Makers a district-wide meeting was held simultaneously with three other districts in 1953. The caste had retained southern marriage regulations, and at these meetings it undertook to substitute practices more like those of Maharashtra. This is a very old process in India. What was probably new about the phenomenon was the simultaneity of the meetings and their geographic scope. Instead of traditional caste leaders, men with a western type of education presided at the meetings. I have no evidence, however, that a permanent, formal caste organization was established.

It should be observed that by 1937 caste organizations of this type, fairly noticeable elsewhere in India, had not yet made an appearance even in Poona city, which is one of the first places we would expect to find them in Maharashtra.[16] By 1954 there were indications, albeit feeble ones, that the

[16] D. R. Gadgil, *Poona: A Socio-Economic Survey*, Pt. 2 (Gokhale Institute of Politics and Economics, Pub. 25), Poona, 1952, p. 185.

new kind of organization was appearing among some castes of Mot and Gaon.

One outcome of changing conditions in the area was an increase in antagonism among some castes. The anti-Brahman movement, especially as embodied in the Satyaśodhak Samāj, had some effect. In the recent past, villagers said, Brahmans had been disliked. However, all agreed that hostility had not been very great within Gaon itself. Village Brahmans had always been used for ceremonies in the village, whereas it was reported that in other areas many castes, particularly "Marathas," had taken to using their own priests. This had some effect in the *tālukā,* but not much. A number of castes in Vādi used their own priests in 1954; none used those from Gaon. However, Vādi had no Brahmans in it, and it was essentially separate from Gaon. Brahmans in Gaon were sensitive to possible hostility from other villagers—the stereotype of Deśastha Brahmans held them to be "haughty" —and they were careful to refrain from overt displays of superiority. In fact, in 1954 anti-Brahman feeling was slight.

As indicated, some mutual rejection between Scavengers and higher castes was probably a long-standing phenomenon in the village. The stereotype of the caste as given to violence, e.g., as cattle poisoners, was an old one. Informants of Scavenger caste and higher castes asserted that Scavengers and others had managed to get along in the past, but that there had always been some hostility. Congress' egalitarian ideals, along with the related movements started by Ambedkar, probably aggravated the existing hostility. In 1954 a few young Scavengers were imbued with the idea that they were equal to others. They were, of course, not being treated as equals, and they reacted by expressing antipathy to "Marathas," Brahmans, and other high castes. These young men were more conscious than most of political movements, and

they were markedly hostile to the Congress Party. They felt
that the party had done too little for Harijans, that it really
represented the higher castes. According to them, in 1946
Poona District Harijans had held a mass protest meeting for
equal rights, instigated by Ambedkar. Harijans, mostly Scavengers, had gone to Poona city in order to enter Hindu temples en masse. This was against the law at the time; as these
informants saw it, the law had been enacted by the British "to
please the Hindus." Many had been jailed, including about
ten Scavengers from Gaon. Some were freed after having
apologized. According to these informants, Congress leaders
had instigated the apologies.

Scavengers identified the Congress Party with Hinduism,
and, following the new Buddhist movement, a few young
men of the caste had come to reject Hinduism. Older men of
this caste were willing to accept whatever came about, to follow the trends in their caste; but these younger people were
vigorous in their denial of Hinduism. This was brought out
especially in the celebration of Dr. Ambedkar's Birthday, a
regularly celebrated event by 1954–1955. In 1955 there were
about thirty present for the celebration (held in the Mariai
temple). Most were Scavengers, but a few Rope Makers and
Leather Workers, two Rajputs, one Maratha, and two Brahmans were also there. The Brahmans were the young English-speaking marginal leader and his brother. All were young
men, around twenty-five years old or less. A Scavenger
opened the meeting with a violent attack on Hinduism and an
appeal to everyone to accept Buddhism. He was answered by
others of "touchable" caste to the effect that religion was not
at fault but men, both of Harijan and higher caste, who had
to learn to change their ways. One of the defenders of Hinduism said: "Harijans must help themselves. Note that many
have not attended this meeting. . . . Religion, as such, I do

not know—you may follow any religion, but then you should practice it. In every religion there are good principles. There is no need to criticize any religion. . . . Do not say one religion is good and another bad. You should follow your own religion. It will do you no good merely to utter Dr. Ambedkar's name. You must improve yourselves. All men are liable to err. Do not point out their mistakes. Improve yourselves."

The Scavenger answered, "Hinduism is based on castes. In Buddhism there is no caste," and then went on to explain some of the main features of Buddhism.

Most Scavengers were not intimately involved in this movement and continued to identify with the village. Even the young men who had been affected by it stayed on good terms with young men of higher caste and persisted in giving respect to individual villagers of "touchable" caste. But it is clear that the idea of equality had begun to have an effect on the group, and the result was an increase in hostility.

The Rope Makers had also become more hostile to higher castes in the village. This was unrelated to Ambedkar's movement, for they did not associate themselves with it. In large part it was due to a weakening of the *bālutā* system, a matter which will be taken up in more detail later. Because so many Rope Makers were landless, they were more dependent on *bālutā* than any other caste. In 1954 many of them were getting less *bālutā* than in the recent past, and a few were getting almost no *bālutā*. Many were forced to sell rope items in Mot, where only a meager income could be earned. They had attempted to adjust to the situation. Some people of the caste visited Poona and saw other Rope Makers using diesel-operated rope-making machines. With such machines, they said, they could not only make better rope in less time, but could also manufacture thread sufficiently fine to weave cloth.

They wanted a machine and had heard something about government loans for the purpose. However, they were told that in order to get the loan they needed the signature of the village *pāṭīl*.[17] They turned to him and were refused. He said he would be financially liable if the Rope Makers defaulted. He feared that they would use the money for other purposes, such as weddings. But the Rope Makers explained his refusal differently. They contended that the *pāṭīls* wanted to keep them impoverished "so they can get cheap labor at harvest time." The *pāṭīl* was symbolic for them of all important village landowners, the very ones who had started giving less *bālutā*. Thus their hostility was extended to the entire village.

That this antagonism was recent had been agreed by everyone, both Rope Makers and others. But it was acute. The Rope Makers felt apart from the village and had few loyalties to it. When I was about to leave Gaon in 1955, the village as a whole planned a send-off celebration. The Rope Makers were the only ones in the community who, as a group, started to organize a separate celebration. (They were dissuaded by some village leaders.) The caste still attended major village ceremonies and public functions, although they were not so well represented as others, and most of them still operated in the *bālutā* system. But their ties to the village had been attenuated.

A similar process was taking place with Rope Makers in other villages of the *tālukā,* but the outcome was different. It was reported that landowners had started to decrease *bālutā* payments to Rope Makers, but that in some cases the caste had struck back. They had destroyed crops and animals and

17 I do not know whether the headman's signature was legally required, but this was the way the Rope Makers and the headman understood it. His signature was not required in 1961.

sometimes even attacked individuals. But in Gaon, it was said, "Rope Makers are good."

It should be observed that the Leather Workers showed none of the antagonism found among Scavengers and Rope Makers. They did not associate themselves with the Scheduled Caste Federation or the Buddhist movement. Eleven of the thirteen households had withdrawn from the *bālutā* system, and the remaining two had all of the patrons they required. Their withdrawal from the *bālutā* system was probably partly due to their efforts at upward mobility, although the decline of the system was probably also a factor, for a number of Potters had also stopped participating.

VILLAGE POLITICAL LIFE

Formal political institutions had been changed in recent years. The introduction of a village *pancāyat,* having jurisdiction over both Gaon and Vādi, was one such change, but it was of relatively little importance. It was composed of thirteen members at the start and later increased to fifteen. One seat was reserved for a Harijan, another for a woman. The *pancāyat* elected its own chairman and deputy chairman. It elected two committees, a judicial committee and a school committee. Its expenses were dependent upon government aid and a number of local sources, for example, taxes on all village houses, on all weddings held within the village, and on items such as raw sugar, pottery, and so on, that were manufactured in the village.

The duties of the *pancāyat* had to do with such matters as repair of village roads, inspection of water facilities, maintenance of hygienic conditions, and provision for security against theft and violence. The school committee supervised schools in the community, but its powers were only advisory. The judicial committee had the power to try civil cases involving sums up to 100 rupees and criminal cases involving the theft of sums up to twenty rupees. It also was supposed to investigate and fine violations of the compulsory education regulations and misuse of common village lands.

However, the *pancāyat* did rather little. It was supposed to meet once a month, but for lack of a quorum it had missed twenty-eight per cent of its meetings since 1947.[18] Villagers' interest in it seemed slight. It had called a meeting of all adult villagers in 1951, and only twenty-two people were present. It had hired a village servant, who lit the village lamps at night and did other odd jobs, and a woman to sweep the village streets. A considerable part of the discussion at *pancāyat* meetings involved the suitability of these employees; it repeatedly fired and hired people. When it did take action, which was infrequent, it was in terms of the old power hierarchy. The well, constructed—inconveniently for most villagers—beside the home of a village leader, is an example. Inaction was more usual. The village leader left the community, and in time the well became polluted. It was therefore useless, although it could have been used despite its position. The *pancāyat* made resolutions to have the well cleaned in 1950 and again in 1952, but it remained unfit for use. Many of the deserted houses in the village had fallen down, and large areas were covered with heaps of stone. This was recognized as a health menace; the stones housed a fair population of rats and, to a lesser extent, snakes. In 1949 the *pancāyat* resolved that the owners should remove the stones; they made a similar resolution in 1950; in August of 1955 the stones still remained. Most of the owners were fairly well off, and there was considerable hesitancy in issuing an ultimatum to them; this would precipitate conflicts.

18 This information and much of what follows was taken from the official minutes of the *pancāyat*.

Many of the owners themselves agreed that strong action
should be taken, but there was little action. People said that
the government should do the job. They cited a Marāṭhi
proverb to the effect that when a kinsman pierces a baby's
ears it hurts, but when the Goldsmith does so it does not.
Action by a fellow villager would be taken as offensive,
while that of an outsider would not.

This was the approach to almost all affairs. Attendance
at school was legally mandatory, but many farmers kept their
children away for work, and many others, especially Harijans,
did not even enroll their children. The *pancāyat* was ineffectual. In 1952 it instructed its judicial committee to do something about this; by 1955 nothing had been done, and the
pancāyat appointed a separate committee to look into the
matter. The *pancāyat* made no efforts to secure the village
against theft or damage to property, although farmers were
concerned about these subjects. The cattle pound, intended
for trespassing animals, was not much used. The parties involved preferred to argue the matter out among themselves.

The judicial committee of the *pancāyat,* which was em-
powered to try cases, was used but once. A Potter had constructed a kiln on what was alleged to be someone else's land.
The dispute was brought before the committee, but a decision was never reached. Interpersonal disputes were either
resolved quietly by arbitration, using leaders in an informal
capacity, or through the courts in Mot. The *pancāyat* members preferred it so. Records had to be kept of *pancāyat* proceedings, and decisions were supposed to be made imper-
sonally. Personal factors, the whole background of each man
involved in a dispute, could be taken up in informal arbitration, and the problem could be settled with a minimum of
publicity.

It was required by local authorities, in accordance with

the law, that at least one member of the *pancāyat* be a Harijan. The man selected was the Scavenger on permanent village *bālutā* duty. He was held in little esteem, disrespected even by members of his own caste. One Scavenger complained, "He carries things for the *pāṭīl*—*javari* and *bājari*—so he can get some for himself." He was said to have stolen food at weddings, an action allegedly often taken by Scavengers and Rope Makers, but in fact only done by those least respected. Some Scavengers asserted that village leaders had put him up for election precisely because he was known to be a man of no account.

Most of the others on the *pancāyat* were village leaders. Yet they chose to act in the old way, through informal channels. They ran for *pancāyat* office because it demonstrated cooperation with the Congress Party, with whose program they said they identified. To cooperate with Congress showed "patriotism" and gave leaders an additional rationalization for the informal power they exercised. The actions of the *pancāyat* were not important, but membership on it served the purpose of enhancing the social and political positions of informal village leaders.

A change of greater significance was the substitution of a government-appointed official called *talāṭhi* for the Brahman *kuḷkarṇi* in the post of village accountant. The duties of the accountant did not change much. He still kept village records of land and similar matters and still helped collect taxes. He was somewhat more dependent upon the revenue headman than was the *kuḷkarṇi,* for he did not know who the villagers were nor where their lands lay, but his greater knowledge of financial matters and government procedures kept him in a position superior to the headman. Like the *kuḷkarṇi* he was sometimes called upon to arbitrate disputes, but he knew less about the people and was less used. Furthermore, because

he was not a member of the village, he was not so much concerned with the esteem of villagers; he did not usually remain
in one village for more than a few years. As a result his
power was greater than that of the *kulkarni*. It could be used
for personal economic advantage, and it could be used to help
produce change.

One *talāthi* created a furor over his demands for particularly large "tips"—up to two rupees from most people who
came to him for records. An educated young Brahman who
was marginally a leader complained of this (in English): "He
takes nothing extra from the powerful or educated, only from
the poor and ignorant. Even Harijans. For educated people,
he may even have records delivered to [their] doors. He delivered to me. Normally *talāthis* take about eight annas. This
man takes too much. People are speaking about it." Actually
the accountant did take "tips" from most of the wealthy, and
they did not trouble to complain. They preferred to placate
him. One of the village leaders encouraged others to pay
what was asked. The *talāthi* took nothing from the Brahman
because he knew of the man's objections and feared that he
might protest to the Revenue Department. The informant
tried to have the *talāthi* removed from the village. "Three,
four people complained to me about the *talāthi*," he said. "I
asked them to sign an affidavit [against him], but they said
'Why affidavit?' But I know they are too afraid to complain.
They are afraid to sign the affidavit, and they will be afraid
to complain, surely. So nothing will be done."

There were, of course, limitations on what the *talāthi*
might do. Where he offended the poor and powerless, little or
nothing was likely to be done. But when he offended the village leaders, he was removed. Around 1950 the *talāthi* had
been a Scavenger. This in itself probably annoyed some people of high caste. Furthermore, he attempted to encourage

solidarity among Untouchables. The public celebration of Ambedkar's birthday was being practiced by Scavengers in Mot and elsewhere, and he talked village Harijans into holding it in Gaon. Then, using his status as *talāṭhi,* he went around to others in the village and "suggested" that they make some financial contribution toward the event. They did, and the ceremony was held. However, the village leaders were incensed at his actions. A number of them, along with other villagers, went to his superior and complained. They asked to have him transferred, and their request was granted. Despite his transfer, his efforts had some effect, for the event was celebrated every year through 1955.

The effects of the *talāṭhi* are, in part, unpredictable. They must vary with the personality and opinions of the man who fills the office. Most did not attempt to alter village relationships, but the fact that they existed as agents of the government within the borders of the village helped to alter people's attitude toward the government. This matter will be discussed subsequently.

The patterns of informal leadership described earlier were extant in 1954. There had probably been some changes in emphasis. The positions of active leaders had probably been slightly weakened, for a number of recent immigrants, particularly farm residents, tended to ignore them, especially in regard to the arbitration of disputes. However, most old residents continued to give them respect and deference. Another shift in emphasis involved the Bal group. In the past the alliance between the ancestors of the Bal group and the "disreputable" Harijan element had had no conceivable justification. It was simply accepted as a part of the power network of the community. Recent ideological changes gave some sanction to the Bals' activities. In 1954 it was, in theory, quite proper to protect and defend Harijans. Bal could openly defend them and refer to Congress ideals in doing so. In the event described earlier, where Bal had invited Harijans into a Brahman's courtyard for water on Independence Day, he had taken advantage of the new ideology and of the symbolic nature of the occasion. Brahman sensitivity to anti-Brahmanism was also involved, but it was less important. Active leaders other than Brahmans had been present, and they were angered by Bal's act. Yet, even after Bal had left the scene, they made no public protest. After everyone had left excepting one young Scavenger, a village leader reprimanded him. The Scavenger answered, "First wash your heart with water from the well, then tell me what to do."

For a Scavenger to have "talked back" to an important village leader was a rare thing, especially in the recent past. The ideological change was at least partly responsible for greater Harijan boldness in this regard. The young Scavenger was educated, had been much affected by Ambedkar's campaign, and bitterly resented the stigma on his caste. He made efforts to gain the respect of other villagers. For example, he offered to coach, free of charge, schoolboys—Harijans and others—who had difficulty in their studies. (None accepted.) Although a fairly aggressive person, he was usually courteous and mild mannered with others. He had answered the village leader, but with restraint, even with a certain elegance of speech. He took pride in his education and often let others know of it. He wanted to be a leader, especially of Harijans. It was his leadership that had kept the celebration of Ambedkar's birthday going after the Scavenger *talāṭhi* had left. He was at the forefront of the Buddhist movement within the village. It was he who had overtly argued for Buddhism before Brahmans, Marathas, and Rajputs, as well as Harijans.

Yet he was accepted as a leader by only a few young Harijan men, most of them Scavengers. Older members of his caste occasionally asked his advice on affairs that required a western type of education but did not follow his suggestions on other matters. Older men, for example, did not attend the Dr. Ambedkar's Birthday celebration. People were accustomed to the leadership of mature men of some wealth or of some formally defined status. This young man was in his early twenties and was no wealthier than other Scavengers, much less well off than some Leather Workers. As a result he was not in a position to have many followers.

It was similar with a Brahman of about twenty-five years of age. He was the best educated man in the village, the only one who was very competent in English. He was strongly in favor of Congress ideals (although not of the party itself). Because of his education he was usually among the speakers on Harijan Day and Independence Day. He was the only speaker to mention the condition of Harijans. He exhorted them to take advantage of the opportunities offered by government. He and his brother were among the few non-Harijans attending Dr. Ambedkar's Birthday.

The Brahman's sphere of leadership was much limited. When people required assistance in technical matters where literacy, arithmetical ability, or knowledge of "modern" ways was required, many went to him for advice. He was the informant quoted earlier to whom people protested about the *talāṭhi's* exorbitant demands. He was respected for his education, but, like the Scavenger, he was not followed in other respects and he was never asked to arbitrate disputes. Only one man, a Harijan, named him as a leader. He was considered too young. While fairly well off economically, he was not within the top economic bracket in the village, and he did not make a display of what wealth he had. He was a new resident; his family's brief history in the village may have contributed to his unacceptability as a leader. In addition, he was thought to be an extremist. Many villagers spoke against the Congress Party, but not publicly, certainly not before village leaders; it was known that he was against the Congress Party because he had formerly been a member of the R.S.S., the militant Hindu nationalist organization. Furthermore, he was not aggressive. He feared antagonizing powerful villagers. "After all," he said, "we must live with these people." Though he influenced some people in the community, his power was not great.

THE DECLINE OF VILLAGE SOCIETY

As might be expected, the economic and demographic changes described earlier resulted in a weakening of village ties. The emphasis on cash led to land being conceived less as a traditional heritage and more as a marketable commodity. Fifty-seven of those registered as owners of village land were identified by informants as absentee landlords. Five not known to the informants were probably also absentee owners of land in Gaon or Vādi. Many of the new residents were but loosely bound to the village. Some had simply bought land and worked it; others had gone to wherever a job could be found. A considerably higher percentage of new than old residents lived outside the main settlement on farms, seventy-five per cent of new residents as against forty-eight per cent of the old. Many of the new residents, especially those living outside the main settlement, had little interest in village affairs. They did not conflict with others; they were, by and large, apathetic. If a new-resident landowner was approached by a village leader for a contribution for a village ceremony, something was usually given, but it was often only a token sum. The new residents on farms rarely came in for ceremonies, except sometimes the new secular ceremonies. They came in for Hanumān Jayanti not infrequently, but outsiders also attended the ceremony in order to watch the procession and the wrestling matches. They were observers of the spectacle, not participants. Fewer of them took part in the *balutā* system than did old residents. About sixty per cent of the new-resident landowners did not participate, or participated little.[19]

The *balutā* system was in the process of declining. This was not only because of the new residents, but also because of other innovations that have been mentioned. People had more cash than they had had in the past and were able to purchase things in Mot without difficulty. *Balutedārs* were slow and unpredictable, and, as was noted, people were more time-conscious. The increase in the price of grain during World War II had resulted in many landowners selling much of their produce and giving less *balutā*. The inflation was not of fundamental importance, however, for in unirrigated villages, especially those distant from Mot, the *balutā* system remained strong in 1954. But in Gaon even some old-resident landowners were withdrawing from the system. Twenty-eight per cent of them participated little or not at all. Others who gave *balutā* to most *balutedārs* were now giving less. *Balutedārs* reacted by giving fewer services. For example, Rope Makers were supposed to give a full complement of ropes on Bāil Poḷā and at any other time they were needed. In 1954 rope was given to most farmers only on Bāil Poḷā. The farmers were buying additional rope in Mot, and Rope Makers were selling their wares there.

The Rope Makers, as has been observed, were hardest hit by the decline, because they were nearly all solely dependent upon their craft. But others were also serving fewer farmers

[19] Those who gave *balutā* to fewer than six castes are here considered to have participated little. This information was taken, in the course of my census, from individual landowners. Seven questionable cases, one a new resident, are omitted.

and getting less *bālutā* from them. It was this as well as the mobility of the Leather Workers that probably accounted for eleven households withdrawing from the system. It probably applied to the Potters as well. Five of the nine Potter households had given up *bālutā* work. These were fairly large landowners by village standards. Their craft took much time and interfered with agricultural activities. As it had become less profitable, they had retired from the system. Furthermore, metal pots were coming into vogue, and the wealthiest landowners, the best patrons, had started purchasing these in Mot. Hence even the remaining four households were getting a little less *bālutā*. The two remaining Leather Worker households, however, were little affected. Farmers' fear of Scavenger violence resulted in that caste getting adequate payments. The main village Barber also had all the *bālutā* trade he required. But the Blacksmith who had recently returned to the village had difficulty in getting *bālutā* patrons. The larger part of his trade was on a cash basis. Most people washed their own clothing or had their servants do it. The village Washerman still took *bālutā* for ritual services, but in less quantity. The village Muslims got slightly less *bālutā* than in the recent past, as did the Goldsmith, whose payment had in any event always been small. The entire system was, as it were, infected by the innovations. Thus the Watchman, whose services were not readily purchasable, said he was getting less *bālutā*. "Some people say government has given lands, so I should not ask for *bālutā*." Similarly the Temple Priests said they got less *bālutā*. However, according to these *bālutedārs,* their payments had not been much reduced. During the past ten years or so Brahmans had stopped going for *bālutā;* what they received was sent to them. Their *bālutā* payment had always been small and their *dakṣiṇā* relatively large. In 1954 they received *bālutā* from very few; *dakṣiṇā* was usually considered adequate recompense for their services.

One village leader, the Maratha resident, was claiming in no uncertain terms that *balutā* was not a right. He would give *balutā,* he said, but *balutedārs* could not insist upon it. While other landowners were not overtly saying this, some were acting appropriately, and some *balutedārs* were beginning to accept it, however unwillingly, as the norm. As one Rope Maker put it, "Once we had *balutā* as a right; now it is up to the landowner whether to give or not." There was a little defensiveness among *balutedārs* regarding the payment. For example, a Temple Priest said, "Most people give *balutā,* but I wait until I am called." Among Rope Makers and Scavengers *balutedārs'* prerogatives were losing clarity of definition. It was a Rope Maker's right to perform a ritual for his patrons on Bāil Poḷā, for which he received a little money and some clothing. Scavengers had started doing this also; they were given no clothing, but a small coin. In other villages of the *tālukā,* unirrigated and more distant from Mot, Rope Makers were shocked when I told them of this. "We would beat them [the Scavengers]," one said.

Although the system was declining, it was still in operation. Most men who wanted prestige continued to make payments of much the same size as in the past. The majority of old-resident landowners continued to give *balutā,* although a number of them had reduced the size of the payments.

The decline of *balutā* was one factor that weakened village identification. There were others. The community was in the process of being caught up in a network of relationships extending beyond its borders. There was more interaction with people in Mot. This in itself was not a great change; some interaction had always taken place, for example, on market day in the town. But there had probably been a slight increase in recent times. One member of Gaon was on the Marketing Committee and four were on the Tālukā Development Board; both organizations were recently formed and met in Mot. The decrease in *bālutā* resulted in more buying and selling in Mot. However, this was usually restricted to market day, although a few Rope Makers went in two or three days a week.

The most important expansion of relationships had not been spatial; the encroachments of government were broadening people's worlds in a psychological sense. Ceremonies sponsored by the government and by the Congress Party were celebrated. Their representatives not infrequently made speeches in the village when these ceremonies were held and on other occasions. Government was present within the borders of Gaon in the form of the *talāṭhi.* The *pancāyat* was government instigated and responsible to the government. No matter how ineffectual, it meant that government was *here.*

The *pancāyat* was a part of the government's plan to resuscitate "ancient Indian polity." Another new institution intended to effect this was the Cooperative Credit Society. Although not so ineffectual as the *pancāyat,* it was far from realizing its aims. It had a number of powers, as noted earlier, but the only one it exercised was the granting of loans. In this matter it was supposed to operate in accordance with individual needs. But the old patterns of village life were not excluded from society meetings. Many people refused to join the society, despite the advantage of low interest rates. These and some who did join were dissatisfied with the organization. Favoritism was the main complaint. Powerful villagers, it was said, could get loans more easily than others, and they were more likely to use them for non-agricultural purposes. Fellow villagers were "supervisors," and these, of course, would not act against the powerful. Such men were said to be slow to repay. Non-repayment of loans resulted in the closure of the society by the central bank in Bombay; the 1954 society was named Cooperative Credit Society Number Two. There was said to be much conflict and intrigue in the society over who was to get loans and how large the loans should be, and especially over election of officers. Marathas and Rajputs, Annas and Bals (though Bal, himself, was not in it) were said to be constantly at odds with one another. As a result the society had but ninety-seven members—forty per cent of the 242 residents of Gaon who were registered landowners and, hence, eligible.

Thus the aims of this part of the government program were not succeeding. But the constant presence of government had resulted in people adjusting to it. The headman in 1955, a man of about forty years of age, said that in his childhood, when people heard of an impending visit by a government official, they went home and bolted their doors, waiting until he left before showing themselves. Those whose duty it was to report to the officials, the headman and Water Carrier, for instance, were servile and circumspect. "Now," the headman added, "people are more rational; they know their rights." The headman possibly exaggerated the frailties of the past and surely he overestimated the "rationality" of 1955. Many people in 1955 still feared government officials, and the headman himself still acted, whenever possible, to shield the village from outside agencies. But he exaggerated what was, in fact, occurring. Village leaders identified with the government, at least overtly, and others stood less in dread of it.

This does not mean that all were favorably disposed toward government. Apart from village leaders, many people were hostile. They referred to Congress advocates derisively as "white caps," after the hand-spun gandhi cap that symbolized party allegiance. All the ills they suffered were blamed on "the new government." Some praised the pre-independence regime. Yet their hostility seemed tinged with a feeling of disappointment in something they took to be closer to them than the old political institutions, something less awesome, from which they felt they could expect much but from which they thought they got little.

The changes we have discussed were bound to have an effect on village solidarity. The over-all weakening of *balutā* had influenced the attachment of some villagers to Gaon, as had probably the expansion of the sphere of interaction with government and with other forces from without the village. We have noted the increase in antagonism among Scavengers, due largely to Ambedkar's campaign, and the increase in hostility among Rope Makers, primarily a result of the decrease in *balutā* payments. The influx of newcomers probably exacerbated the situation; as might be expected, newcomers showed least attachment to the village. There were also signs of apathy among some old residents who lived out on their farms, Marathas, of course, but also a few others, even including Rajputs. A number of such people said, with some conviction, that they wanted nothing to do with village squabbling. These rarely came into the village, even staying away from some important ceremonies.

The sharpest break involved the Anna hamlet. In response to the antagonism of the Bals, some Annas were avoiding the main settlement. Around 1952 the Annas stopped coming to the main settlement for the celebration of Bāil Poḷā. In part, this may represent the beginnings of the long-term process of "budding" by which new communities were formed, just as Vādi had been. The formation of Vādi probably had little relation to recent innovations. But the Anna hamlet was different, for it had strong traditional ties to the village. The residents of the hamlet were mostly Kokes with traditional rights to the status of village *pāṭīl*. (In 1961 an Anna held the position.) A number of them were informal village leaders. Their traditional bond to the village had resulted in their having attended Bāil Poḷā in the past and in their helping to organize it and other ceremonies despite the recurrent conflicts. Vādi contained no Kokes. The beginnings of the formation of a separate social entity in the Anna hamlet were no doubt partly due to physical separation and conflict; but a general decrease in village solidarity was probably also a factor.

Identification with the village was still unmistakably present. Most of the signs of cohesion mentioned earlier had been observed in 1954. A few of the village ceremonies were poorly attended. This was especially true of New Year's Day, when forecasts of village crops were made. Only about forty people were present. It should be mentioned, however, that crop forecasts were less important since irrigation had lessened most of the farmers' dependence upon rain. Hoḷi was not held in 1954; the government had passed a law against it. But most other village ceremonies were still well attended. Almost everyone, even those on distant farms, came in for Āmbīl Ghugriya, which was one of the most significant ceremonies for village unity. Dasarā and Hanumān Jayanti still drew most people, many not only as observers but as participants. Practically everyone came to the village for the new secular ceremonies, particularly Independence Day. Nearly all village leaders were present at the ceremonies, and many of them made speeches on the secular occasions. Thus we see that, while village solidarity had been weakened, it had not been destroyed.

13

The Changing Village, 1961

THE most noticeable innovation since 1954 was an intensification of government activities. The institutions observed in 1954, the Tālukā Development Board, for example, remained. The multiplication of government activities took place partly within the old organizations. Officials of the Revenue Department had increased contacts with the local population. They visited villages for inspection and propaganda more frequently than in 1954–1955. In the interval the work of the higher officials had become so much greater that two men instead of one now headed the Poona District department. One was called by the old title of collector, the other "additional collector." The addition of one office was in order to facilitate travel for inspection and propaganda. The additional collector visited Gaon while I was there—a surprise visit, hence the audience was small—and spoke on a number of topics such as birth control, education, and increased production. The emphasis in his talk was on the need for the local population to cooperate, to help themselves, if the government was to help them.

The intensification of Revenue Department activity and the emphasis in the collector's talk formed part of a general movement. The theme was, in the words of another government official, "Now *you* start. Form a committee. See what kind of equipment you need. Save some money and pool it. Then come to government." If a group of men, a minimum of eleven, was able to save a stipulated sum of money for what was deemed a worthy project—housing, for example—government gave them additional funds, usually much more than the sum saved, as well as advice. There were variations in this "self help" program, but government officials repeatedly emphasized the necessity for cooperation, democratic action, and, if possible, local initiative in effecting improvements. This was found even in the government's efforts to reduce land fragmentation. The land consolidation program had started in the late 1940's in this area and reached Gaon in August of 1961, when the first steps were being taken to consolidate fragmented holdings. These involved the formation of committees of villagers to suggest fair land redistribution. The committee members were elected by a general meeting of village landowners chaired by a consolidation officer.

The most notable cooperative ventures were two government-sponsored sugar factories started in the *tālukā*. In 1955 they had been in the planning stage; they were now fully operating cooperative societies, and an additional society of smaller scale was being started. Each member owned at least one share in a factory, no one more than fifty. Ownership of one-half an acre of canal-irrigated sugar-cane land [1] gave elligibility, so all members were not necessarily well off. Members participated in regular meetings to elect officers and discuss policy. Each member had one vote. Membership in the cooperative societies was profitable, for members could sell cane to the factories at good prices, and they had a number of other economic advantages, such as use of society equipment at a low rent. Those who had not joined at the start had difficulty in doing so later. The only way was for a farmer to purchase canal-irrigated sugar-cane land from a member. He could then be admitted after consideration by a committee.

[1] The government restricted sugar-cane growing on canal-irrigated land to designated blocks.

The largest single government program started in the six-year period was an extension program begun in October of 1959. It was a part of the general community-development movement taking place in India, the intent of which is social and economic "uplift." The *tālukā* was classified as a "block," headed by a block-development officer. It was in a pre-extension phase in 1961, preparatory to an intensive phase to begin in April 1962. The 1961 phase was already fairly intensive. Apart from the block-development officer, there were five extension officers, one in charge of *pancāyats,* two for agriculture, and two for cooperatives (including the sugar factories). There were ten village-level workers, about one for every six villages in the *tālukā.* The main work done by the extension program thus far had been to encourage cooperative societies.

The cooperative movement and the more intensive government activity I have outlined had been going on for some years in other parts of India. But by 1955 they were little known in this *tālukā,* hardly at all in Gaon. In 1961 nearly everyone was talking about them.

CHANGING CASTE

There was possible evidence of a more overt acceptance of Congress principles on caste in 1961. In 1954–1955 most speakers at the new secular ceremonies avoided the topic of untouchability. The celebration of Independence Day in 1961 was different in many respects. There were but two speakers, one a young Scavenger (the marginal leader mentioned earlier), the other a Brahman, a former government employee who had recently retired to his home in the village. One of the emphasized points in the Brahman's speech was the need to help Untouchables. This and the presence of a Harijan speaker were departures from the tenor of the 1954–1955 ceremonies. But the meeting is difficult to interpret. Most village leaders did not attend the ceremony, and none spoke. Yet the program plan was subject to supervision by the village headman and other leaders. The meeting may be an indication of a more overt acceptance of Congress principles, but it may be merely a sign of apathy on the part of village leadership. It may be both.

Apart from this, the shortness of my 1961 stay prevented me from making systematic observations on ritual pollution. Not long after I arrived in Gaon, I had a village Brahman perform a Satyanārāyaṇa Pujā ("good luck" ceremony) in my house. Among those distributing sweets to the guests was one Scavenger. Two Brahman guests, known to me as religious men, accepted sweets from him and ate them. This was no doubt done in deference to what they assumed (correctly) to be my egalitarian values. I think it probable that they underwent ritual purification when they returned home. But it was an indication that they understood the practice of untouchability to be not unequivocally respectable. My impressions of conditions in 1961 were that there may have been a further decrease in the practice of untouchability, that certainly there was no increase.

The condition of the traditional type of caste meeting remained the same as in 1954. The Goldsmith, Water Carrier, Washerman, and Watchman castes still held meetings on some occasions. For example, a *soyare* of Gaon's Washerman had been "tried" in 1959 or 1960 for keeping a woman of lower caste. He confessed his offense, agreed to give up the woman, and feasted the group.

The cooperative movement had some direct effect on caste organization in Gaon, but not much. Caste was related to the village Cooperative Credit Societies, to be discussed later. An effort had been made by the extension office to form a cooperative among Scavengers in the village. Their *inām* land, traditionally inalienable, had been converted into ordinary land. An extension officer tried to get them to pool their land and work it cooperatively—with substantial financial aid from the government. The effort failed, probably in part because some owned much more land than others and refused to make the "sacrifice." However, even these larger land-owners could have been expected to gain from the cooperative. The failure was probably also due to the fact that if a cooperative were established, everyone would have had to share in the actual working of the land; the steady labor involved in farming was objectionable to some Scavengers. Hence, despite the financial advantage to be gained, the necessary enthusiasm was lacking. Furthermore, local leadership did not act with sufficient vigor. Within the caste it was practically absent, as we shall see, and few village leaders applied the necessary pressure or encouragement. According to some informants—three Scavengers and a Brahman—one village leader had helped to undermine the effort. He was renting land from some Scavengers and did not want to lose it, so, it was said, he had spread rumors that the Scavengers would lose their land if the plan were adopted. The three Scavenger informants held that this village leader had convinced the *talāṭhi* to delay giving the necessary land records. In any event, the scheme did not materialize. Some Scavengers had since leased their land for long terms, breaking up the single block required for a cooperative. In another village, where leadership in the Scavenger caste was strong, I observed a similar plan put into effect with considerable efficiency.

Although their efforts to get rope-making machines had failed, Gaon's Rope Makers were, in 1961, in the process of forming another cooperative. This involved the construction of new housing for the group. They had saved most of the required sum, and it was anticipated that building would soon start. Their future plans were to save an additional sum, 500 rupees, to which they anticipated the government would add 3000 rupees, in order to form a cooperative dairying society. With profits from this, they hoped to purchase rope-making machines on their own.

Apart from the sugar factories, which I will discuss later, these were the only new efforts at forming cooperatives in which traditional village castes were involved. However, in the *tālukā* as a whole many localized caste groups, especially Harijans and low castes, had taken advantage of the cooperative movement. The Bāgḍis of Gaon were forming a cooperative housing society in 1961. The Rope Makers of Mot had a rope-manufacturing cooperative. Only a few of these societies had existed in 1954. In 1961 it was impressive to observe the alacrity with which such cooperatives had been formed and were in the process of being started. The formation of such cooperatives obviously resulted in a solidification of caste interests on the local level and a greater measure of independence from village ties.

The widespread modern caste organizations and movements, feebly seen in this region in 1954–1955, were more marked in 1961. The Scavenger campaign had been intensified, although it had little effect on interaction among Scavengers in Gaon. Young men of this caste no longer spoke of the Scheduled Caste Federation; they said it had been changed into a political party, the Republican Party,[2] which emphasized advantages for Harijans. Like the Scheduled Caste Federation, only Scavengers gave allegiance to it, and only a few of the young men showed much interest. Even these were less enthusiastic than in 1954. These young men

[2] I believe that this party is much older than villagers thought. However, they did not know of it in 1955.

also spoke of the Bharati Boudha Mahasabha, an organization devoted to converting Indians to Buddhism. Ambedkar, the Scavenger leader, had been officially converted to Buddhism in 1956 along with many other people, probably mostly Scavengers. Mass conversions to Buddhism had taken place among Scavengers in a number of villages of the *tālukā* but had not yet reached Gaon.

The exclusive, primarily social, type of caste organization had clearly increased in importance. The Rope Makers' efforts at organization were almost forgotten in 1961, but formal caste organizations were now familiar to members of six traditional castes in the village. The Potters and Rajputs of Gaon participated actively in newly formed caste organizations. A Barber organization existed in Mot, but as it had been started as recently as 1960, it had not yet extended to the villages. The Mot officers were planning to take in all Barbers in the *tālukā*. Organizations of this type existed in the *tālukā* for the Leather Worker, Water Carrier, and Goldsmith castes. Villagers of these castes knew of them, and some of their kinsmen participated in the organizations, but they had not yet joined.

The organization of caste associations of this type tended to follow administrative divisions. Communication among members was effected through the mails or by way of meetings held at regular intervals. The Potters of Maharashtra, for example, were scheduled to meet once a year, and an elected committee of the association met once a month. The organizations had as their purposes to "modernize" caste custom, to gain more respect for their caste in the eyes of the larger community, and in other ways to benefit members of the caste. Education, often including campaigns for student boarding houses and scholarships, was always a feature of the programs. A boarding house for Rajput schoolboys was constructed in Mot in 1958 or 1959. Another feature of the new association was assistance to members in their trade. For example, Barbers were attempting to fix prices and to improve tools and techniques. The plan was, according to the secretary of the Poona District Barbers' organization, so to improve work as "to show people that our trade is not lowly, but essential." Potters wanted to improve brick and pot manufacture and to get good clay at fair prices. The Potters' organization was also intended to get members to cooperate and, through cooperative groups, to get government aid in the construction of brick factories. Other caste societies were also concerned with government programs. Thus the secretary of the Barbers' society commented: "Government gives privileges to backward classes. We are not a backward class, but we are not equal [to Marathas, e.g.]. We need help too. . . . We need help like that given to backward classes." The Barbers were not seeking aid through the government's cooperative program, but by means of organization they were trying to help themselves. At meetings of Rajputs, almost all of whom were farmers, the discussion often centered about the cooperative sugar factories.

Involved in these formal organizations there was, of course, a tendency to measure the privileges and position of one's own caste by reference to those of others. The statement by the official of the Barbers' organization is illustrative. The organizations were concerned with social mobility, and in this respect were similar to the old type of caste meeting, although secular features were more emphasized. Below I give part of a speech presented at a Sagar Rajput meeting by the man who was primarily responsible for founding the organization:

We have come here to make men [human beings] of our-

selves; with the same motive we have started this organization. . . . Since we do not know from where we came, who
we are, and so on [others will not accept us as real human
beings]. Hence I planned to start making men out of us. In
this I have not thought of caste. No political and social
leaders bring this castism into their work. As an experiment
I tried this organization.

Our scholar, Dāji Hāri Koke, studied much and worked
for the people in general. From his studies it has been revealed that during the regime of Śivāji there were thirteen
sardars under him. Of these Bhagvānrāv Ātoḷe was one—a
very honest, brave, and able man. These thirteen *sardars* developed into fifty-two during the Peśvā regime. All of them
pleased the Peśvās except the Ātoḷes, and hence they [the
others] retained their titles. Among the *sardars* only Hoḷkār
was Dhangar, others Marathas. One of them [the Marathas]
was Ātoḷe [a Rajput surname]. We call ourselves "Sagar
Rajput." Who are they? Sagar was born seven generations before Rāvaṇ, who lived ten thousand years [ago]. Remember
you are all [descended] from Rajputs—Marathas. From Sagar
the word Śegar came. Dhangar means one who has no knowledge. We have no knowledge, hence we are known as Dhangar.
Well, let me ask you whether Dhangars have the surname
Ātoḷe in their caste!

[The audience] No!

Then who was this *sardar* Ātoḷe?

[The audience] Maratha!

Then tell everyone that you are Marathas!

There was thus a generalized rejection of "castism" and
at the same time an effort to achieve mobility for one's caste.

Caste organizations of this type are not new in modern
Indian history. But, as I have mentioned, they were probably

unknown in the deccan region of Maharashtra in 1937. Only feeble signs of them were seen in Mot or Gaon by 1955. Now suddenly, in 1961, they were rapidly gaining ground in Gaon and its environs, and this was coincident with a considerable increase in government activities. It seems probable that these activities gave an example, a psychological blueprint for action in formally constituted organization, that hastened the process of diffusion.

Although there is evidence that castes, as social groups, were gaining in strength, there were fewer signs of intercaste hostility. The Rope Makers, who had been very antagonistic to higher castes in 1954, were less so in 1961. One reason for this is probably that they had just been refused assistance by the village *pāṭīl* in 1954; by 1961 they had adjusted to this. Furthermore, in the later period they had renewed hope of bettering their condition through government aid. They still rejected village leadership when this subject was brought up, but, contrary to their attitude in 1954, they did not themselves bring up the subject. Their attitude toward leaders was often phrased, "They do not help us, and they do not hurt us." The Rope Makers were much concerned about the government program, apathetic toward village leaders and, to a considerable extent, toward the village as a whole.

There was still some antagonism between a number of Scavengers and other villagers, but my impression in 1961 was that it was less than in 1954. This was due partly to the fact that the young Scavenger who had been attempting to lead his caste and other Harijans toward greater unity was now less active in this regard. Dr. Ambedkar's Birthday was not publicly celebrated in 1961. The caste seemed less solidary than earlier, the members less conscious of themselves as a group. Their *bālutā* payments were nearly gone, and a number of mature men had turned to agriculture. In 1954, of approximately sixty-six acres owned by Scavengers, forty-four per cent lay fallow, forty-three per cent was cultivated, and thirteen per cent was leased or rented. In 1961 less than one per cent lay fallow, and twenty-nine per cent was leased or rented. A few Scavengers took jobs in Mot or Gaon. A considerable number of young men of the caste were engaged in a *tamāśā* performance given every week in the village. *Tamāśā* is a traditional show involving singing and dancing, often somewhat bawdy. In this case, villagers said, it was not a "real" *tamāśā* at all, but merely a smutty show. Two alleged professionals, a man and a woman, performed along with the Scavengers. Villagers said that neither were genuine *tamāśā* performers, that the woman was merely a prostitute, the man a procurer. The Scavengers involved in the *tamāśā* practiced singing and dancing almost every night, often well into the morning, and during the day usually did nothing. The general impression given by the group was one of aimlessness.

VILLAGE POLITICAL LIFE

The *pancāyat* remained relatively ineffectual. In 1958 it had passed yet another vain resolution to have owners remove the stones from the village. Their efforts regarding school attendance in 1955 had had no effect. The most important action taken in the six-year interval was the construction of a new school building with the aid of government funds. Many villagers asserted, correctly, I believe, that the funds had been wasted, that the old buildings had been adequate. They purchased a battery-operated radio, allegedly to keep people informed on national and international affairs. The radio was kept in the *pancāyat* office, which was locked and rarely visited. The batteries died and were not replaced. The last meeting, held in the summer of 1961, took up the problem of the sale of the radio. In a few villages of the *tāluka* there were no *pancāyats* in 1961; they had destroyed themselves in their efforts to take positive action.[3] It was by avoiding significant action that Gaon's *pancāyat* preserved itself.

The *pancāyat* was given even less respect by villagers than in 1954. It had called two general village meetings since 1955. In one there was not even a quorum of *pancāyat* members; in the other only fourteen villagers appeared. One villager, like many others, said, "They do nothing. There is much to do . . . water supply, drainage, but they do nothing." According to the 1961 *pāṭīl*, "They do not take interest. . . . They do not work in a proper way, and they will not in the future." Village leaders showed less interest in membership on the *pancāyat*. In 1954 most members had been leaders; in 1961 there were only two leaders on the *pancāyat* and two sons of village leaders. The recent chairman of the *pancāyat*, a village leader's son, was little esteemed. He was accused of absconding with *pancāyat* funds, about twenty-five rupees, and, after some persuasion, resigned. The deputy chairman assumed his duties; the *pancāyat* was without an official chairman.

The small number of village leaders on the *pancāyat* was indicative of a new attitude on their part. They were less concerned with village affairs. One active leader was explicit. "If I try to help, I lose time from work. They do not listen anyway." Some leaders attended only to private affairs. Others showed interest in running for offices on the sugar-factory boards, while one wanted an office in Mot Tālukā. As was noted, in the 1961 celebration of Independence Day very few leaders attended, and none gave speeches, although many of them had given speeches in 1954. Of course, they had not entirely given up their primacy in village affairs. For example,

---

[3] This information was given me by an extension officer in charge of *pancāyats*.

village leaders were elected to the committee to oversee land consolidation. But their interest in village life had declined.

Even the young Scavenger who had been able to lead some Harijans in 1954 was less concerned now. He had taken a job outside the village for a time, was disillusioned with it, and resigned. Upon his return to Gaon, he was disillusioned with all of his prospects. He lost his ambition, although he was still an efficient organizer. It was he who had, in 1960 or early 1961, turned his efforts to the organization of the *"tamāśā"* performance in the village. In 1954 his standards of behavior had been considered good by people of higher caste who knew him, while in 1961 he was said to have degenerated. He was much less active in the campaign to raise the status of Harijans than he had been.

The only men of some importance who exhibited any interest in village affairs were Bal, a wealthy *soyare* of Bal, and the English-speaking Brahman. Bal and the Brahman had been the only men of any importance in the village who had attempted to facilitate the Scavenger cooperative-land scheme. The Brahman had brought officials of the extension office to the village. He and Bal had encouraged the Scavengers and attempted to discredit the rumor that the land would be lost if the plan were effected. Bal's *soyare*, a man of some wealth and importance, had encouraged the Rope Makers in their housing and dairying projects. However, he was primarily interested in affairs outside of the village. In 1961 he was on the Marketing Committee. Bal, himself, had become less aggressive since 1961. "He is [somewhat] better now, more quiet," as one informant put it. This was probably due to the fact that the Annas were avoiding the main settlement, possibly also because Bal wanted to improve his reputation. In any event, he had never been looked upon as a proper village leader, however much his power had been respected. Similarly, the Brahman had been only marginally a leader.

If the old sanctioned leaders were to have responded to the pressures of 1961, they would have led people in the direction of opportunities created by the government. They did not do this. The Scavenger cooperative scheme is an example. If they had acted in accordance with the new conditions, they would have been moving contrary to the old scheme of village organization; they would have acted, for example, to better the lot of the Scavengers without simultaneously creating greater dependence upon themselves—indeed, there would have been more independence. Consequently, they either retired from leadership or attempted to adapt in a broader sphere of activity.

THE DECLINE OF VILLAGE SOCIETY

Village identity had been further weakened by 1961. The same factors were at work—an increase in cash, in immigrants, and so on. The *bālutā* system was nearly entirely destroyed. Even the Scavengers, who had received what they considered satisfactory payments in 1954, were getting very little *bālutā* in 1961. As has been pointed out, many more were making use of their land, either renting it or farming it themselves. A few of the wealthiest villagers continued to give *bālutā*. Some of these called it charity. Others continued, although with smaller payments, because, they said, they needed *bālutedārs* for rituals. But most had stopped completely. This was the case in most of the heavily irrigated villages of the *tālukā,* especially those close to Mot. In distant villages that had little irrigation the system continued, although even in these communities a few farmers had started giving little or no *bālutā*.

Another severe outbreak of conflict had very nearly completely severed the Anna hamlet from the main settlement. This occurred once again on Hanumān Jayanti. On the day of Hanumān Jayanti, prior to the evening procession, it was customary to erect a pole (*malkhāmb*), which the young men of the village used for calisthenics. In 1956, one year after I had left the village, the Annas wanted a separate pole for themselves, and they paid two young Leather Workers to erect one. The main-settlement people objected, especially the Bals. The two Leather Workers were beaten when they persisted, and the extra pole was taken down. The Annas fled, but the next day, after the wrestling matches, some of them were caught by the Bals and beaten. From that time on, most Annas avoided the main settlement. Almost all celebrations were held in their hamlet. Excepting the on-duty *pāṭil,* who was an Anna, they even stayed away from the 1961 celebration of Independence Day. Some Annas went to Vādi for Independence Day, which they had never done for secular or religious ceremonies in the past.

A separate Independence Day was held at Maratha hamlet I for the first time in 1961. It was attended also by members of Maratha hamlets II and III, as well as by neighbors, some of them not Marathas. The occasion of the separate celebration of Independence Day was the opening of a new school building, but the participants said they planned to continue to hold a separate ceremony.

The weakening of village solidarity was probably hastened by the government program, especially the Cooperative Credit Society idea. In 1954 the village society included only forty per cent of the registered landowners; conflict and mistrust kept people from joining. But, as government propaganda reiterated, the advantages of membership were considerable. Eventually the program resulted in the formation of more than one society in most villages of the *tālukā*—

despite the development-program formula of "one society to one village and one village to one society." [4] Gaon now had four societies. There were 246 members, fifty-four of whom were residents of other villages. This gives 192 members from the village, about sixty-three per cent of the registered landowners residing in the village (about 320).[5] Judging from the number of outsiders in Gaon's societies, it was probable that some people in Gaon belonged to societies in other villages, but I did not investigate the matter. Table 13 gives the caste composition of village societies.

TABLE 13

Composition of Cooperative Credit Societies by Caste

A		B		C		D	
Maratha	22	Rajput	46	Maratha	26	Maratha	30
Rajput	14	Maratha	6	Blacksmith	1	Rajput	7
Scavenger	9	Brahman	3	Outsiders	1	Mali	6
Leather Worker	4	Scavenger	2			Potter	5
Brahman	3	Outsiders	17			Outsiders	8
Mali	2						
Basket Maker	2						
Other	4						
Outsiders	28						

The category "Other" in Society A refers to members of four castes—Temple Priest, Goldsmith, Watchman, and Leather Worker. Society A is the old 1954 organization. People who joined other societies did not always resign from the old one; fifty people had double memberships, at least on

[4] *All-India Rural Credit Survey, Report of the Committee of Direction,* Vol. II, *The General Report,* Bombay, 1954, p. 450.

[5] The figure of 320 may actually be too low. It is based on the 1961 land records. The man who copied them for me was a villager, and he marked the names as residents of Gaon or of Vādi. Nineteen names were unidentified. These may have been residents of either community or absentee landowners.

paper. (These have not been counted twice, but have been assigned to the second society joined.) Although not a majority, the core of the society, its most unified power block, consisted of the Bals. Apart from Scavengers, most of those not in the Bal group remained in the society in the hope that, by inaction, they could avoid commitment to a faction. Many remained because they lived in or near the main settlement, where the Bals were located. Only five Rajputs not in or openly allied with the Bal group belonged to this society to the exclusion of membership in another organization.

Society B was dominated in numbers and power by the Annas. Those in this society who were not Annas lived in or near their hamlet, sympathized with them, or had quarrels with people in other societies. The split between these two societies was clearly based on the Rajput feud.

Societies C and D were Maratha dominated. Society C was headed by the Maratha leader. This society was only about one year old and had not had time to develop. The Marathas of Society D were from hamlets I, II, and III. All other castes in the society lived in their vicinity. The split with Society C was partly due to distance and partly to the fact that the Marathas of C had had a history of involvement in village affairs, while many of those in D had been aloof for a long time or were new residents.

Despite the multiplication of cooperative societies, dissatisfaction and conflict remained, especially in Society A. The English-speaking Brahman, with the support of the Bal group, had been elected as joint chairman of the society along with a Maratha. His election had been contested by two Annas, men of considerable power, who were also members of Society B. By a subterfuge, his official appointment had been blocked, almost certainly by these men. Because they had double memberships, it should be observed, they did not need

Society A for loans and so could risk others' resentment. Oddly enough, the Brahman had sympathized with the Annas and disapproved of the Bals' disreputable activities. After his appointment was blocked, he was invited to join Society B by one of the very men who had probably acted against him. He, along with his brother, joined Society B but kept at least nominal membership in A.[6]

Whatever the motives behind this intrigue, it was evident that the conflicts and intrigues of village life persisted in the societies. This may have been the reason for the high incidence of outsiders in Gaon's societies. People may have joined the societies of other villages in order to avoid the conflicts of their own and thus to secure more impersonal treatment for themselves. It seemed probable that further shifts in membership would take place in Gaon's societies, and that additional societies would be formed.

An important outcome of the division of the cooperatives was an increase in the tendency, already present in the past,

---

[6] The Brahman was the main informant for these events, although the general outlines were confirmed by others. He was sympathetic with the Annas, not with the Bals, and was completely bewildered over the motives for the Annas' actions, hence I think it likely that the details he gave me were accurate.

Like the Brahman, I do not know the Annas' motives, but I offer a conjectural explanation. Although leaders were not much concerned with village affairs, the Annas and Bals remained hostile. It seems possible that Bal had lately been making a bid for respectability. His family's history of alliance with Harijans now had some sanction. Most of the Annas were avoiding the village. Village leaders, including Annas, were less concerned with village affairs. So the main stimulus for Bal's former violence was lessened. Note that he was said to be quieter. His support of the Brahman, a respectable though not a powerful man, may have been an effort to gain some esteem, possibly an ally. He had already worked with the Brahman in an effort to put through the Scavenger cooperative. The Annas' actions may have been intended simply to thwart Bal. They were sensitive to Bal's alliances or potential alliances, and sometimes tried to break these. The invitation to the Brahman to join their society might be interpreted as an effort to keep him away from Bal.

toward village disunity. The existence of four cooperative societies forced people to choose membership in one or another group. In the past, caste conflict and feud could lie beneath the surface of day-to-day affairs. Many were neutral in the Maratha-Rajput dispute, even many members of these castes, and many stayed out of the Rajput feud. Most of the neutrals stayed in the old society. But a number of villagers, especially those living in or near the hamlets concerned, were under pressure to join another society. Neighbors were, in fact, much dependent on one another's good will, and the data show that this sometimes overrode caste antagonism. Thus the fragmentation of the village had been worsened.

The failure of village-wide organizations contrasts with the relative success of more broadly based ones. The Tālukā Development Board was still in operation and still functioned adequately. Possibly because of competition with other new cooperative ventures, it had not expanded. The two sugar-factory cooperative societies, on the other hand, were large, flourishing industries. In one of them the annual budget statement gave an income of Rs. 15,793,358 and expenditures of Rs. 15,347,605. Membership in the societies was held by seventy-nine landowners in Gaon, four of whom owned shares in both societies. One was a manager at one of the factories. Those landowners in the village who were not members and who were well enough off to think in these terms were making every effort to join.

The sugar-factory cooperatives functioned with relatively little reference to the old social factors of caste, feud, or neighborhood. Conflict existed within them, as should have been expected, but it did not threaten the existence of the organizations. In meetings I witnessed there were heated arguments from the floor, in the course of which relatively poor and clearly uneducated farmers participated along with wealthier, better educated ones. Parliamentary procedure was minimized, thus allowing for maximum, if not especially orderly, discussion. The points discussed were often relevant for the economic interests of types of individuals, rather than for the interests of individuals aligned in terms of the old social groupings. For example, a much debated subject at one meeting was the purchase by the factory of tractors to be rented to members at low rates. Some were for immediate purchase, although this would mean second-hand machines bought for the same price as new ones. Others wanted to wait for new ones, even if this meant a long delay. The alignment in the issue was between the relatively well-off farmers and the poorer ones. The latter wanted immediate purchase, while the former could afford to wait and rent tractors at higher prices. Such a discussion could hardly have involved caste friction or village feud. The individuals were in too large an organization, and divisions of economic interest crossed the lines of the old groups. Old loyalties affected behavior to some extent. For example, discussion came up of whether to allow new members to enter the society, and I suspect that those who were for it were trying to help people related to them via old groupings. But the antagonisms and alignments of the past were only one of many more determinants of behavior on this level, and they could not be so important as they were in the localized context of the Cooperative Credit Society.

Sheer power could not influence policy as much as it did in the village. It still existed, to be sure. In the tractor case discussed the general membership had voiced its wish for immediate purchase at a previous meeting. They were complaining that their board of directors, who were mostly wealthy, had not followed their wish. Simple expansion in size of a society does not eliminate extralegal action by the powerful. Checks on this kind of thing were government supervision, which could usually be circumvented, and the holding of general meetings and elections. It should be emphasized that the board was being called to task by members. They owed their positions to election by members. Members were too dispersed, relations too impersonal, for extralegal pressure to be applied with as much effect as in the village, so the board had to attend to their wishes to a greater extent than did leaders in the localized societies.

Cooperatives, whether efficient or not, were an important part of peoples' lives, and, partly because of this, government in general figured more significantly in their eyes. It was also conceived differently. In the traditional past it was something to be avoided. In 1954–1955 this was beginning to change; government was feared less, but it was often disliked as much or more. In 1961 there was a less antagonistic attitude. Most people rarely referred to government when they spoke of their ill fortune, as they did in 1954. I interviewed some of the identical individuals (in groups and alone) that I had interviewed before, and in almost every case in which these people had complained about the government in the past, they made more favorable remarks in 1961. There was a feeling that government was more accessible, that one could "talk back" to it. Villagers expressed opinions more frankly to government officials—to the officers of the extension program, for example. During the visit of the collector, a figure of extraordinary and inaccessible position in the past, villagers expressed their ideas freely. Some disputed with him, others protested about alleged ill treatment. Government in 1961 was not so much something to fear or avoid or hate as something with which one could interact—possibly to advantage.

The mental outlook of villagers was, therefore, being expanded. The same held true of their sphere of interaction. The two sugar-factory cooperatives are an example, for they included people from a number of different villages of the *tālukā*. The presence of government offices in Mot, old ones like the Revenue Department and new ones like the block development officer's, also encouraged this. Some members of some of the service castes, now nearly entirely deprived of *bālutā,* often went to Mot to sell their wares, not only on market day, but several times a week. Many others went to Mot frequently, some daily, for business or amusement. The 1961 *talāṭhi* established his office in Mot rather than in the village, an unprecedented move. One of the Cooperative Credit Societies moved its office to Mot, "because people come here all the time. It is more convenient." As I have observed, village leaders with sufficient means and ambition now sought outside political office. Thus, while the village tie was losing its hold, a larger geographic area was increasing in importance.

Part IV · Summary and Conclusion

14

Summary and Conclusion

IN THIS study we have isolated the system of interaction of the traditional village and have shown this system to have been composed not only of political forces but also, and at least equally importantly, of social ones. The social identity of the village persisted despite—and in part because of—conflict and despite the disruptive potentialities of class-based inequality in the distribution of power and of the caste system, with its juxtaposition of solidary, sometimes opposed, groups.

The bonds of caste membership were compelling. They were assimilated to kinship ties in the minds of members. Caste allegiance and caste organization, sometimes clearly structured organization, extended well beyond the boundaries of the village. Even where organization was loosely structured, castes maintained fairly effective control over members due to the ties of the bilateral kindred, which tended to have consistent composition through time for each *bhāuki*. Moreover, caste rank pervaded Hindu values. The concept of *vitāḷ* (pollution) tended to produce alienation and dehumanization where large differences in rank existed. Where rank was not very disparate, it still held disruptive potentialities. Caste mobility was always a possibility. Castes close in rank could become competitors, especially as caste rank was not perfectly clearly defined; hence group was posed against group in the system. Thus, in a multi-caste community like Gaon, the caste system was, latently at least, a centrifugal force.

As we have seen, the disruptive force of caste had some

effect. Aloofness regarding caste rank helped minimize this. But Marathas and Rajputs conflicted. Rope Makers and Scavengers were antagonistic to higher castes, although the extent of it was probably recent, especially among Rope Makers. These were the very groups in which one would have anticipated hostility. Marathas and Rajputs were opposed because they were similar; status was secularly based—both had the same traditional occupations, and both were dominant castes. Moreover, Rajputs were upwardly mobile, hence all the more readily seen as competitors by Marathas. The antagonism shown by some Scavengers and Rope Makers was due, in part at least, to their ritually and secularly low rank. They were the most polluting castes in the community, and they were given the least esteem. They were so distant in status from the dominant that their value as an "audience" for wealth display and as social "creditors" was lessened. Because valued less than others, there was a tendency for some of them to be hostile to others.

Moreover, the distribution of productive wealth in the village was unequal, and the wealthier tended to be dominant. This was recognized in the belief that the goods and services produced in the community were produced *for* the "owners" of the village, the landowners, especially the main *bhāuki* of Rajputs, the Kokes. Almost all village leaders—all sanctioned leaders—were among the very wealthy. Most were Kokes. Village politics tended to isolate the community from outside forces and helped maintain the asymmetry of power and privilege. Class-based power like this can hinder group identification; if it is a predominant factor, interaction is little more than a process whereby some people command the passive obedience of others.

One of the most decisive factors that prevented caste and class from destroying village unity was the existence of cross-cutting lines of cooperation and conflict. Neighborhood created dependence among people who might otherwise have conflicted; Marathas and Rajputs, Scavengers and members of high castes sometimes farmed contiguous land. More important, conflict, which divided the whole village, also divided its parts.

The genesis of conflict among kinsmen has been discussed. Some kinship relationships were usually conflict-free because statuses were clearly ranked, as for example between *soyare* and between father and son. Harmony was furthered by the process of merging, whereby distant kinsmen were assimilated to closer ones, thus reinforcing the tie and clarifying rank differences. Merging, however, was often inefficacious among brothers. Intimacy, social similarity, and approximate equality of total social status resulted in a tendency toward competition in this relationship, which was probably exacerbated because the society was pervaded by rank. The conflicts among brothers were often inherited by other close patrilineal kinsmen; and these *"bhāu bandaki"* were, in turn, passed on to the *bhāuki,* where they usually took the form of vague tension and distrust, and in one case—the Bal-Anna factionalism—involved overt hostility. The Koke *bhāuki* is the very group in which we would anticipate intense competition; dominance resided in the group at large, not in this or that particular member, hence each had to compete in order to exercise it.

The traditional castes of the village, apart from Marathas, were composed primarily of members of the same *bhāukis.* While this helped provide a basis for common action, the inheritance of *bhāu bandaki* resulted in the fact that castes were less clearly posed against one another as unified groups. The opposed interests of classes were divided both by caste and by faction. Maratha-Rajput hostility involved both small and

large landowners of both castes; Rope Makers and Scavengers, both fairly poor groups, did not act together because
caste allegiance divided them. Most important, the Bal-Anna
feud disrupted the unity of the Rajputs, who were the most
powerful group in the community. The Bals and others
affected by them lent support to the politically weakest elements in the village, whose rights were thereby given some
political backing.

It was perhaps because rivalry was especially acute among
the wealthy that some large landowners preferred a relatively
passive role as leaders. Passive leaders were accepted as
neutral by most elements in the community and hence could
act as "judges" whose decisions would naturally be less subject to accusations of bias against one or another caste or
faction.

The position offered here is not that conflict necessarily
augments cohesion. On the contrary, persistent and marked
hostility often helps to destroy it. For example, when parties
involved in sharp conflict are geographically separated, this
can lead to apathy toward the larger community. The original Maratha hamlets are illustrative; spatial separation combined with Maratha-Rajput hostility probably resulted in the
fact that they remained, in part, socially isolated from the
community. But conflict is probably to be found in all groups
that are cohesive; for cohesion is ultimately based upon likeness, which promotes rivalry, or complementarity, which
paves the way for haggling. Conflict is thus likely to be present, and it may—I think often does—function to maintain
cohesion.

Intragroup conflict in Gaon functioned in a negative sense;
it mitigated the effects of centrifugal forces. But this in itself
could not have produced solidarity. Other factors were present. One of these was the cycle of village ceremonies, wherein

solidarity—or, at times, conflict—was reflected and thus reinforced. The *bālutā* system was another, probably more important, factor. It coincided neither with class nor caste interaction, but much economic and ritual activity was channeled by the system. Rights as well as duties were assigned to service castes, and these were conceived as binding. Furthermore, continued operation of the system presumed the existence of mutual trust and helped foster it. It also helped promote the notion of mutual debt, but gave greater emphasis to the debt of the service groups to landowners, thus converting a potentially class-organized relationship into a social "debtor-creditor" relationship. Moreover, because *bālutā* payments were related to crop size, the economic security of service groups, even of those owning little or no village land, was dependent upon village land; hence they, as well as landowners, had a stake in the system of relationships bounded by the village.

This last point deserves some emphasis. Technics, the process of producing and exchanging goods and services, is probably one of the most important phenomena behind village cohesion. Contiguity along with common and complementary economic activities always gives a potentiality for social cohesion. It need not come about, of course—there are some territorial groups, in India and elsewhere, in which the systems of interaction are more political than social—but it often does, and it did in Gaon. It was mentioned in the introductory chapter that the Hindu great tradition, which probably reflects most of the central values of Indian civilization, contains few references to the territorial group. Notwithstanding this, we have seen that the territorial bond has social reality; the material circumstances of the Indian peasant usually promote village solidarity, and this is reflected in the symbols of the little tradition.

In 1954 the traditional system of social organization was undergoing rapid change. Some of the old norms had weakened, and new ones were in the process of replacing them. The concept of pollution in caste interaction had been attenuated, and the traditional type of caste meeting was declining. But identification with one's caste remained, and castes, as interacting groups, persisted in the form of bilateral kindreds. Despite government efforts to bolster village solidarity, it was declining, due to such factors as immigration, dispersion to the fields, the impact of government, and, related to these, a weakening of the *bālutā* system. The lessening of solidarity was evident, for example, in the apathy of some farm residents, especially new residents. It was seen in the beginnings of the social separation of the Anna hamlet from the rest of the community; conflict and spatial separation had, no doubt, contributed to this, but traditional ties to the village were strong; the decline of general village identification was probably the most significant factor.

One of the clearest indications of a weakening of village social identity was observed in the increased hostility of the Rope Makers. Their low status in the village, the unequivocal position of "debtor," was not being fully compensated for by guaranteed *bālutā* rights and by consistently satisfactory payments. The right to *bālutā* payment was now being questioned; the norm was changing to one in which payment was not obligatory. Gaon's Rope Makers did not dispute this redefinition of the norm, but many of them reacted with marked hostility. In some other villages Rope Makers took issue with the change in rule and openly attacked landowners.

Similar to this was the increase in Scavenger hostility, although there were differences in the causes. The Scavenger position in the *bālutā* system had been little changed. The increased resentment of some members of this caste was due to the new egalitarian values. These had affected others too, but, because of the Ambedkar campaign, a number of Scavengers had been more deeply affected than members of other castes. While caste restrictions had been lessened, they had by no means been obliterated; Scavengers were considered very low, and they knew it well—thus the increase in hostility. It should be observed that their hostility, because generated by a rapid change in values, was different in some respects from that of the Rope Makers; it included the village, but it extended well beyond it. The disaffected members of the caste reviled not only the village and its leaders but also the government and Congress Party and, indeed, even Hinduism.

The increased hostility and/or conflict among Scavengers and Rope Makers in Gaon and its environs differed from the antagonisms of traditional village society. The latter took place within the rules of social interaction; these were over the rules themselves. This kind of conflict is basically asocial.

The Leather Workers may be contrasted with Rope Makers and Scavengers. Their connection with the *bālutā* system had become even more attenuated than that of the Rope Makers. But this had been primarily voluntary; hence, unlike the Rope Makers, they felt no hostility over the alteration in *bālutā* norms. The households that remained in the system, probably because few in number, received *bālutā* payments which they considered satisfactory. Unlike the Scavengers, the Leather Workers had been no more affected by egalitarian values than others. Furthermore, their withdrawal from the *bālutā* system was probably partly in order to disassociate themselves from their highly polluting traditional occupation. They had a reputation for being economically well off—much better off than they were in fact—and were less thought of as "debtors." They were upwardly mobile, both ritually and secularly, and received more esteem from fellow villagers than would be anticipated for a caste as low in rank as theirs. The Leather Worker adaptation was primarily in terms of the old status values, and it allowed for continued identification with the village.

That the Leather Worker's traditional kind of adaptation allowed for their social integration is an indication of the persistence of traditional village identity. Although it was weakened, we have seen that in 1954 village solidarity had not been fundamentally shaken.

The phenomena that had been changing village organization in 1954 continued through 1961 and some were more active. New factors had appeared, with deeply felt effects. *Bālutā* was now nearly completely extinguished. Formal caste organizations were catching hold in the area. Government activities impinged upon the village to a much greater extent, for example, the extension program with its associated self-help cooperatives, including the sugar factories.

One of the effects of the innovations was a greater fragmentation of village society, a contraction of the individual villager's range of interaction. When communities decline in solidarity, the conflicts and alliances contained by the old rules and loyalties are likely to assume more importance. It cannot be said to what extent this would have taken place in Gaon without the government's cooperative program, but it clearly had taken place, at least partly due to the self-help movement. It was seen in the beginnings of the cooperative housing and dairying societies being formed by the Rope Makers. This aspect of the government's cooperative movement, which emphasized the "Scheduled Castes," was not especially effective in Gaon, but in other villages where it had been more successful a number of castes formed their own localized self-help cooperatives, in this way creating more independence from village ties. Fragmentation was evident in Gaon in the Cooperative Credit Societies, which had increased in number from one to four, and which showed signs of possible further splintering in the future. Partly as a result of this, there was an acceleration of budding, seen in the distant Maratha hamlets (I, II, and III) and especially in the Anna hamlet. Thus caste, neighborhood, and faction, stimulated by the cooperative program, promoted the formation of relatively separate social entities within the borders of the village.

Paradoxically, another effect of recent innovations had been an expansion in the villagers' sphere of interaction. Government agencies and those sponsored by government, most especially the sugar factories, as well as the new formal caste organizations, brought about wider contacts and subsumed more people who knew less of one another; they involved a more highly formalized, less personalistic application of rules than obtained in traditional social organization. The failure of the *pancāyat* and the Cooperative Credit Society in 1954 was due in part to the fact that they were supposed to act impartially, to involve a formal, impersonal administration of regulations. In traditional village organization, still clearly in evidence in 1954, rules were administered informally and flexibly. The whole person was taken into account—his caste, family background, and personal reputation. Privilege and asymmetrical justice obtained; but in dispute resolution the headman or informal leader could consider such factors as who was most likely to lie, who had a grudge against whom, and so on. Formal, "rational" administration clashed with such methods, but was more readily applicable in the new, wider spheres of interaction.

The new system of interaction involved less social domination, though it was likely to allow for more political domination. The conspicuous display of wealth and the social debtor-creditor relationship were of less consequence in these conditions. The potential audience for a man's display and his potential "creditor" are, under such circumstances, less relevant because more impersonal; he needs persons "to act back upon *him*," in Simmel's phrase,[1] if they are to be relevant audiences and relevant creditors.

Thus, as might be expected, village leadership was less active in 1961. To be dominant in the past was to be a creditor. Villagers of lower status were now less important to former leaders. Moreover, if the pressures of 1961 were met, giving assistance, advice, or encouragement was likely to create not debtors but more independence on the part of the recipients.

Conflict and hostility were rarer in 1961. They continued as acute as in the past only within the Cooperative Credit Societies, where social interaction was still intense. But social conflict, such as that between Bals and Annas, was less frequent, because interaction was less frequent and socially less meaningful. The asocial hostility of Rope Makers against landowners was much lessened, partly because the issue was resolved; *bālutā* was nearly gone. In addition, the Rope Makers' aspirations were less than ever focused on the village, where they felt they could get little aid, and more on government, especially the extension program, from which they felt assistance might be forthcoming.

Neither the Rope Makers nor most other villagers could be said to be anomic; the rules and ties of kin and caste persisted. The one group in which people most clearly approached anomy was the Scavenger caste. The bond to caste remained, but this gave less support than it might, for they

---

[1] *The Sociology of Georg Simmel,* K. Wolff, transl. and ed., Glencoe, 1950, p. 181.

were ambivalent about their caste. They knew the larger society held their caste in low esteem as pariahs, an allegation founded on traditional, deep-rooted values, which even they could not quickly set aside, but which many of them consciously repudiated. They identified the larger society with Hinduism and the Congress Party, and the impulse was to reject these. A vigorous action of this kind could have enhanced the solidarity of the group. In 1954 there were the beginnings of an appropriate movement. But by 1961, though the movement was still extant—possibly even more active in other villages—in Gaon it was feeble, for Scavenger leadership in the village, to the extent that it existed, was not moving in this direction. The Scavengers' rejection of Congress and Hinduism was more a gesture than a vital protest. Again because of weak leadership, along with other factors, they were unable to overcome the obstacles necessary to meet the conditions laid down by the Congress-dominated government for integrating themselves with its programs. Thus, unlike the Rope Makers, hope of betterment did not bind them to the larger society. Their own group identification in this case being insufficient, they were, by and large, aimless.

For the others, there were not only the ties of kin and caste, but also the link with the larger society. The bond to government was becoming firmer—their attitude not only involved less distance, but was more positive—and government regulations, albeit less well understood than those of the traditional village, were becoming more acceptable. Most villagers were, indeed, becoming apathetic, but not toward all social ties, only toward the village tie.

Social organization was not being completely westernized. The traditional kind of kinship pattern persisted and showed no signs of decline. Caste also remained and was, indeed, growing stronger in some respects. However, apart from kin-

ship, a drift toward impersonality, formality, and seculariza-
tion pervaded not only the local, territorially delimited sphere
of interaction but the caste system itself.

Thus we see that while the Maharashtrian village had
been, in fact, a solidary community in the not very distant
past, there was a recent tendency toward "rationalization,"
accompanied by a decided trend away from the social significance of the village toward that of more broadly based
territorial units.

Appendices and Index

 A

Kinship Terminology

THERE were significant differences in terms of reference between Brahmans and other castes in the village. Some non-Brahman informants gave a few Brahman terms; these will be mentioned later. Wherever an asterisk is employed, the relationship was designated by alternative terms and will be repeated in the list. "Generation O" indicates ego's own generation, "Generation −1," the first descending generation, and so on.

BRAHMAN TERMINOLOGY

GENERATION +3

panjobā: fa fa fa, fa mo fa, mo fa fa, mo mo fa
panji: fa fa mo, fa mo mo, mo fa mo, mo mo mo

GENERATION +2

ājobā: fa fa, mo fa
āji: fa mo, mo mo

GENERATION +1

bāp, vadīl: fa
cultā: fa bro*
māmā: mo bro
kākā: fa si hu, fa bro,* mo si hu*
māvaśā: mo si hu*
sāsarā: hu fa, wi fa
āī: mo

ātyā: fa si
māvaśi: mo si
culti, kāki: fa bro wi
māmi: mo bro wi
sāsu: wi mo, hu mo

GENERATION O

bhāu: bro
culatbhāu: fa bro so
ātebhāu: fa si so
māmebhāu: mo bro so
māvasbhāu: mo si so
mehuṇā: wi bro, si hu, hu si hu
sāḍu: wi si hu
dīr: hu bro
culatmehuṇā: fa bro da hu
ātemehuṇā: fa si da hu
māmemehuṇā: mo bro da hu
māvasmehuṇā: mo si da hu
vyāhi: so wi fa, da hu fa
kārbhāri, navarā: hu
bahīṇ: si, wi bro wi
culatbahīṇ: fa bro da
ātebahīṇ: fa si da
māmebahīṇ: mo bro da
māvasbahīṇ: mo si da
mehuṇi: wi si
bhāuje: bro wi
nanand: hu si
jāū: hu bro wi
culatbhāuje: mo bro so wi
atebhāuje: fa si so wi
māmebhāuje: mo bro so wi

māvasbhāuje: mo si so wi
vihīṇ: so wi mo, da hu mo
bāiko: wi

GENERATION −1

mulgā: so
puṭnyā: bro so (male ego), hu bro so
bhācā: bro so (female ego), wi bro so, wi si so, hu si so, si so
jāvai: da hu
culatjāvai: bro da hu (male ego), hu bro da hu
bhācejāvai: bro da hu (female ego), wi bro da hu, si da hu
mulgi: da
puṭni: bro da (male ego), hu bro da
bhāci: bro da (female ego), wi bro da, si da, wi si da, hu si da
sūn: so wi
culatsūn: bro so wi (male ego), hu bro so wi
bhācesūn: si so wi

GENERATION −2

nātū: so so, da so
nāt: so da, da da

GENERATION −3

paṇṭu: so so so, so da so, da so so, da da so
paṇṭi: so so da, so da da, da so da, da da da

NON-BRAHMAN TERMINOLOGY

The terms are identical to the Brahmans' in the second and third ascending and descending generations.

GENERATION +1

bāp, vadīl: fa
cultā: fa bro
māmā: mo bro, fa si hu*
māvalā: fa si hu*
kākā: mo si hu
sāsarā: hu fa, wi fa
āī: mo
māvalaṇ: fa si
māvaśi: mo si
culti: fa bro wi
māmī: mo bro wi*
sāsu: wi mo, hu mo, mo bro wi*

GENERATION O

bhāu: bro, hu si hu,* fa si da hu*
culatbhāu: fa bro so
mehuṇā: fa si so, mo bro so, wi bro, si hu
māvasbhāu: mo si so
sāḍu, sāḍubhāu: wi si hu, fa si da hu,* mo bro da hu
dīr: hu bro
culatmehuṇā: fa bro da hu
māvasmehuṇā: mo si da hu
nandava: hu si hu*
vyāhi, evay: so wi fa, da hu fa
mālak, kārbhāri, navarā: hu
bahīṇ: si, wi bro wi, fa si so wi, mo bro so wi, co-wi*
culatbahīṇ: fa bro da
mehuṇi: fa si da, mo bro da, wi si
māvasbahīṇ: mo si da
bhāuje: bro wi
culatbhāuje: fa bro so wi

māvasbhāuje: mo si so wi
nanand: hu si
jāū: hu bro wi
vihīṇ: so wi mo, da hu mo
savat: co-wi*
bāiko: wi

GENERATION −1

mulgā, lyok: so, bro da hu (female ego), si so (female ego),
     hu bro so,* wi si so,* bro so (female ego),* si da hu*
puṭnyā: bro so (male ego), hu bro so*
bhācā: bro so (female ego),* so wi bro, si so (male ego),
     hu si so, wi bro so, wi si so,* si da hu*
jāvai: da hu, bro da hu (male ego)
culatjāvai: bro da hu (male ego)
bhācejāvai: si da hu*
mulgi, lek, porgi: da, bro da (male ego),* hu bro da,* si
     da (female ego), wi si da,* bro so wi (female ego), si
     so wi (male ego)
dhavdi: bro da (male ego),* hu bro da*
bhāci: bro da (female ego), so wi si, si da (male ego), hu
     si da, wi bro da, wi si da*
sūn: so wi, bro so wi (male ego), si so wi (female ego)

These lists do not cover all terms used, for I neglected to
make enquiry about some relationships for which terms probably existed, for example, spouse's sister's children's spouses.
The term *"navarā"* for husband, given in both lists, is literary;
it is not used in everyday speech. The term *"sasu"* for
mother's brother's wife was given by but one informant, a
Scavenger. The Brahman use of *"kākā"* for reference to
father's brother is uncertain. It is the regular term of address,
and a normally reliable informant insisted that it was also

sometimes used as a term of reference. The same informant gave the term of address for father's brother's wife, *"kāki,"* as the term of reference for that kinsman. Brahmans sometimes dropped qualifying prefixes in referring to cousins, cousins' spouses, siblings' childrens' spouses, and spouses' brothers' children's spouses. Non-Brahmans sometimes did this in referring to parallel cousins and wife's sister's husband. They frequently did so in referring to parallel cousins' spouses, mother's brother's daughter's husband, sister's daughter's husband, and brother's daughter's husband (male ego). Among non-Brahmans only one informant gave *"sāḍu"* for father's sister's daughter's husband; others gave *"bhāu,"* or said that there was no term but that "the relationship is that of brother." In fact, some non-Brahmans said that there were no terms for any cross cousins' spouses, that the relationship was similar to the sibling tie. Much the same was said by some non-Brahman informants of sister's son's wife (male ego), brother's son's wife (female ego), and wife's sister's children, in which instances the relationships were likened to own children.

In a few cases non-Brahman informants gave Brahman terms, either in place of or as alternatives to the regular non-Brahman usage. One Goldsmith informant (not the regular village Goldsmith) gave Brahman terms as alternatives to non-Brahman for all cousins and their spouses, and substituted the Brahman term for non-Brahman in reference to sister's son's wife. A Temple Priest informant gave the Brahman term as an alternative for the regular non-Brahman usage in referring to father's sister, and he substituted Brahman terms for brother's daughter's husband (female ego) and brother's son's wife (male ego). A Rajput gave Brahman usage as an alternative in referring to father's sister and husband's brother's daughter, and he employed the Brahman term alone for brother's daughter (male ego). A Leather Worker substituted the Brahman usage for brother's daughter (male ego), and a Scavenger gave Brahman usage for wife's sister's daughter. It is possible that these are examples of an on-going process of sanskritization. Brahman terms, it should be pointed out, were used in school text books, so their use by other castes may be increased in the future, if education is more widely spread.

 B

Caste Rank

WHEN questioned on caste rank, individual villagers rated castes relative to one another or said that one or another were about equal. The end result in each case was a total hierarchy for all castes in the village. These systems of ranking are of considerable use in constructing a general system for the village. But, as was mentioned in Chapter 8, people were not very firm in their convictions regarding the relative rank of many castes. Additional data are needed, therefore, to supplement these.

In the course of ranking castes, informants often stated their beliefs as to who they thought would take food from whom. For example, when undecided on the relative rank of two castes, informants frequently said that they refused to take food from one another. (In fact, in such cases they usually did take food from one another.) In ranking Leather Workers above Scavengers, a point on which everyone agreed, it was often said that Scavengers would take food from Leather Workers, but that the latter would not reciprocate. Informants were sometimes wrong in the matter. They were, in fact, ranking castes on their own beliefs as to who was higher than whom, but expressing their beliefs in terms of how they thought other people acted in commensal taboos. In this context each person was consistent and firm regarding his own behavior; he had a clear idea from which castes he would (or should) accept food and from which he would not. It appears to me of use in constructing a general scheme of caste rank to take into consideration how people said they themselves acted in commensal relations with others. Most household heads in the village were asked from which castes they would refuse food. A list of village castes was read to them to be sure that none was forgotten. Their tabulated responses I call a "summation rating," in contrast to the systems of ranking held by particular individuals, which I call "individual ratings." Both of these sources of information, as well as others, went into the construction of the all-village view of caste rank given in Chart II.

Summation ratings have a number of defects. One is that ritual interdictions had been weakened in recent times, if not in fact, at least in what people said they would do. Some people claimed they would accept food from all castes (though many of these did not in fact do so). These have been omitted from the tabulations. In other cases people were probably more lax than they had been in the past. For example, it is improbable that any Temple Priests, being vegetarians, would have admitted accepting food from Marathas in the recent past. Similarly, probably no Scavengers would have said that they took food from Rope Makers in the past. A number of Rope Makers reported that they had once refused food from Scavengers but that they no longer practiced any taboos. However, this can only affect the ratings very seriously in the lowest ranks, where their relative rank is fairly easily determined by means other than summation ratings.

Another defect in summation ratings is that individual judgments are emphasized at the expense of positions that castes, considered as wholes, might take on the matter. For example, Marathas and Rajputs, who have large populations, are counted more heavily than Brahmans or Water Carriers.[1]

[1] This defect and others like it could be more readily handled in studies less restricted than this. A more accurate summation rating would have to take in a number of villages in a region. Even then, as will be evident from the following discussion, individual ratings will also be needed.

To help correct for this, I have computed the percentage of each caste refusing to accept food from every other. If we add these percentages, which I admit is an unusual statistical device, we get an approach to the total of castes' "judgments" of other castes. This figure cannot be relied upon alone, for here one man's judgment, possibly an idiosyncrasy, is given great weight, as, for example, the Water Carrier's of the Blacksmith caste in the table. Both types of summation ratings must be considered together, and then only as a first step in the construction of a general view of caste rank.

There are other faults with summation ratings. Idiosyncratic opinions may deeply affect relative rank even where castes' percentage totals are not involved. For example, in the table below, the judgments of one Leather Worker and three Marathas considerably depress the rank of Goldsmiths. Moreover, while a refusal to accept food from others is usually indicative of a belief in the inferiority of the latter, this is not invariable. For example, Goldsmiths traditionally refused food from all other castes, including Brahmans, yet no Goldsmith ranked his caste above Brahmans, and some ranked themselves below Marathas. This kind of interdiction probably represents a caste's organized effort to assert high rank by, as it were, overstating its case; individual members of the group may persist in "being realistic," that is, in accepting the ranking of the majority. This is most serious when ranking Harijans. Scavengers and Rope Makers, perhaps to assert ritual exclusiveness vis-à-vis some group, often said they refused food from Basket Makers, who, being "outsiders" of low rank, constituted a convenient group for this purpose. The irregularities that obtain in summation ratings because of such phenomena can be corrected only by considering individual ratings and other information.

In Table 14 I give the tabulated summation ratings. The

left-hand column, entitled "Interdicting Castes," gives caste membership of individuals refusing food from others. The column heads, "Castes Interdicted," give the castes from whom food was said to be refused. The bottom row, as I have explained above, gives totals of the percentages of each caste refusing food from each other caste, and is an attempt to summarize "judgments" by castes of other castes.

The totals contain contradictions and anomalies which can partly be resolved by reference to individual ratings. As was noted, the way in which individuals ranked castes varied from person to person. A few varied much. For example, one Rajput ranked Leather Workers above Washermen. This was probably due to the fact that he was very friendly with one Leather Worker, while, like many others, he did not consider the village Washerman to be "respectable." On another occasion the same informant said that the Barber would shave the Washerman but not Leather Workers; thus he seemed to recognize that his own ranking was not that of the larger community. In part the way people ranked castes was related to their own caste rank. Brahmans and Temple Priests strongly emphasized purely ritual criteria, and they ranked the first four castes in this order: Brahman, Temple Priest, Goldsmith, Maratha. Rajputs often ranked themselves, along with Marathas, just below Brahmans, though some placed Temple Priests above themselves. Some Marathas and Rajputs ranked Goldsmiths very low. However, in many respects all or most people shared views, and where this was the case, we can employ the data to advantage.

A considerable number of villagers were asked to rank a few castes, generally those closest in rank to themselves. In addition, a number of informants were asked to rank all castes of the village. In all cases, the method used was to read out caste names, two at a time, and enquire which of the two

TABLE 14

Caste Rank: Summation Ratings

CASTES INTERDICTED

INTERDICTING CASTES	Brahman	Temple Priest	Maratha	Goldsmith	Potter	Rajput	Water Carrier	Barber	Blacksmith	Muslim	Washerman	Watchman	Basket Maker	Leather Worker	Scavenger	Rope Maker
Brahman	—	5	5	5	5	5	5	5	5	5	5	5	5	5	5	5
Temple Priest	0	—	2	1	2	2	2	3	3	3	3	3	3	3	3	3
Maratha	0	0	—	3	0	1	1	2	15	20	23	25	32	32	32	32
Goldsmith	1	1	1	—	1	1	1	1	1	1	1	1	1	1	1	1
Potter	0	0	0	0	—	0	0	2	6	7	7	7	8	8	8	8
Rajput	0	0	1	0	0	—	0	3	22	28	30	32	38	38	41	41
Water Carrier	0	0	1	0	0	0	—	0	1	0	0	1	1	1	1	1
Barber	0	0	2	0	0	0	0	—	0	0	0	1	1	1	1	1
Blacksmith	0	0	15	0	0	0	0	0	—	0	1	1	1	1	1	1
Muslim	0	0	20	0	0	0	0	0	0	—	0	0	2	2	2	2
Washerman	0	0	23	0	0	0	0	0	1	0	—	0	1	1	1	1
Watchman	0	0	25	0	0	0	1	1	1	0	0	—	2	2	2	2
Basket Maker	0	0	32	0	0	0	1	1	1	2	1	2	—	5	3	3
Leather Worker	0	0	32	1	0	0	1	1	1	2	1	2	5	—	5	5
Scavenger	0	0	32	0	0	0	1	1	1	2	3	0	24	4	—	20
Rope Maker	0	0	32	0	0	0	1	1	1	2	0	1	6	4	8	—
Total	1	6	8	10	8	9	9	16	53	64	75	81	130	106	114	126
Total of Caste Percentages	100	200	267	162	267	270	270	339	576	528	776	963	1468	1360	1500	1483

the informant thought higher.[2] In some cases two men were interviewed simultaneously. In one case a group of Scavengers was interviewed. However, most interviews were of single individuals, held in private. In Chart III six fairly representative individual rankings are given in numerical order, highest rank first. The Brahman, like most others of his caste, refused to rank Muslims. Where castes were ranked as equal, I have grouped them after a single number. The column heads give the castes of informants.

Individual ratings are of considerable use in resolving contradictions between the two totals in summation ratings. One contradiction involves Scavengers and Rope Makers and is easily resolved; all villagers, including Rope Makers, agreed that Scavengers were higher. Another relatively simple problem involves Blacksmiths and Muslims. When people spoke of "Marathas" in a general sense, they usually included Blacksmiths, never Muslims. In individual ratings, Blacksmiths were almost always ranked above Muslims. It is only the Water Carrier's statement that results in Muslims being higher when caste percentages are totalled. In this case the best general summary of village opinion is to place Blacksmiths above Muslims, although their positions were close.

A more serious contradiction between the two totals is between Goldsmiths and four other high castes. Opinions given in individual ratings were variable. Some people, most often Marathas and Rajputs, ranked Goldsmiths as very low. But many people ranked them high, usually above Potters. Brahmans and Temple Priests rated them above Marathas and just beneath Temple Priests. The village Goldsmith,

---

[2] At the time these data were originally collected, in 1954–1955, I did not have the benefit of other anthropologists' technical suggestions regarding the collection of such information. However, by reading caste names, two at a time, in a calculated disorder, I was able to arrive at satisfactory individual ratings.

CHART III

Caste Rank: Individual Ratings

Brahman	Maratha	Rajput	Goldsmith Rajput	Watchman	Scavenger (group)
1. Brahman	1. Brahman	1. Brahman	1. Brahman	1. Brahman	1. Brahman
2. Temple Priest	2. Maratha	2. Rajput, Maratha	2. Maratha	2. Temple Priest	2. Temple Priest
3. Goldsmith	3. Temple Priest	3. Temple Priest	3. Rajput, Goldsmith, Temple Priest	3. Maratha	3. Maratha, Goldsmith
4. Maratha	4. Rajput	4. Potter		4. Goldsmith	4. Rajput
5. Blacksmith	5. Potter	5. Water Carrier	4. Potter, Water Carrier, Barber	5. Rajput	5. Potter
6. Rajput	6. Water Carrier	6. Barber		6. Potter, Water Carrier, Barber	6. Water Carrier
7. Potter, Barber, Water Carrier	7. Barber	7. Blacksmith	5. Blacksmith, Muslim, Washerman		7. Barber, Blacksmith, Muslim
	8. Blacksmith	8. Goldsmith		7. Blacksmith	
8. Washerman	9. Goldsmith	9. Muslim	6. Watchman	8. Muslim, Washerman, Watchman	8. Washerman
9. Watchman	10. Muslim	10. Watchman	7. Basket Maker		9. Watchman
10. Basket Maker	11. Watchman	11. Washerman	8. Leather Worker	9. Basket Maker, Leather Worker	10. Leather Worker
11. Leather Worker	12. Basket Maker	12. Basket Maker			11. Basket Maker, Scavenger
12. Scavenger	13. Washerman	13. Leather Worker	9. Scavenger	10. Scavenger	
13. Rope Maker	14. Leather Worker	14. Scavenger	10. Rope Maker	11. Rope Maker	12. Rope Maker
	15. Scavenger	15. Rope Maker			
	16. Rope Maker				

however, ranked his caste below Marathas, not only in the presence of a Rajput, but also in a prior interview, when alone. However, he ranked his caste above all others, excluding Brahmans. It seems a fairly accurate summary of village opinion to place Goldsmiths below Marathas but, following many individual ratings and the total percentages of each caste in summation ratings, above other high castes.

There are other anomalies in the summation ratings, not involving contradictions between the two totals, that can also be resolved by reference to individual ratings and additional information. One of these is the relative rank of Marathas and Temple Priests. Many villagers' individual ratings placed Temple Priests above Marathas, as do the summation ratings, but a considerable number reversed the order. The latter were those who emphasized secular criteria. While by traditional sacred criteria Temple Priests were doubtlessly higher than Marathas, the secular dominance of Marathas gave them much prestige. I have placed them on an equality with Marathas in Chart II, the general chart of caste rank in Gaon, although it must be kept in mind that an emphasis on different criteria was involved.

The position of the Basket Makers in the summation ratings is clearly not indicative of the general opinion. It gives very great weight to Harijans' stated practices. In individual ratings no one in the village, not even Harijans, ranked them as lowest in the village, and far the majority of members of the "touchable" castes ranked them above Leather Workers. Furthermore, Leather Workers, Scavengers, and Rope Makers, but not Basket Makers, were treated as literally untouchable in the recent past; in 1954 they were still barred from village temples. Hence it is an accurate reflection of most villagers' opinions to place the Basket Makers above Leather Workers.

Index